LONDON

WORLD CITIES SERIES

Edited by
Professor R. J. Johnston and Professor P. L. Knox

Published titles in the series:

Forthcoming titles in the series:

Other titles are in preparation

LONDON

MORE BY FORTUNE THAN DESIGN

Michael Hebbert

JOHN WILEY & SONS

Chichester • New York • Weinheim • Brisbane • Singapore • Toronto

Published in 1998 by John Wiley & Sons Ltd, Baffins Lane, Chichester, West Sussex
PO19 1UD, England

National 01243 779777. International (+44) 1243 779777

e-mail (for orders and customer service enquiries): cs-books@wiley.co.uk.

Visit our Home Page on http://www.wiley.co.uk or http://www.wiley.com

OTHER WILEY EDITORIAL OFFICES

John Wiley & Sons, Inc., 605 Third Avenue, New York, NY 10158-0012, USA

WILEY-VCH Verlags GmbH, Pappelallee 3, D-69469 Weinheim, Germany

Jacaranda Wiley Ltd, 33 Park Road, Milton, Queensland 4064, Australia

John Wiley & Sons (Asia) Pte Ltd, 2 Clementi Loop #02-01, Jin Xing Distripark, Singapore 129809

John Wiley & Sons (Canada) Ltd, 22 Worcester Road, Rexdale, Ontario M9W 1L1, Canada

BRITISH LIBRARY CATALOGUING IN PUBLICATION DATA

A catalogue record for this book is available from the British Library

ISBN 0-471-97399-8 cl
ISBN 0-471-98237-7 pb

Typeset in 9/12pt Caslon 224 from authors' disks by Mayhew Typesetting, Rhayader, Powys
Printed and bound in Great Britain by Bookcraft (Bath) Ltd, Midsomer Norton

This book is printed on acid-free paper responsibly manufactured from sustainable forestry, for which at
least two trees are planted for each one used for paper production.

For Shirley and John

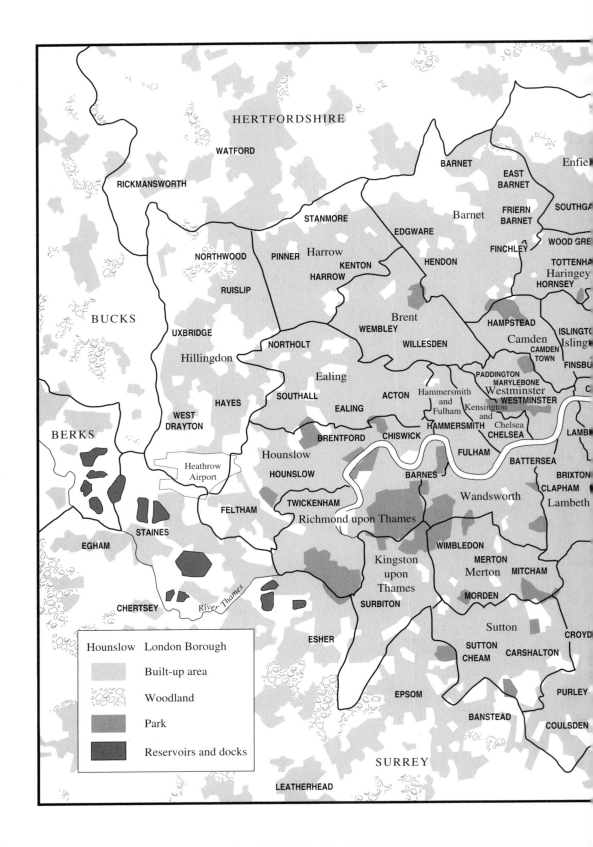

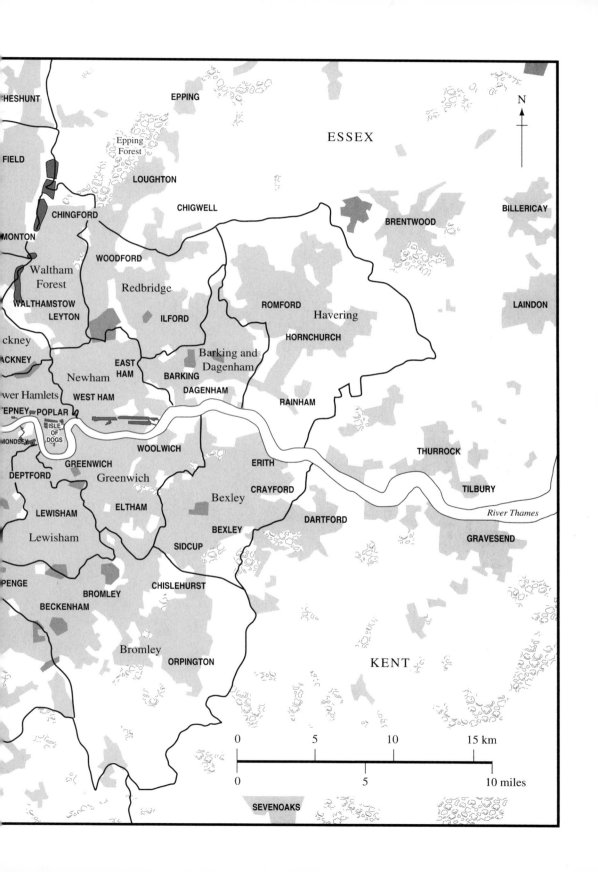

CONTENTS

PREFACE

For those of us who enjoy urban portraits – painted, written, photographed or filmed – a series of world city profiles has always seemed an inspired publishing idea. 'Up-to-date authoritative and challenging profiles of the world's main urban centres,' ran the original cover blurb to this series, 'each book blends urban history, sociology, ecology, economics, politics, transport, architecture and built environment into a fascinating portrayal of the contemporary urban scene'. The key word here was 'blend'. Contributors were told they must research eclectically but smooth out the jargons and specialised discourses in their material into an account that could be read with equal interest by scholarly experts, compilers of in-depth background reports, and the serious-minded tourist. That is quite a tough brief.

At the time of asking, I was working on a 'London' entry for the *Encyclopedia Britannica* with a similar list of headings, and thought at first the one could be a scaled-up version of the other. On reflection, the assignments were very different. A reference entry has to give factual answers to disconnected questions. A book needs to present London as a whole – and give an interpretation. What could it be? What themes stretch round such a bundle of topics as the editors wanted in their 'fascinating portrayals'? Further reflection, most of it pedalling around the streets of London – so badly equipped with cycle-ways, despite much planning – led to the themes of fortune and design, chance and intention, spontaneity and plan, muddle and pattern. All city histories combine these elements, but in London they were written into the basic structure of the city, producing a place that really looks and functions like no other.

The problem of this or any perspective is what it leaves out. There is little flavour in these pages of the ceremonial London of state events, or the arena for mass joy, grief, or anger. The book all but omits the political economy of the capital's relationship with its mother country and the geographical significance of its regional setting in south-east England. It draws less than it might on comparative studies of globalisation, life and labour in world cities. There is scant discussion of current public policies for urban regeneration or economic development. The coverage of demography is rudimentary. The treatment of places and spaces in London rather takes for granted a detailed topographical knowledge which it was perhaps this book's task to provide. Sport and popular culture are almost completely absent. So is the housing market. Where are Geoffrey Chaucer, Marie Lloyd and a thousand other famous Londoners? And why is there so much here about the history of town planning?

But that way madness lies. A book has to have a focus, and this one reflects the interests of an author who happens to be a historian and town planner. The reader can judge whether that is a useful vantage point for making sense of London's 'contemporary urban scene'. I do believe it is.

So to a list of acknowledgements, long but incomplete, and always with the usual disclaimer that responsibility for errors lies with the author alone. These ideas developed during 15 years spent at the London School of Economics. I joined the school in 1979 to help with, and later to direct, its unique masters programme in urban and regional planning. The course is taught by economists, geographers and political scientists on an equal footing. It recruits students from all over the world and from every type of disciplinary background, many with professional experience. My first debt is to those 15 cohorts of masters and doctoral students, perhaps particularly the Americans whose alert, puzzled questions about London were often so very difficult to answer. One way and another the metropolis provided our staple topic for theses, dissertations, seminars, study visits and evening sessions in the Beaver's Retreat bar. Dan Graham and Andre Sorensen deserve special mention, as well as Hazel Johnstone who administered the programme, and Michael Wise, who has provided such a genial and wise element of continuity over nearly five decades of planning studies at LSE. Almost all the academic contributors to the Urban & Regional Planning programme were actively involved in researching and debating London policy issues through the seminars and projects of the Greater London Group. These colleagues were superb by any standards: Derek Diamond (a true mentor), Patrick Dunleavy, Stephen Glaister, Chris Husbands, George Jones, Mark Kleinman, Judith Rees, Yvonne Rydin, Peter Self, Nigel Spence, Tony Travers (him especially), Christine Whitehead. LSE epitomised metropolitan centrality. From my present office in an a pleasantly landscaped inner-city campus university I look back with nostalgia to everyday encounters with colleagues from other departments in the corridors, bridges and communal spaces of the School's dense cluster of buildings around Houghton Street and Clare Market. Those 15 years were a turbulent time for London, and LSE was always close to the heart of things, intellectually as much as physically. It was a privilege to get to know the city from that vantage-point.

On joining LSE we moved house from a terrace near the rural Thames at Wallingford to another within sight of the river in Limehouse in the heart of the East End of London. The West India and Millwall Docks were still operational, and the sounds and smells of the neighbourhood were industrial: the clunk of scrap metal being shipped for Spanish and German foundries from George Cohen's quay at Limehouse Basin, the pulpy odour of Hough's Thames Paper Board Mills on Narrow Street. The house looked out onto a patch of wasteland surrounded by corrugated iron, one of a vast and still-increasing stock of derelict sites, mostly publicly owned, which seemed blighted in perpetuity by the decline of the dockland economy, the shortage of public funds, the lack of private sector interest, and a pervasive climate of restriction and no-can-do traceable (as a member of the

Labour Party soon learned) to union control. Though only a 5-minute drive from the City, it was off the map for cabbies.

As our children grew up, the area underwent an extraordinary transformation. Lavish central government aid – some of it well spent, some not – persuaded the private sector to venture east of Tower Bridge into the E1 and E14 postcode areas. One by one, the derelict sites were sold off for development. The opportunities and struggles of regeneration in an inner-city neighbourhood provided another education into London and its ways. I learned about parish communities and historic buildings conservation working with the Reverend Christopher Idle, Prebendary John Pearce and John Chesshyre and architect Julian Harrap on the restoration of Nicholas Hawksmoor's church of St Anne Limehouse: about community networks in a (not completely unsuccessful) campaign to save Limehouse Basin, which among others, involved Nick Wates, Dave Chesterton, Eric Reynolds and the redoubtable Illtyd Harrington.

The Limehouse Basin Cooperative and the Greater London Group led me into the wider networks of amenity organisations across the metropolis. With Nicholas Falk, Esther Caplin and Rob Cowan I became involved in launching the organisation *Vision for London* to provide a forum for debate on architectural and policy issues in the capital. It was one of several such initiatives in the curious decade of interregnum after the abolition of the Greater London Council. A shared sense of metropolitan crisis – largely illusory, as it turned out – brought politicians, industrialists, amenity activists, consultants, designers, academics, property developers, media types, local government officers and environmentalists out of their separate orbits. I was fortunate to be involved in this uncharacteristic moment of civic *rapprochement*. Those ephemeral debates, public lectures, exhibitions and seminars of the early to mid-1990s have not been referenced in the Bibliography, but they did provide an important source of inspiration for the book, and specifically for the revisionist view of abolition and its legacy offered in Chapter 5. One wonders whether any British city has seen such a spate of well-attended public meetings on topics of civic concern since the 1880s. Of the scores of articulate Londoners who furthered the London debate from the platform or the floor, or backstage in the committee-room, let me just note the contributions of Tony Aldous, Alan Baxter, Walter Bor, Richard Burdett, Michael Cassidy, Judy Hillman, Simon Jenkins, George Nicholson, Anne Page, and my old PhD supervisor Professor Peter Hall of the Bartlett School.

Peter Hall uniquely combines policy leadership with outstanding academic eminence, as the Bibliography shows. Much of his work has been historical, and he has played an important role in writing the history of twentieth-century city planning. He was a key speaker at the 1994 conference of the International Planning History Society celebrating the fiftieth anniversary of the *Greater London Plan*, which I organised with Robert Home of the University of East London. The conference attracted a splendid set of papers, due to be published in book form before too long, confirming the importance of Sir Patrick Abercrombie's wartime plans not only for London but as international exemplars. The revisionist streak in this book crystallised at that conference.

The late Gordon Cherry, founder and president of the International Planning History Society, supported the conference with his usual enthusiasm, and I should also thank his successor Stephen Ward, David Massey (Secretary-Treasurer of IPHS), and Patricia Garside who chaired the programme committee. She deserves another acknowledgement in her role as editor of the *London Journal*, that most valuable resource for any researcher whose interests range over the metropolis past and present. Another fructifying network was the *London Seminar*, meeting monthly in the Vera Anstey room at LSE with financial support from the Economic and Social Research Council. Mark Kleinman, Michael Harloe, Ian Gordon and Peter Hall (again) have won the gratitude of many London researchers by giving space for good, robust seminar debate that crosses the usual disciplinary and institutional boundaries. The contributions of the writer Paul Barker deserve special mention. Chapter 9 began as a paper for the London Seminar.

Though the book had a long gestation during my time at LSE, most of the writing was done in a semester's sabbatical leave from the Department of Planning & Landscape at the University of Manchester. I am indebted to Christopher Wood and our departmental colleagues who provided the opportunity of leave and to Philip Ogden and Nigel Spence for offering a hospitable writing base within the Department of Geography at Queen Mary College. The companionship of another sabbatical visitor, the cultural and social geographer Stanley Waterman, was an agreeable bonus. Edward Oliver's football map is a cherished souvenir of the six months on the Mile End Road; he also contributed, at very short notice, the main topographical map. Back in Manchester, Peter Burton and Michael Pollard conjured wonderful images out of my indifferent rolls of film, and Nick Scarle of the Department of Geography went out of his way to prepare the maps as the Cartographic Unit closed for summer redecoration. At the final write-up two home computers collapsed and I was indebted to a colleague, the architectural historian Frank Salmon, for his kind loan of a Macintosh powerbook.

During the autumn of 1996 I was assisted in one way and another by librarians at Queen Mary and Westfield, the British Library of Political and Economic Science, the British Library, the City Business Library, the Bishopsgate Institute, the Tower Hamlets Local History Collection at Bancroft Road, and (above all) the Guildhall Library: thanks to them and to the collections in their stewardship. Another tranche of acknowledgements is due to the many people who responded uncomplainingly to questions that were generally put over the telephone and out of the blue: Joe Bacon of Richard Ellis; Robin Clement, Giles Dolphin and Abigail Warren of LPAC; Michael Von Clemm of Merrill Lynch Capital Markets; Philip Davies of English Heritage; David Ellis and Simon Murphy of the London Transport Museum; David Goode of the London Ecology Unit; John Hall of the London Pride Partnership; Jenny Hall and Oona Wills of the Museum of London; Chris Hamnett of King's College London; Alison Harker and Maknun Gamaledin-Ashami of the City

Parochial Foundation; Martin Howell of LB Wandsworth; Angela Jeffrey of the Port of London Authority; Andrew Lainton of LB Brent; Sir Peter Levene, formerly of Canary Wharf; Charlie Mason of LB Ealing; Nick Matthews of TCPA; Bruno Rost of Experian Goad; Martin Mogridge of Martin Mogridge Associates; Julie Scott of the Association of London Governments; David Tau of Westminster City Council; Richard Wainwright of BAA; Andy Wood of *East End Life*; Max Dixon of the London Research Centre; Jim Thomas of the London School of Economics; and Andreas Vedung of the Office of National Statistics. Duncan Fallowell kindly granted permission to end the book with his words.

To return to the *World Cities* series, I would like to acknowledge the role of Iain Stephenson, who conceived it under the Belhaven imprint. He launched this volume and was patiently supportive when it got becalmed by my move to Manchester and the distractions of new projects in the north-west. His successor at Wiley, Tristan Palmer, adeptly steered the book home. Ron Johnston, co-editor of this great series with Paul Knox, offered characteristically concise, positive feedback on drafts: I suppose I am not the only dilatory academic to be amazed by his power of instantaneous response.

Last and greatest thanks are due to Flip, Frank and Kay Hebbert, who bring so much back from their London perambulations.

Department of Planning & Landscape
University of Manchester
September 1997

CHAPTER 1

THE KNOWLEDGE

CHAPTER 1

THE KNOWLEDGE

A moped weaves through the traffic at Bank junction, on its handlebars a clipboard with a list of addresses and an *A-Z* street map in a plastic wallet. The rider peels off down a side-street, finds a building, checks it on the clipboard, consults the map, and rides off in search of another street and another address. It looks like a treasure hunt but it is an apprenticeship. The moped rider is training to be a cabbie. He or she is 'doing the Knowledge' (Figure 1.1).

The driver who plies for hire in a black London taxicab must pass an examination set by the Public Carriage Office of the Metropolitan Police. The syllabus, which has hardly changed in a hundred years, is set out in the blue book called *LIST OF QUESTIONS similar to those put to applicants for Licences to act as CAB DRIVERS at examinations held to test their knowledge of London*. The blue book consists of 26 sets of 18 routes or runs. The total 468 runs, together with the quarter-mile radius to either end, form the framework of the Knowledge. For example:

LIST NO 15
1 Phillimore Gardens, to Royal Oak Railway Stn.
2 Marylebone Stn., to Regent Palace Hotel.
3 London Library, to Abercorn Rooms.
4 Oasis Pool, to Royal Veterinary College.
5 St Martin's Theatre, to Tufnell Park Stn.
6 Maitland Park, to Public Trustee Office.
7 Farringdon Stn., to Lordship Road, N 16.
8 Salisbury Square, to Hornsey Central Hospital
9 Myddelton Square, to Hackney Downs Stn.
10 Clarence House, to Loughborough Junction Stn.
11 Kennington Cross, to Basinghall Street.
12 St Bride's Institute, to Thames Magistrates' Court.
13 Companies House, to Long Lane, Bermondsey.
14 Guy's Hospital, to Wandsworth Bridge.
15 Clapham North Stn., to West Side Clapham Common.
16 Chelsea Police Stn., to West Side Clapham Common.
17 Sth Western Magistrates' Court, to Nevern Square
18 W. London Magistrates' Court, to Westminster Council House.

Runs are tested in batches of 90 (that is, five lists at a time) at intervals of 56 days. The complete 'Knowledge' covers every street within the 6-mile radius of

Figure 1.1 Doing the Knowledge. *Behind the trainee cabbie is the magnificent screen wall of the Bank of England, designed by Sir John Soane and built 1795–1826*

Charing Cross, and all the main destinations within the Metropolitan Police District, a radius of just over 12 miles. The literary cabby Maurice Levinson compares this heroic accomplishment to learning the works of Shakespeare by heart (1963: ch. 2).

For London is a legendarily difficult city to get to know. A dense, irregular street network extends over 600 square miles, joining a hundred or so local centres into a continuous built-up mass with 7 million residents. It is a messy map with few unifying features: no ring road (except the outer orbital M25 motorway), no axial boulevards, no consistent street grid, and no clearly defined 'downtown'. Buckingham Palace has the grand approach route of The Mall but all the other landmarks are tucked informally into the street plan.

London's strongest morphological feature is the River Thames. Flowing through the heart of the city, from west to east on the ebb tide and east to west on the flood, it divides north from south, and provides – what the street layout does not – a long-distance setting for its greatest monuments: St Paul's and the City churches, the Palace of Westminster, the Tower of London. In the terminology of Kevin Lynch's classic study of *The Image of the City* (1960), it is a strong 'edge' feature, a reference point or axis for building your mental map of London. But orientation to the river can be tricky – perhaps only cabbies fully appreciate the effect of its twists and turns. The Thames enters at the far south-west of London beyond Hampton Court Park and winds north for 7 miles around the gravel terraces of Richmond Hill. Its eastward course from Kew Bridge to the Erith salt marshes is a sequence of meanders, 20 miles as the crow flies but 30 by boat. As it loops, the river bends the space around it, playing strange tricks of disorientation. When you look across the river at Big Ben from the South Bank (Figure 1.2) you are not seeing the south face, as commonsense suggests, but the north, and from a train leaving Waterloo Station parallel with the river towards Vauxhall all four faces of the famous parliamentary landmark come into view in sequence.

Images of cities also rely on administrative geography. Unlike Parisian *arrondissements*, or Tokyo's *to* and *ku*, local governments and public services in London follow a variable geometry with little coterminosity. The system of 120 postal districts, often used for purposes of orientation, is unique and esoteric. It splits the dense urban core into east central (EC) and west central (WC) zones and the rest of the metropolis into six compass sectors, north (N), east (E), south-east (SE), south-west (SW), west (W) and north-west (NW), each containing up to 28 numbered districts. The district nearest the centre always has the number one, so that N1 (Islington), E1 (Stepney), SE1 (Southwark), SW1 (Lambeth) and NW1 (Kensington) form a ring around the central area. Then logic breaks down. While the Parisian *arrondissements* are numbered in a neat clockwise spiral from the centre, London postal areas scatter randomly around their sector according to the alphabetical order of sorting office names. N16 abuts N1; SE2 lies in the distant suburbs east of Plumstead while SE11 is a stone's throw across the river from Westminster; E4 reaches out into the nursery gardens of the Lea Valley north of London while E14 is

Figure 1.2 The Palace of Westminster. *From the South Bank, the northern (sic) aspect of the Houses of Parliament, rebuilt by Sir Charles Barry in 1835, and of Westminster Abbey (1375–1400, towers by Nicholas Hawksmoor added in 1735)*

the Isle of Dogs business district close by the City. The name systems are even more elusive than the numbers, leading the American political scientist Hank Savitch (1988: 171) to conclude that 'technically there is no London'.

MULTIPLICATION AND DISCONNECTION

At the heart of London's complex administrative geography sits a 1000-year-old municipal nucleus, 'the City'. Its chartered boundaries have remained constant for centuries; their constancy explains the surrounding variation. Figure 1.3 shows the lines of the Roman walls, the medieval walls, the administrative boundary of the Corporation of London, and the limits of the traffic cordon, with police guards and security cameras, which has controlled vehicle access into the City since the IRA bombs of 1994 and 1995 (the City of London runs its own police force, in blue shirts and brass badges: London's Metropolitan Police have white shirts and silver badges). The physical intactness of the municipal nucleus, over hundreds of years, has protected it from the forces of constitutional evolution centred a mile and a half upstream at Westminster: the consolidation of monarchy, the rise of parliamentary democracy, and the evolving apparatus of the British state. As the City of London stayed within its walls, Westminster matured into a city in its own right. The two

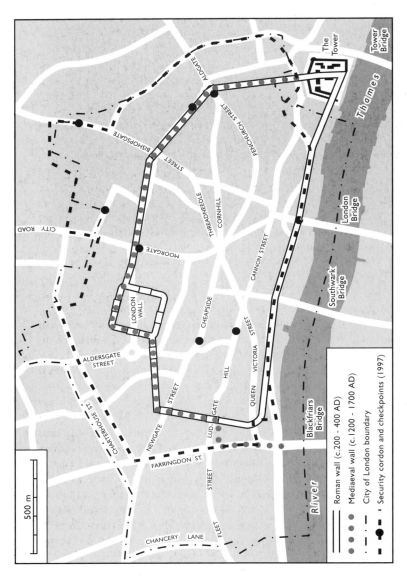

Figure 1.3 City in a Ring (1). *The Square Mile's three defensive shells. The line of the Roman Wall, laid out around AD 200, was incorporated into the mediaeval fortifications which remained in place until the eighteenth century. The Police Commissioner's 'ring of steel' was introduced under traffic legislation in 1995. The continuity of London's enceinte is unique*

Legend:
Roman wall (c.200 – 400 AD)
Mediaeval wall (c.1200 – 1700 AD)
City of London boundary
Security cordon and checkpoints (1997)

500 m

Map labels:
CHARTERHOUSE ST.
ALDERSGATE STREET
CITY ROAD
CHANCERY LANE
FLEET STREET
FARRINGDON ST.
NEWGATE STREET
LUDGATE HILL
QUEEN VICTORIA STREET
CANNON STREET
CHEAPSIDE
LONDON WALL
MOORGATE STREET
THREADNEEDLE STREET
CORNHILL
BISHOPSGATE
ALDGATE
FENCHURCH STREET
The Tower
Tower Bridge
London Bridge
Southwark Bridge
Blackfriars Bridge
River Thames

cities formed a compound nucleus around which metropolitan London grew in a polycentric, dispersed fashion, without unifying municipal government. Plurality of governance explains irregularity of topography.

So, the 2000-year-old boundary separating the City from Tower Hamlets still separates a financial district of dark suits, marble floors and clicking heels from an East End of street markets, municipal tenements bedecked with the washing of large immigrant families, the clatter of sewing machines in sweatshops, the street names evocative of class struggles or lurid Victorian crime. Small wonder the sites of the old gates in the City's moated wall – Bishopsgate, Aldgate – are among the most popular starting points for walking tours of the modern metropolis.

The contrast with Paris could not be more complete (Lees 1973). There, the French state worked from the heart of the medieval city, enlarging its *enceinte* and modernising the fabric to make the city a symbol of national unity and indivisibility, and cultural *point d'équilibre* for the world at large. The history of Paris is a history of absorption and incorporation into a progressively higher organic unity. London's is a history of multiplications, not just of local governments but every aspect of metropolitan life. In music, art, sport, religion, local government, hospital provision (Rivett 1986), business, London sails as a flotilla with two, three or more flagships. Three examples which make the point are music, sport and learning.

For symphony orchestras, Berlin has the Berlin Philharmonic, New York has the New York Philharmonic, Amsterdam has the Amsterdam Concertgebouw. In London, five orchestras compete for primacy (and a further thirty are listed in the *Performing Arts Yearbook for Europe*). They manage to co-exist because of the multiplication of centres of patronage and venues. Royal patronage created the Royal Albert Hall in South Kensington where the great annual festival of Promenade Concerts is led by the BBC Symphony Orchestra, itself a product of state patronage. Municipal patronage, first of the London County Council and later of Greater London Council, developed former industrial and warehousing land on the Waterloo riverbank into the South Bank arts complex around the Royal Festival Hall, performance venue of the London Philharmonic and the Philharmonia Orchestra. The London Symphony Orchestra is resident at the Barbican, the arts complex created by the Corporation of London inside a high-density urban renewal scheme on bomb-sites within the central business district (Figure 4.2). Three major symphony halls and two opera houses provide the setting in which five full-scale symphony orchestras vie for audiences and funding.

In sport, the pattern is inverted. Nobody plays for or cheers for London in rugby union, rugby league, hockey, basketball, athletics, cricket or football. Cricket has been played since 1845 on the Oval Cricket Ground only a mile from the Palace of Westminster, but the home team has always been the Surrey County Cricket Club, and modern Surrey is the greenest and wealthiest sector of suburbia beyond the south-west boundary of London. North of the river is Lord's, home of the Marylebone Cricket Club (MCC), the game's national regulating authority since its foundation in

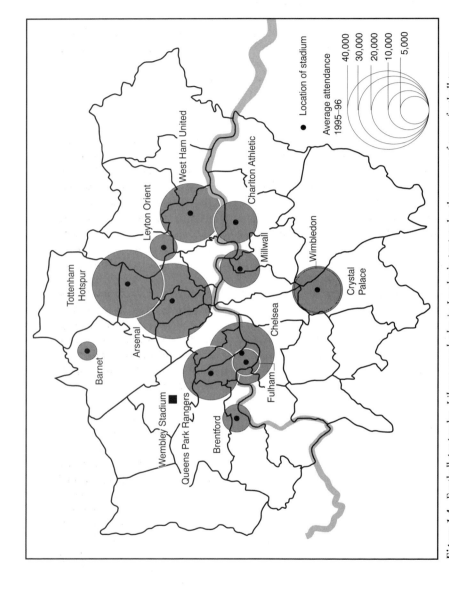

Figure 1.4 Football geography. Like so much else in London's geography the names of some football teams have been displaced with the passage of time

1788. Also there since 1877 is the Middlesex County Cricket club, though the administrative county of Middlesex disappeared 30 years ago. Football teams do represent real places, though often not the places where they play, and none belongs to London as such. The capital has 13 clubs: Arsenal (named after the Woolwich Arsenal in south-east London, but based in the north in Highbury), Barnet, Brentford, Charlton Athletic, Chelsea, Crystal Palace (based in nearby Norwood), Fulham, Millwall (based in Deptford), Leyton Orient, Queens Park Rangers (based in Shepherd's Bush), Tottenham Hotspur, West Ham United, and Wimbledon (also at Norwood).

In higher education London has had a university to its name only since 1836, centuries after the universities of Paris, Rome and Madrid. Despite the imposing monumentalism of its administrative buildings in Bloomsbury, it is a weakish federation of 50 institutions ranging from small specialised schools to institutions such as Imperial College, University College, King's College and the London School of Economics which act as universities in their own right. London has eleven other universities besides the federal University of London, including the universities of Westminster, City of London and Guildhall. The pattern, or rather the lack of it, reflects once again, the diverse springs of initiative in London – ecclesiastical, secular, royal, municipal – and the absence of an organising impulse within the city.

'There is no logic to London' writes the novelist A.N. Wilson, introducing his *Faber Book of London*: 'it is both a collection of villages slung chaotically together and it is an idea, almost a metaphysical entity in the minds of those who contemplate it' (1993: ix). For creative writers this kaleidoscopic quality has always been a stimulant. In Walter Bagehot's famous phrase, what drew Charles Dickens to London as a source of inspiration was the fact that it is 'like a newspaper. Everything is there and everything is disconnected' (Collins 1973).

BOOK KNOWLEDGE

Our task in this London volume of the Wiley *World Cities* series is to search out the connections of history and geography which explain the distinctive character of London and account for its pre-eminence as a world city. The topic and its immense specialist literature (see Creaton 1994; Garside 1995) are equally daunting. London's best interpreters are either novelists – Charles Dickens, H.G. Wells, Doris Lessing, Elizabeth Bowen, Martin Amis, Peter Ackroyd, Ian Sinclair – or surefooted professional writers such as the journalists Simon Jenkins, Tony Aldous and Michael Elliot, biographers such as Christopher Hibbert or Michael Harrison, or academics with a literary touch (Peter Hall and Roy Porter are outstanding examples). London is well suited to patchwork books which mirror its variegation, like recent anthologies by A.N. Wilson (1993), Andrew Saint and Gillian Darley (1994) and Paul Bailey (1995), or the indispensable *London*

Encyclopedia of Ben Weinreb and Christopher Hibbert (1983). Walter Besant's *Survey of London* (1909–12) was wonderfully true to its subject: immense, in ten volumes and – 'to turn to another subject' – kaleidoscopic.

A good starting point for the searcher after London knowledge is the Bishopsgate Institute (Figure 1.5). This was founded in 1891 with the funds accumulated over 500 years by the ecclesiastical parish of St Botolph, Bishopsgate, and its entrance, an Art Nouveau archway flanked by towers, makes the most of a narrow frontage site just north of Liverpool Street Station. Inside the Institute are meeting rooms, a lecture or recital hall seating 450 people, and a remarkable London reference library. Charles Goss, Bishopsgate Librarian from 1897 to 1941, amassed an important collection of maps and prints, making the Institute the headquarters of the London Topographical Society which has been producing high-quality facsimiles of historic London maps since 1890. Goss was a vigorous collector of books and pamphlets on the history and topography of the capital, its schools, churches, businesses, families and social organisations, and on Londoners' contributions to the labour and cooperative movements, secularism, anarchism, and distributism. A cordial, old-fashioned library, with a card index and typed subject index list, Bishopsgate's material is shelved inside high glass-fronted bookcases with more books piled against the doors or parked in front on trolleys under newspaper to protect them against the drips from the Institute's leaking roof (under repair in 1996–7). The library claims to hold a million items – a million! Vertigo is an occupational hazard in London studies.

The epicentre of London scholarship lies half a mile south-west from Bishopsgate, in the Library of the Guildhall of the Corporation of London. First founded in 1423 by a bequest of Sir Richard (Dick) Whittington, Lord Mayor of London, the library was re-established in 1828 and today has a quarter of a million books, 28 000 maps – including Ralph Agar's rare and enormous aerial view of Tudor London engraved in woodcut – besides 30 000 prints and drawings of London scenes, 17 000 topographical photographs and a huge collection of the ephemeral output of London printing presses over five centuries: trade cards, menus, tokens, theatre programmes, diagrams, directories and membership lists. The Guildhall Library is also the municipal archive of the Corporation of London, holding the charters and records of 900 years' civic continuity. It is an outstanding place to pursue research and has pride of place in the acknowledgements of most books about London, including this one.

Half a mile to the north again in a converted Clerkenwell warehouse are the London Metropolitan Archives, where the papers of the London County Council (1889–63), the Greater London Council (1963–86), the Middlesex County Council (1888–1963) and all their historic predecessors are held in the stewardship of the Corporation of London. Its 31 miles of shelving hold more than one and a half million photographic images of the buildings and streets of the metropolis, unparalleled collections of architectural and engineering drawings, and the former Members' Library – established for the wise government of the metropolitan area –

Figure 1.5 The Bishopsgate Institute. *The side door of the Institute is behind the boom of the crane. Looming over it is the Broadgate Centre, an air rights development above the railway tracks leading into Liverpool Street station; behind, the National Westminster Tower. New trading floors have been developed on the site since the view was taken in 1996*

with another 100 000 volumes on all aspects of London. Then, a mile to the west lies the higher-education quarter where the libraries of the London School of Economics, University College and Senate House each have strong collections of London books and material. Their neighbour, the British Library, only recently moved from its historic home beneath the domed Reading Room of the British Museum to red-brick and slate premises on the site of the St Pancras Potato Yards. Its holdings include approaching 1 750 000 titles responding to the catalogue keyword 'London'.

And all this is just a start. Following the lead of McBurney (1995), Dolphin, Grant and Lewis (1981) and Marcan (1993), the library crawl can stretch indefinitely through the specialist collections of central government departments and agencies; academic collections in London's many other universities; the specialist local studies libraries – many excellent – in the 32 Boroughs which share the government of London with the ancient Corporation; the libraries of London's 300 museums or its learned societies, professional organisations, religions and denominations; or private subscription libraries such as the Highgate Literary and Scientific Institution. In the last category, the London Library in St James's Square is the source that wins more acknowledgements than any other from professional writers: in Simon Jenkins's words, 'no bibliography can do justice to its contribution to any book about London'.

Like dogs, libraries resemble their owners. The libraries of this ancient and vast capital city have sprung from many sources of patronage and collective action. All human life is on those shelves. If the Guildhall collection attests to continuities of wealth and power, Bishopsgate's pamphlets reflect the equally persistent awkward streak in Londoners. The fact that nobody knows if there are really a million books in the Bishopsgate Institute is nicely symbolic in itself.

GETTING A GRIP

Only cabbies carry the Knowledge round in their heads. The rest of us rely on the *London A-Z* published by the Geographer's A-Z Map Company. The story of this map and company is superheroic. First published in 1936, the *London A-Z* was the work of one woman, Phyllis Pearsall, an artist and author of Irish–Italian–Hungarian–Jewish extraction who died in 1996 at the age of 89. In 1935 she covered the city on foot, 3000 miles in all, rising at five and walking for 18 hours a day, to compile the first accurate and complete street guide to London. The 23 000 street entries were stored in shoeboxes in her bedsitter in Horseferry Road, the maps were drawn by a single draughtsman, and Pearsall herself compiled, designed and proof-read the book. The retail trade were uninterested until she persuaded the buyer at W.H. Smith to accept 250 on a sale or return basis, delivering them in a wheelbarrow. The *London A-Z* was an immediate success and remains indispensable.

The London Underground network diagram is from the same vintage as the *London A-Z*, and just as indispensable. Displayed in stations, distributed in leaflets, printed in the back of diaries and guidebooks, including the *London A-Z*, the diagram is much more than a route guide to Tube travellers – it is the foundation on which most people organise their spatial knowledge of the city. Ken Garland (1994) has written the history of this great cartographic icon. The diagram was conceived by Harry Beck, an engineering draughtsman who had just been laid off by Underground Railways. Management were at first reluctant to believe that the public would accept a purified diagram of horizontals, verticals and diagonals, disconnected from topography. Beck persisted, the map was issued and – instantly successful – has remained in use ever since. Its designer rejoined the publicity staff of the Underground and supervised the evolution of the diagram over the following decades in which it grew in status as a seminal work of twentieth-century graphic design (Figure 1.6).

The 1930s were a critical decade for London, a period of very rapid growth and of strong disillusionment. Harry Beck and Phyllis Pearsall provided visual keys enabling Londoners to get to grips with the growth and complexity of their city. At the same time, and with a linked inspiration of modernism, others devised plans to manage the growth of the city and impose on it the missing elements of pattern, order and administrative coherence. War and reconstruction gave the opportunity to pursue this agenda. The second half of the twentieth century saw sustained

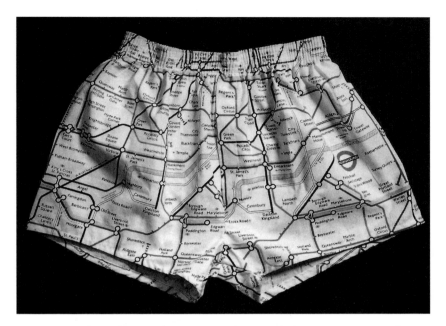

Figure 1.6 The Underground Map. *Boxer shorts with the current version of Harry Beck's classic diagram, supplied by courtesy of the London Transport Museum.* © *London Transport Museum*

efforts to impose a planned order upon London. Their main legacy was a broad green belt of countryside around the sprawling metropolis. It remains to this day, framing the street network in the *A-Z* and the limits of the London Underground system. Like the works of Shakespeare, London is vast but unlike New York or Tokyo it does have a tangible limit: that is the knowledge to be explored in the chapters which follow.

A-Z GUIDE

We begin chronologically with the growth of London from its Roman origins to the late nineteenth century. Chapter 2 shows why the city developed as a cluster of settlements without overall government, explaining the part played by private landlordism in making and maintaining the fabric of London, the delayed reform of local government in the exploding Victorian metropolis, and the eventual establishment of a single government for London in 1889. Physical growth continued to run strongly through the first decades of the twentieth century until the Second World War. Chapter 3 describes the interwar development which doubled again the size of the continuously built-up mass to a 12–15-mile radius. It describes the political reaction, and the momentous debates over reconstruction after the Second World War, culminating in ambitious plans to modernise the capital through town planning and administrative reform.

The middle section of the book traces their outcomes. Chapter 4 reviews the planning and development of modern London. It contrasts the immediate impact of the green belt around London with the checks which frustrated designs on the actual fabric of the city. We show how planners shifted, fortuitously for London, from the intended task of modernising and remodelling into a more conservative, regulatory role which echoed their nineteenth- and eighteenth-century predecessors, the private landlord-developers.

Chapter 5 considers the government of London, the second great object of reform. We see how the green belt assisted the consolidation and reform of a miasmic metropolitan governance system. We follow the creation of London-wide government in 1964, its abolition in 1986, and its resurrection after the Labour victory in 1997. We consider how paradoxically a decade without common government served to strengthen the sense of commonality within the metropolis.

The measure of a city's success is given by the vitality of its economy and by its quality as a place to live, Chapter 6 reviews the economic performance of contemporary London, and Chapter 7 examines the ethnic and social diversity of Londoners and their spatial distribution within the city. To pull these strands together, we return to the interplay of fortune and design in what claims to be the world's largest urban regeneration project, the 6-mile tract of London Docklands due east of Tower Bridge. Beginning with the decline and demise of the world's greatest port, we follow a sequence of unsuccessful attempts at planned regeneration, through the abandonment of planning, to the fortuitous arrival of the North American developers of Canary Wharf, a project large enough to shift the entire centre of gravity of the metropolis eastwards, counterbalancing Edward the Confessor's Westminster developments of a 1000 years earlier.

When academic urbanists compare notes on London and discuss reading lists for students coming fresh to the city, one book tends to stand out among the recommendations. *London: The Unique City* was written in the 1930s by a Danish architectural historian, Stein Eiler Rasmussen. It seems to have been in print ever since. Rasmussen could as easily have provided the starting point for this book as a cabby doing the Knowledge. Instead we will come to him last. Motorisation, ethnic immigration, deindustrialisation, globalisation, tertiarisation, the environmental revolution: so much has changed since the Dane drew his affectionate portrait of the 'unique city'. What remains of the qualities he found there?

Chapter 2

The First Six Miles

CHAPTER 2
THE FIRST SIX MILES

To begin as a geographer should. The River Thames drains to the sea through a shallow elliptical basin formed by a downfold in the chalk of south-east England, filled with thick deposits of grey clay. Terraces of gravel, rising 300 or 400 feet to either side, contain and deflect the river as it meanders eastwards through the flood plain. Soon after the invasion of AD 79 Roman military engineers recognised the dual potential of a site in the centre of the basin as a bridge point and deep mooring (Figure 2.1). The logistics for the invasion of Wales required a Thames crossing for supplies from the south coast to join the main line of communication east–west from the capital in Colchester. The supply route struck across the low marshes of south London on a causeway, meeting the north bank at the slight elevation of Cornhill. Scouring of the gravel terraces alongside the bridge site had created a natural mooring, the Pool of London. The crossing, the crossroads and the mooring had evident urban potential. Beginning as a straggling bridgehead settlement, *Londinium* soon developed into an administrative centre with a strategic command of the road connections to all parts of Britain. It superseded Colchester as capital of the province, acquiring an amphitheatre, baths, forum, procuratorial palace, and the full complement of public buildings, a circuit of walls (fragments of which still survive) and a planned street grid.

Recent archeology has revealed an impressive sequence of waterfront quays along the north bank of the Thames, over which passed 'an extraordinary range and quantity of imported food and goods, ranging from cereals, wine and other commodities carried in ceramic amphoras, to table-ware pottery, glass, metal-work, stone and timber. Although some materials such as Kentish Ragstone and Purbeck Marble were imported from elsewhere in Britain, the majority of the traffic originated from Gaul or the Rhineland' (Fulford 1995). Domestic capital of Britain and gateway to the global economy of the empire, London continued to grow in the second century. The controlling roads which radiated from its Forum across Britain are still instantly visible in satellite images as the only straight lines amid the great post-Roman tangle: clockwise, the Old Kent Road to Dover (Dubrae); Clapham Road, leading to Chichester (Regnum); Bayswater Road, defining the straight northern edge of Hyde Park on its way towards Silchester (Calleva) and Winchester (Venta Belgarum); Edgware Road, the southern end of Watling Street, the highway to Wroxeter (Virconium), Wales and the north-west; Kingsland Road, which becomes Ermine Street and leads to Lincoln; and Roman Road in the East End, the original route to and from Colchester (Camulodunum).

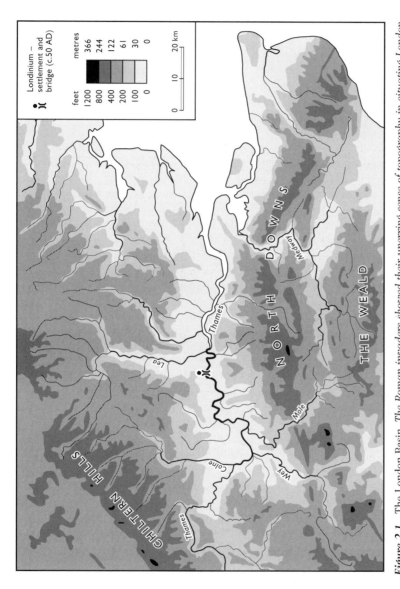

Figure 2.1 The London Basin. The Roman invaders showed their unerring sense of topography in situating London Bridge, the land link between their initial camps at Colchester and Dover. The bridgehead settlement, Londinium, was a by-product

The partition of the province of Britain in the third century marked the first step towards the eventual disintegration of the island into a patchwork of kingdoms after the collapse of Roman power. London lost its administrative primacy while keeping its place in the second rank of eccesiastical centres through the foundation of St Paul's Cathedral and see in 604. The port remained strong. Anglo-Saxon London was a prosperous trading city with connections throughout northern Europe and the Baltic – a 'mart of many peoples', according to the Venerable Bede around 730. Recent archeological finds have revealed a commercial suburb stretching all the way west from the Fleet to the modern site of Trafalgar Square (Keene 1995). Sacked during the Viking raids of the ninth century, the Anglo-Saxon city was re-established by King Alfred of Wessex as part of a strategic system of walled strongholds against the Danes who began to ravage England in 793. Whereas the grid of the Roman city had been submerged beneath irregular accretions, the modern street plan (Figure 1.3) does still have a family resemblance to other fortified Anglo-Saxon *burghs* such as Nottingham, Oxford, Wallingford and Winchester. The burghal system stabilised the Danish incursions and laid the basis for an eventual unification of England under the kingdom of Wessex. The final years of Anglo-Saxon London, from 1000 onwards, saw a strong revival of European trade, conspicuous wealth, and the first documentary evidence of collective civic identity (Keene 1995; Brooke and Keir 1975).

WESTMINSTER

The final legacy of the Anglo-Saxon kingdoms was the decision of Edward the Confessor (died 1066) to rebuild an abbey by the shallow braided gravels a mile upstream from the walled city. Towards the end of his life Edward moved from a royal palace inside the City walls to be near his chosen burial place in the new west minster. 'Mighty consequences flowed from the royal flitting to Westminster', writes G.M. Trevelyan (1959: 101): on account of his 'pious whim' the monarchy struck root outside London but close to its walls. And there it remains.

After the Norman invasion in 1066, Westminster was where William the Conqueror chose to be anointed, crowned, and make his seat of court. The mercantile City of London, a mile downstream, surrendered to him without seige or sack. In a charter still held at the Guildhall, William agreed to respect the liberties of the City, but he also put it under the armed guard of two formidable fortresses, Baynard's Castle, now disappeared, by Blackfriars on the west, and the Tower of London on the east (Figure 2.2).

The Tower was built of Normandy stone, with walls up to 3.7 metres (12 feet) thick. By location and design it unambiguously expressed the relationship, watchful but aloof, of Crown to City. London was the most remunerative tax farm in Britain and its citizens were left at liberty to run their affairs and pursue trade on the provision that the revenue stream flowed regularly, supplemented from time to

Figure 2.2 The Tower of London. *The Norman invaders built the keep – the White Tower – immediately after the Conquest. Corner turret tops were added 300 years later*

time by 'gifts' from the Sheriffs. The accommodation reached in the aftermath of the Norman Conquest proved durable. The feudal power of the monarchy was balanced against the wealth and independence of the mercantile City. The Tower expressed the Crown's advantage of military power, but dynastic uncertainty (for example, after the death of Henry I in 1135), war, or courtly extravagance would shift the balance of advantage to the mercantile community, yielding charter concessions and grants of privilege. Richard I's crusades brought a double advantage. Having loaned him the money to go, London took advantage of his absence to back the rival claim of his brother John, winning charters in 1191 and 1199 that recognised the autonomy of the commune and its right to elect Sheriffs (Brooke and Keir 1975). When the crown was strong it might try to rescind earlier concessions or, more subtly, seek to undercut the City by confirming special jurisdictions within the walls. In due course the immunities of these precincts attracted craftsmen and traders from outside London and overseas – French, Dutch, German and Scottish – a mixture which further reinforced the economic strength of the merchant city.

From accidental beginnings in Edward the Confessor's move to Westminster the give and take between Crown and City laid the basis of the British Constitution. Londoners, with their charters and liberties, were at the forefront of the rise of municipal consciousness in Europe, but they were also the economic engine behind the British crown, allowing the monarchy to consolidate its hegemony and create at Westminster a seat of royal power and ceremonial ritual to rival the splendours of the Paris of St Louis. The relation between the two poles was itself ritualised in the later Middle Ages in the mayor's annual barge procession from London to Westminster, and the monarch's coronation eve procession from Westminster to London (see opening page of Chapter 5).

So, within the spacious natural basin of the Thames, two settlements took shape, their physical separation expressing a fiscal nexus between wealth and power. Upstream at Westminster, the Court, feudal authority, and the evolving apparatus of the state, legislature and executive. Downstream in the City of London, mercantile independence and prosperity, international trade, markets and manufactures. In between and all around, a girdle of great palaces and seats of feudal dignitaries, beginning with the Archbishop of Canterbury in Lambeth Palace, just over the water from Westminster. All the bishops, abbots and other great men of England, wrote William FitzStephen in 1173, 'are as it were citizens and dwellers in the City of London, having their noble edifices, where they stay, lay out lavish expenditure, when they are summoned to the City by the King or Archbishop to Councils or other large gatherings, or to attend to their own affairs' (Brooke and Keir 1975: 116).

GEOMETRY OF ABSOLUTISM

The pattern established in the early Middle Ages remained intact for five centuries (Schofield 1993). The Tudor period brought sustained economic growth and a physical expansion fuelled by the stripping and sale of eccesiastical lands, none more covetable than those 'noble edifices' and estates around the city. Shakespeare's London was a boom town, surrounded by building activity. In 1580 Elizabeth I proclaimed a ban on house construction within 3 miles of the gates of the City of London. Though the decree was reissued in 1593 and 1602 and again by James I in 1605, the momentum of the boom was irresistible. The great *Survey of London* published by the antiquary John Stowe in 1598 describes the approach roads to town 'pestered with cottages and alleys'. His minutely detailed topographic descriptions, the giant woodcut plan engraved by Ralph Agar around 1580, the comic banter of Falstaff and his men, and the musical setting of street-vendors' cries by Orlando Gibbons, all provide a most tangible sense of the life of Tudor London: a city of crooked buildings in crooked streets, dense, timber-built, overhung, as vibrant as a Moroccan *souk*.

Towards the end of the reign of Elizabeth I the vision of an alternative urban world begins to appear in the background of portraits and in the scenery of theatrical productions: the city of classical symmetry, built of stone and marble, geometrical and rational in plan, and laid out with serene piazzas and arcades. In Italy this vision was becoming reality. Through town planning, Renaissance rulers made themselves participants in the divine act of creation. The great projects in

Rome of Pope Sixtus V (1585–90) were familiar to the well-travelled English, as was the assertion of kingly power in Henry IV's vast, symmetrical Place Royale in Paris, built in 1605–12 (today's Place des Vosges). Town-planning projects were a necessary part of the absolutist conception of monarchy. Could their geometry be applied to London, higgledy-piggledy, timber-built, straggling from Chelsea to Limehouse? The answer would depend on the direction of the relationship between the City and Westminster. In the great constitutional struggles of Britain's century of revolution, London was not just the cockpit of action, but also the prize.

Inigo Jones (1573–1652) was a theatrical scene painter, London-born but Italian-trained, who introduced the elaborate masques of the Medicis to the court of James I in Whitehall. In 1613 he was appointed Surveyor of the King's Works, returning to Italy soon afterwards with the Earl of Arundel to refresh his familiarity with best practice on the Continent. On a budget ten times larger than that of his predecessors, he began to tackle the modernisation of the royal palaces. The Queen's House at Greenwich (1617), in the manner of a Palladian villa, was the first strictly classical building in Britain, and later in the century became the centrepiece of London's greatest architectural ensemble, the Naval Hospital. In 1619 Jones began work on a new Palace at Whitehall, designed on a scale that would, if built, have surpassed Greenwich, the Louvre, and even the Escorial, with a 280-metre (900-ft) frontage onto the Thames (Summerson 1966). But the Stuart monarchy was never able to complete the project: all that was built was Jones's magnificent Banqueting House in Whitehall, with its ceiling painting by Rubens of *The Apotheosis of James I*. From its window (Figure 2.3) Charles I went to his death on the scaffold erected by a victorious Parliament after the Civil War of 1642–8. The Roundheads' victory was largely financed from the City. London played a critical part in crushing the Crown: Roy Porter (1994) recalls the words of the philosopher Thomas Hobbes, 'but for the City the Parliament never could have made the war, nor the Rump ever have murdered the King'.

Charles I had been keenly interested in town planning. Besides continuing Inigo Jones's works at Whitehall and at Old St Paul's Cathedral, he renewed the efforts of his predecessors to control the location and materials of new building, encouraged demolition of medieval slums, and in 1636 established a 'Corporation of the Suburbs' in an unsuccessful attempt to establish some overall control over development in the parishes where three-quarters of the population by now lived, beyond the jurisdiction of the Lord Mayor and the Court of Aldermen. The disruptions of the Civil War depressed the London economy but they did not slow the pace of demographic expansion; if anything, they quickened the influx of migrants to the sprawling capital, which grew from 200 000 to 375 000 population in the first half of the sixteenth century (Porter 1996a). But the ambition to impose some physical order on the metropolis went into abeyance until the restoration of the monarchy with the return of the Stuart Charles II in 1660.

Meanwhile, the French monarchy continued to remodel the streets and buildings of Paris in the image of absolute kingship. In his pamphlet *The State of France*

Figure 2.3 The Banqueting House. *By Inigo Jones, 1619–22, this chamber for banquets and masques is all that survives of James I's ambition to enlarge and remodel the Palace of Whitehall in the Italian manner*

(1651) the diarist and arboriculturalist John Evelyn compared London's 'poor nasty cottages' with the splendours of the French capital – *'a city in a ring'* – 'so incomparably fair and uniform that you would imagine yourself rather in some Italian Opera, where the diversity of Scenes surprise the beholder, than believe yourself to be in a real city' (Rosenau 1970: 38). Evelyn returned to the same theme in a satirical essay *A Character of England* (1659), supposedly written by a French visitor to London, reporting scornfully on this city of wooden houses with no fountains, vistas, or paved streets:

> In general the buildings are as deformed as the minds and confusions of the people, for if a whole street be fired (an accident not unfrequent in this wooden city) the Magistrate has either no power or no care to make them build with any uniformity, which renders it, though a large, yet a very ugly Town, pestred with *Hackney-Coaches* and insolent *Carremen*, *Shops* and *Tavernes*, *Noyse* and such a cloud of *Sea-Coal*, as if there be a resemblance of *Hell* upon Earth, it is this Vulcano in a foggy day (de Beer 1938).

THE CITY BURNT AND REBUILT

Evelyn mentions street fires as a common accident, but there was nothing common about the four-day conflagration started by a fire in a baker's shop in Pudding Lane on 1 September 1666. It destroyed 89 churches, 13 200 houses, 400 streets, and four-fifths of the area of the walled City.

The Mayor and Corporation were defeated by the catastrophe: it was King Charles and his brother James Duke of York who rode up from Westminster, organised firefighting, and (on the third day) brought in the Royal Navy to blow up blocks of property as firebreaks. As soon as the fire was out Charles took prompt and decisive measures to stabilise confidence, prevent loss of trade, and set ground-rules for the reconstruction. Within a week he had proclaimed a 7-year tax break from the property rate known as 'hearth money' for owners rebuilding their plots. New houses were to be built in brick or stone, and streets would be widened, with due compensation paid for land taken. As a preliminary to the replanning, six Commissioners were appointed – three by the King (including Dr Christopher Wren) and three by the City – to complete a cadastral and land survey, and prepare a reconstruction plan. Beadles' Booths were set up in every Ward with powers to requisition information from owners and tenants. Charles II's decisive role in the reconstruction is commemorated in the massive bas-relief and inscriptions on the plinth of the Great Fire Monument by the head of London Bridge, completed in 1676. It shows him in a Roman breastplate and toga, London in the figure of a weeping, fallen woman (Figure 2.4).

The king had inherited his father's interest in town planning. He had persuaded André le Nôtre to visit London and enlarge St James's Park between laying out the palace and park of Versailles for Louis XIV and extending the immense linear

24

Figure 2.4 The Monument. *Designed by Sir Christopher Wren and Robert Hooke, and erected in 1671–6 on Fish Street Hill near to where the conflagration began*

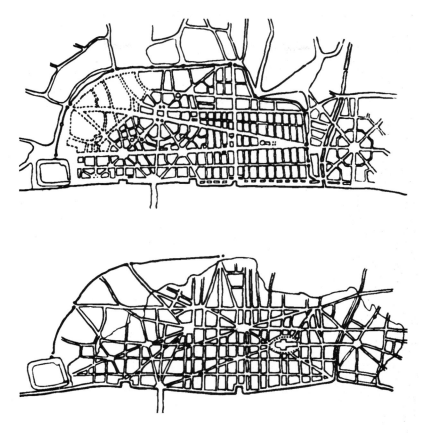

Figure 2.5 Reconstruction Plans, 1666. *Above, the layout proposed by Sir Christopher Wren: under the influence of Bernini's Rome, two avenues radiate out from Ludgate towards the Stock Exchange and the Tower, framing a triangular piazza on the slope in front of St Paul's. Below, one of John Evelyn's modester proposals, regularising the medieval streets into a formal grid. Both plans create open quays along the Thames (Rasmussen 1948: 109). Drawn by Walter Segal for Gibbon (1942: 255) and reproduced by kind permission of John Segal*

geometry of the Parisian *grande axe* from the Tuileries over the hill to the Seine at Neuilly. Now, with the City in ruins all around, here if ever was the chance to realise comparable visions of a 'fair and uniform' Renaissance city by the Thames. Within hours of the fire, John Evelyn and Christopher Wren were both at work on reconstruction plans for the eyes of the King (Figure 2.5). Wren had just returned from Paris and shared Evelyn's admiration for the symmetries, *rond-points* and quaysides of Louis XIV's capital. There were hopes that Commissioners might replan the City in the grand manner, with roads 30 metres (100 ft) wide, larger street blocks, a radical reduction in the numbers of parishes, a realignment of streets onto the principal monuments of the Tower, St Paul's, Mansion House and the Royal Exchange, and a fair new river frontage with quays opening onto the water. But first the survey had to be completed in the face of severe practical difficulties: piles of charred rubble, loss of documents, absent owners, a shortage of labour, and (despite the Beadles' Booths) a general spirit of non-cooperation from citizens fearful that delays over redistributing property holdings would cause trade and wealth to 'flow out of the gates' to Bristol, Southampton, Hull, or – closer to hand – to the unregulated, low-tax suburbs. Parliament shared the City's doubts: England was engaged in a costly war with France and the Netherlands, and could afford neither the direct costs of a total replanning nor the revenue forgone by delay (Reddaway 1940). By November 1666 the survey had been abandoned and the principle of rebuilding on-site accepted. There was to be no baroque master plan. However, Charles II's Act for the Rebuilding of the City of London (1667), commemorated on the plinth of the Monument, left a legacy for town planning just as decisive. It was the system of building control which regulated the great expansions of eighteenth- and nineteenth-century London, and, through the office of the District Surveyors, continues to operate 300 years later.

The central purpose of the Act was to upgrade the quality of buildings and streets, to prevent fire, and to ensure 'the better regulation, uniformity and gracefulness' of new building. The only echo of the grand urbanism for which Wren and Evelyn had hoped was the cutting of King and Queen Streets to make a single axis from the Guildhall porch to the river. For the rest, the approach was regulatory. It established a strict typology of streets, with buildings to match (Figure 2.6):

> Be it enacted:– that there shall be only four sorts of buldings and no more, and that all manner of houses to be erected shall be one of these four sorts of buildings and no other, (that is to say)
>
> (a) the first or least sort of house fronting by-lanes,
> (b) the second sort fronting streets and lanes of note,
> (c) the third sort fronting high and principal streets
> (d) the fourth and largest sort, of mansion houses for citizens or other persons of extraordinary quality not fronting either of the three former ways,
>
> the roofs of each of the said first, second and third sorts of houses respectively shall be uniform (Knowles and Pitt 1972: 31).

The Act laid the basis for a regularised street hierarchy, with High Streets (such as those around the Bank) 40 feet wide, 'Streets and Lanes of Note' 35 feet wide, and by-lanes 14 feet wide. The narrower alleys were to be enlarged to a width of 9 feet, straightened and paved with stone for foot-passages. The regulations prohibited the jutting projections so characteristic of English timber town houses. Thousands of pounds (at 5 shillings per square foot) were paid in compensation to owners to establish uniform frontage lines and turn medieval footways and alleys into lanes.

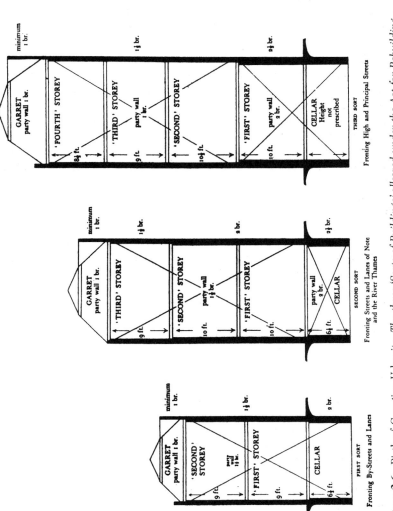

Figure 2.6 Birth of Georgian Urbanity. The three 'Sorts of Buildings' allowed under the Act for Rebuilding the City of London 1667. Freestanding mansions comprised a Fourth Sort. Source: CoL (1951: 153), by kind permission of the Corporation of London

The Act obliged owners to build houses of a uniform height and cornice line appropriate to the street, and it set out the legal basis (which still applies today) for the shared party walls of the resulting terraces. It prescribed materials, ceiling heights, wall thicknesses, and structural requirements such as the placing of joists. In contrast to the colourful individualism of Tudor and Stuart town houses, with their idiosyncratic gables and their flamboyant patterning of brickwork and timber, post-Fire housing would present an even brick facade, confining display to the detailing of door porches and fireplace surrounds.

Five years after the Great Fire, 12 000 houses had been built and the frontage line of the streets was almost continuous again. Work had started on the rebuilding of 44 livery company halls and 51 churches. Sir Christopher Wren designed 17 new churches in 1670 alone, and – with the close encouragement of Charles II – had begun work on the design for the new St Paul's, which he would live to complete in 1710 (Figure 9.4). 'London rises again,' reads the inscription on the Monument, 'whether with greater speed or greater magnificence is doubtful. Three short years complete that which was considered the work of an age.' Poems and ballads celebrated the glorious Phoenix (Aubin 1943), and the comparison with Paris was temporarily forgotten.

For all the vigour of the reconstruction, the Great Fire had permanently altered the relation between the walled City and extramural London. At least a quarter of the refugees never returned, and their numbers included a disproportionate number of nobility and gentry (who went west) and manufacturers (who went north and east). The 1667 Act had already tried to meet labour shortages by temporarily opening up the labour market to skilled tradesmen who were 'foreigners', not having served a seven-year apprenticeship within the City. Despite the protests of the Livery Companies, the open-door policy was extended in 1672 with sales of citizenship ('the freedom of the City') to overseas and provincial tradesmen at a discount price, and gratis to anyone who would transfer residence into the Square Mile.

The new blood, and the reconstruction boom, strengthened the London economy but they also exposed the ancient monopoly rights of the Corporation, prompting the City fathers into a rearguard campaign of writs, legal prosecutions and political opposition against all forms of economic development in the suburbs – markets, new Thames crossings, housing projects. The Fire reinforced both the institutional isolation of the ancient municipality, and its mercantile character. Grandees departed to the West End, where they could park their carriages and live in the correct style under the aegis of the royal court. Sir John Summerson (1988: ch. 4) detects in the architecture of the rebuilt City – with the glorious exception of its churches – the provincialism of 'foreigners' drawn in by the open door policy. A process of polarisation was occurring that would encourage the City's self-perception as a distinct, historically independent, trading republic, turning itself, as Michael Harrison (1965: 162) puts it rather neatly, 'inwards and outwards'.

The institutional culture of separateness and isolation from the other Londons of the court, the gentry and the industrial suburbs was symbolised by the wall and the ancient Bars (barriers) marking the limits of the Corporation's jurisdiction. When the Royalist General Monk entered the City in 1660, he removed the posts, chains and gates and jammed open the portcullises. The Corporation reinstated them and continued to repair the wall until 1760; for a further 80 years tolls were levied at the gates on carts not belonging to freemen. The enclosure was as much psychological as physical (Reddaway 1940). The remainder of London was ignored until it touched on City privileges. The Corporation's opposition to improvements such as the building of a bridge at Westminster in 1740–50 and the creation of the enclosed docks in the 1790s were to give it a curmudgeonly reputation which it has never quite shaken off.

LANDLORDS TO LONDON

Inigo Jones's projects at Greenwich and Whitehall were less significant contributions to London's development than his invention of the basic module for London's expansion for at least two and a half centuries, the classical residential terrace. His client was not the Crown but the Earl of Bedford, one of the select group of families of Tudor and Stuart courtiers who had caught the windfall privatisation of London's medieval green belt of hospitals, abbeys, priories, convents, and ecclesistical palaces. London's prime development land for the next two centuries, in an arc from Chelsea (owned by the Cadogans) to Hampstead (the Mansfields), belonged to a mere 35 landlords. More than the Crown, or the City, or any other authority, the growth of the capital was shaped by these new hereditary elites, the *Landlords to London* whose story is told by Simon Jenkins (1975).

The fourth Duke of Bedford led the way with the redevelopment of the former kitchen garden of Westminster Abbey, the Convent (later 'Covent') Garden in 1630. Inigo Jones, as architect, saw an opportunity to create an urban setpiece in the Continental manner – his models were the Piazza d'Armée in Leghorn (Livorno) and the Place Royale in Paris. Covent Garden was laid out as a piazza, with a church at one end and arcaded frontages around the other three sides. The deep Etruscan portico of St Paul's church still dominates the piazza – all the rest has gone. The most revolutionary feature of the design, in the context of British urbanism, was its use of building leases to impose a regular facade upon a mix of buildings, the Duke's own house and speculative housing of varying sizes, put up by several different builders. The combination of urban design and leasehold tenure allowed the Bedford family to harness the spending power of the new elites in Stuart London without compromising the integrity of their landed estate. Soon afterwards, Inigo Jones repeated the experiment on a smaller scale in the development of speculative housing around Lincoln's Inn Fields, halfway between the City and Westminster. Numbers 59 and 60 are neighbouring terraced houses, whose facades combine to present the frontage of a palace, Lindsay House. Sir John Summerson (1966) calls it proto-Georgian – 'the unacknowledged dictator of whole streets of houses in innumerable cities of the English speaking world'.

The prewar developments of Covent Garden and Lincoln's Inn Fields set a precedent that was vigorously pursued after the Restoration. The Earl of Southampton staked out the building lots for Bloomsbury Square in 1665, the Earl of Leicester started on Leicester Square in 1671, the Duke of Monmouth began the development of Soho Square in 1678, Edward Jermyn, Earl of St Alban's, created his hugely profitable St James's Square in 1684. Grosvenor Square followed in 1695 and Berkeley Square in 1698.

The rise of the aristocratic land developer stimulated in turn that of the speculating master-builder, who would take the ground-lease on a plot and build the shell of a house for sale on the open market to a final client. Most began as craftsmen, but the most active and unscrupulous speculator in the late seventeenth century was the medical doctor Nicholas Barbon (1640–98). He is also remembered for inventing fire insurance and as an economic theorist whose *Discourse of Trade* (1690), admired by Karl Marx, identified the effect of building development as a stimulant of general economic growth, a point well demonstrated by the prolific urban expansion of which he was a pioneer (Summerson 1988).

That suburbanisation of terraced streets and squares (Figure 2.7) was *The Unique City* celebrated by Stein Eiler Rasmussen. In the 1930s he found them despised and neglected. Today the surviving stock is safe under the protection of conservation controls, and its making and maintenance well covered in an extensive literature, notably Sir John Summerson's *Georgian London* (1988), Donald Olsen's *Town Planning in London* (1982), and *London, the Art of Georgian Building* by Dan Cruickshank and Peter Wyld (1975). Rasmussen's original interpretation holds good, with its emphasis on the chemistry of three elements: public regulation under the London Building Acts; private landlordism, in the freedom of landowners around London to develop their holdings; and consumer preference, expressed in the evolution of architectural taste through Palladianism, Roman and Italianate fashions.

Though Charles II's post-fire intervention formally applied only to the City it had as great an effect on the terraces and squares filling the fields westward from the Fleet to Mayfair. The Building Act was formally extended to the City of Westminster in 1700 and its geographical coverage continued to spread as London grew, though not for a further century to the poorer districts of the liberty of the Tower, today's East End (Rose 1951: 60). Successive updatings of the Acts had immediate, visible impacts on building style which can be tracked from street to street as the development frontier advanced outwards. Wooden eaves and cornices were outlawed in 1707. In 1709 a further revision required sash windows to be set back 4 inches into the wall. The legislation was consolidated in the London Building Act of 1774 which introduced the earliest example of a London-wide public agency, a team of 27 District Surveyors responsible for inspecting and approving every new

Figure 2.7 Trinity Church Square, Southwark. *One of the last and finest of the long sequence of 'Georgian' squares, it was built early in the reign of Queen Victoria and is preserved by ground landlordism in mint condition*

construction scheme across the 89 parishes of the metropolis (Cruickshank and Wyld 1975).

For a system conceived in haste as part of the emergency package of measures for the fire-desolated City, the London building control system proved remarkably well suited as a framework for long-term planning: not the direct setpiece design of Continental planning but as Andrew Saint puts it, 'a specifically English model of urbanism, perhaps the only fair one in a mercantile democracy where power is balanced in subtle ways, and the great hidden interests in urban development are those of trade, property and common law' (1991: 49). More by fortune than design, it meshed perfectly with the emerging process of estate development in the West End. Standardised building types allowed master-builders to achieve economies when running off building parts – Nicholas Barbon was a pioneer in mass-production of staircase joinery. Commoditisation eased the flow of capital investment into housing – yet again exemplified by Barbon, whose fire insurance premiums were based on the regulation building materials. The visual regularity of unbroken frontages and cornice lines helped to make a unified street out of the piecemeal efforts of hundreds of small-scale master-builders. As the eighteenth century advanced, estates became more adept at building the rhythm of narrow terraced houses into larger variations on the classical theme, until at Bedford Square (1775) they assembled into four complete palace fronts around central gardens.

The Georgian house expressed the relative fluidity of eighteenth-century British society, a world increasingly open to the talents of a large and prosperous middle class of traders, manufacturers, bankers, lawyers, parsons and office holders. In contrast to Paris, where the great landowners continued to live in palatial detachment of their town houses or *hôtels*, only the very grandest grandees lived in their own compound, the ducal palaces along the Strand, for example, or the mansions that lined the south side of Hyde Park: Colby House, Noel House, Grove House, Kingston House and Rutland House. The London address of the average English county family would be a terraced house of the first rate, handsome in scale and more fashionably located but identical in essential form to the humble fourth-rate home of an Admiralty clerk. In the words of Sir Albert Richardson (1911), one of their first twentieth-century admirers, the smallest houses showed the same intrinsic qualities as the largest: 'good proportions, suitability, direct design'. French eyes accustomed to measure status in terms of command of horizontal floorspace were amused by these vertical towers, whose residents ran up and down stairs and perched on the different storeys 'like birds in a cage' (Summerson 1988: 45). In its simplicity of design and materials, and its homogeneity of form, the house seemed a tangible expression of the English democratic spirit.

Londoners themselves, however, were acutely aware of the nuances of fashion and residence. The essential skill of town planning was, as Olsen (1982) shows, to establish social segregation at the outset by unity of layout and perpetuate it through estate management and eventual rebuilding. Olsen's work on the office records of the Bedford and Foundling estates shows landlords continually preoccupied to maintain the gentility of their areas and avoid the decline that occurred, for example, when the original Inigo Jones piazza on the Bedford Estate was taken over by a produce market. The layout of the squares was exclusionary: they were – until the late eighteenth century – gated enclaves, designed to convey an inner order. Owners were not concerned with the abutments and road connections with neighbouring estates, or with contributing to an overall street plan. Besides, the spread of estate development displaced the less well-off. The London poor, in Simon Jenkins's words, 'oozed into the leftover strips' between the great estates, crowding into the surviving courts and alleys of Holborn, Westminster, Southwark and other parts not purged by the Great Fire. The consequences are still visible on the ground:

> London's main streets today, in contrast to those of Paris or Rome, are visually uninspiring largely because immediately behind them lay such carefully protected graciousness and good taste. So little thought was given to planning these main thoroughfares that they still today follow precisely the wavering lines of the old cart-tracks, lanes and paths through the fields of the Abbots of Westminster (Jenkins 1975: 65).

Thanks to the combined effects of the Building Acts and landlord control, Hanoverian London was no longer unplanned in the sense John Evelyn had criticised, but its jigsaw of disconnected pieces still represented a powerful contrast to the orderly growth of Paris within the circumference of the *enceinte*, where Ledoux's line of fortifications, the sixth, was under development from 1785 onwards. In his *Tour Through the Whole Island of Great Britain* of 1724–7, Daniel Defoe (author of *Robinson Crusoe*) had deplored the amorphousness of London, spreading 'in a most confus'd manner, out of all shape, uncompact and unequal; whereas the City of Rome, though a monster for its greatness, yet was in a manner round, with very few irregularities in its shape'. Systematically surveying the fringe, he concluded London's sprawl had a 36-mile circumference, which could have been 28 miles if developed in a compact ordered manner (Defoe 1974: 321).

The late eighteenth century saw a revived concern with town planning. A leading campaigner, John Gwynne, obtained and published Christopher Wren's plan for the City after the Great Fire, with an emotive (and not altogether accurate) account of its betrayal by City vested interests. His book *London and Westminster Improved* (1766) was essentially the first attempt at an overall development plan for the capital. Its highly practical proposals form a direct link between the seventeenth-century visions for post-Fire London and the process of 'improvements', from the removal of the buildings from London Bridge in the mid-eighteenth century to the building of the Embankments a hundred years later (Summerson 1988: ch. 9).

Gwynn's chief hope, however, was that the overall expansion of London would be checked a new peripheral ring, the orbital by-pass being built around the north of the city in 1756–62 – the Marylebone, Euston, Pentonville and City Roads. The parliamentary bill to construct this toll-road included a provision to prevent residential development for 50 feet to either side of it. But inevitably, its frontages were soon developed, and estates spilling into the fields beyond, with Somers Town, Pentonville, Camden Town and Kentish Town, were already under construction in the 1790s.

Late eighteenth-century London was surveyed over a period of nine years by the cartographer Richard Horwood for the largest map ever printed in Britain – 32 sheets at 26 inches to the mile (Barker and Jackson, 1990). The map combines intimate detail of building plans, street names and even house-numberings with a sense of the immensity of an urban area which by now extended just beyond the New Road to the north, and from Hyde Park in the west to Blackwall in the east. Development was less compact south of the river, where timber yards monopolised the river frontage, and fields were still interspersed with building along the approach roads to London and Blackfriars Bridges. Where the terraces ended, the fields began. North of the river the open country might be half an hour's walk away, but Londoners did still walk out for fairs and sports, and – during the turbulent decades of radicalism – for public meetings such as the mass gatherings of the London Corresponding Society at Chalk Farm, Islington and St Pancras in 1790. Horwood's map shows many surviving traces of the historic girdle of nurseries and market gardens, some with monastic origins and centuries of cultivation. However, the main nurseries were all shifting further out, to locations such as Weybridge,

Turnham Green, Eltham, Hammersmith, Cheshunt, Barnet, Hackney, Leytonstone, and Lewisham, or to the provinces (Harvey 1974). Among them was William Cobbett, the Radical MP, agriculturalist and journalist, who moved his seed farm from Kensington to Ash in Surrey. Cobbett used to liken London to an inflamed and poisonous boil on the fair face of England – the 'Great Wen'. But in the 50 years after Cobbett's death in 1835, London was to grow further and faster than ever before. His Great Wen, the London mapped by Horwood, would soon seem like a lost arcadia.

THE NINETEENTH CENTURY

London took breath at the turn of the nineteenth century. The Napoleonic wars were a time of hiatus, with credit diverted to government stocks and timber to the shipyards. Confidence began to recover after 1805 as the threat of a French invasion receded (Figure 2.8). The curve of population growth began an immense, sustained climb that would continue at 10-year rates of increase of between 16% and 21% for seven decades on end. In 1800 the metropolitan population had just passed the million threshold. At the mid-century it exceeded 2.5 million, and by 1900 6.5 million.

In the previous two centuries London's experience of rapid urban growth had been unique within Britain. In the nineteenth century it no longer was. Higher rates, from lower base-lines, were being experienced in the mining and manufacturing districts of the midlands and the north: they, rather than London, were the main concern of the Parliamentary Commissioners who investigated the 'State of Large Towns and Populous Districts' in 1844–5. The factory system that transformed the midlands and north country was insignificant in London (though see Green 1996). In one of the famous metaphors in economic history the Industrial Revolution was like a storm that passed over the capital and broke elsewhere. But manufacturing did play a considerable part in the expansion of the capital, which was by absolute measures of output and employment the largest industrial region in Britain (Hall 1962; Schwarz 1992). The geography of workplaces and labour markets reflected the basic twin-city structure, with port-related industry to the east and skilled artisanal production of luxury goods to the west. London absorbed the advancing technology of the nineteenth century in a way that tended to reinforce its poly-centric, conglomerate, dispersed character (Sheppard 1971). Its real peculiarity was that deepening dichotomy between the economies of 'city' and 'town', the one with its shipping, trades, finance, and all the infrastructure of production, the other with its royal court, Parliament, home and overseas administration, clubs, social season, and all the Vanity Fair of consumption, each acting upon the other like the pistons of some mighty oscillating engine.

The comparison with Paris continued to fascinate. At the turn of the nineteenth century both cities renewed their interest in planning. For Paris, the stimulus was a post-Revolutionary discovery of the uses of spatial order to legitimate Republic and

Figure 2.8 New Cross. *Early nineteenth-century terraces (disfigured by late twentieth-century satellite dishes) climb the slopes of Telegraph Hill, where a semaphore station carried the news of the Battle of the Waterloo to London*

Empire; on the eve of the Battle of Waterloo, Napoleon was carrying on those monumental axes of the Bourbons, erecting the Arc du Carrousel in the Louvre courtyard and the Arc de Triomphe at the far end of the Champs Elysées. For London there were the less high-minded stimuli of fashion and commerce. Besides, the late Hanoverian monarchy had revived the Stuart interest in urban projects. The future George IV, as Prince Regent, laid out the most ambitious urban setpiece in the city's history, the *Via Triumphalis* or triumphal way from Carlton House by St James's Park, to Piccadilly Circus, Regent Street, Portland Place and into Regent's Park. The scale of the project was on a par with Paris, extending over two and a half miles from Buckingham Palace and Trafalgar Square up to the zoological gardens at the top of Regent's Park, but the style was distinctively English in its combination of the neo-classical and the picturesque. The Prince Regent planned his urban space for fashionable carriages, not marching troops. His architect, John Nash (1752–1835) laid out St James's Park and Regent's Park as informal spaces, and the axis between them bends to left and right as it goes. Regent's Park was by far the largest of the northward obtrusions across the New Road, a garden city the size of the City of London, with its own market, barracks, churches and entertainments. The residential accommodation combined grand freestanding mansions in the park with ranges of terraced housing around the edge, transfigured into white stuccoed palaces; it also included prototype suburban streets of picturesque villas set back from the road with front gardens, clustered as closely as the market would bear (Summerson 1988; Edwards 1981).

The romantic arcadianism of Regent's Park stimulated a scatter of villas and ornamental cottages around London. Unlike Napoleonic Paris, Regency London luxuriated in its openness to the countryside and the opportunity to live, as Dyos (1968) puts it, in 'a state of semidetachment' along the newly metalled roads out of town. But it was found that the lower density exposed both landlord and developer to higher risks. Long private gardens of villas on the Old Kent Road were soon filled up with alleyways, workshops and slums (Olsen 1982: 190). The villas of St John's Wood – London's first semidetached houses – became a raffish bohemia of painters and high-class brothels. Most early nineteenth-century development kept to the well-tried formula of the Georgian terrace. The most important link between old and new was the builder Thomas Cubitt, who built Belgravia, Eaton Square and Pimlico on 19 acres of market garden land between Knightsbridge and the Thames. Cubitt was a new sort of master-builder whose company (still existing) was vertically integrated with its own supply lines of building materials, and an army of 1000 workers on permanent employment. While the production processes were innovative, the product remained the essential London Building Act vertical house, dressed in stucco and composed into palatial terraces (Sheppard 1971).

Cubitt's conservatism was a compliment to the resilience of the great estates of Georgian London. Their tightly defined public domain of terraces, circuses and squares was easier to regulate than looser, more open forms. The leasehold system discouraged piecemeal modification of the building form. As the 99-year leases fell in they tended to be renewed for a second term – and in the twentieth century for a third. Nineteenth-century London developed from a resilient and stable core of privately run estates, with a framework of law and practice for property management which was to some extent – at least in the more favourable locations – able to compensate for the fragmentation of civic authority. In their accounts of the outward extension of estate development in nineteenth-century, Olsen (1983) and Sheppard (1971) convey the increasing uncertainty and risk of the leasehold system, whether of bankruptcy while housing was being built or of degeneration of finished properties into multioccupancy and – at worst – slumdom. The restrictive covenants controlling the use of premises and the positive covenants to ensure upkeep were progressively tightened: a typical agreement committed the lessee to 'repair, uphold, support, sustain, maintain, tile, slate, glaze, lead, paint, pave, purge, scour, cleanse, empty, amend and keep the . . . premises', requiring external paintwork to be repainted (three coats) every leap year and inside walls every seven years. Leases committed residents to pay rates and taxes and to take out insurance, and imposed stringent planning restrictions on the permitted use of buildings. Whether these provisions could be enforced depended partly on the vigour of the landowner, partly on social geography. To keep decay at bay, the public spaces of the more exclusive estates were tightly managed, with public entry controlled by gates, to the irritation of cabbies and other drivers. A conference agitating for the removal of estate gates estimated that there were over 150 such barriers in 1879. Most remained until the 1890s, when Parliament gave the London County Council powers to remove them (Olsen 1982: 145).

Cubitt's Belgravia, behind Buckingham Palace, was instantly and securely fashionable, but the wave of estate development rolled outwards into far less favourably located tracts: the Duchy of Cornwall's lands on the South Bank at Kennington, the Mercers Company's holdings in Stepney, the Bedford Estate's New Town north of Euston Road, Lord Tredegar's estate at Mile End, Thomas Cubitts's estate at Albion Road in Stoke Newington, the De Beauvoir estate off the Kingsland Road. Built in the 1830s and 1840s, these were modest schemes by the standards of the West End, but they showed the same concern to create a stable district that would attract respectable tenants at the outset and keep them for good. The streets are wide, landscaped squares provide focus, the houses are well detailed and the gardens deep. Such generous design in marginal districts could make economic sense only within the long time horizons of the ground landlord system, which judged the success of a scheme not by immediate profit but by reversionary value a century after development (Olsen 1982). Estate owners' concern for an enduring tone made for generous layout and a conservatism of architectural style. Classicism continued to dominate the residential sector half a century after the Gothic revival, giving such visual and morphological continuity between eighteenth and nineteenth centuries that, as Sir John Summerson puts it, Victorian London *was* Georgian London.

London at the time of the Great Exhibition in 1851 was a compact city of some 3 miles radius from Charing Cross. The solidly built-up area which fifty years before had extended northwards just to the City Road now lapped against the new east–west cutting for freight trains from the Docks to Birmingham and the North. River crossings at Blackfriars Bridge (1769), Vauxhall Bridge (1816), Waterloo Bridge (1817), Southwark Bridge (1819) and Brunel's Hungerford Suspension Bridge (1845) were transforming south London from a rural inlier into a symmetrical sector of the fully built-up metropolis.

The compact mid-century city was the nucleus of a larger urban structure whose limits already adumbrated the scope of modern London. Metalling of carriageways in the last years of stagecoach travel had stimulated a ribbon development of terraces, villas, pubs, shops, smithies, stables and nurseries along the frontages of all the main roads out of town. These tentacles – by no means complete – reached to Romford in the east, Orpington and Croydon in the south and Uxbridge in the west. The longest of them, along the old Cambridge road through Tottenham and Enfield, still reaches out beyond the edge of modern London a century and a half later – the E4 postal district mentioned above on page 4. In 1850 the hero of Charles Kingsley's novel *Alton Locke, Taylor and Poet* trudges along it impatient for the end: 'Each turn of the road opened a fresh line of terraces or villas, till hope deferred made the heart sick, and the country seemed – like the place where the rainbow touches the ground – always a little farther off' (1852: 107).

THE INSTITUTIONAL ANOMALY

The tentacular early nineteenth-century metropolis saw the first initiatives of institutional reform since Charles I's Corporation of the Suburbs. In 1829, an area of nearly 700 square miles – corresponding to the parishes within a 15-mile radius of Charing Cross – was established as a single police district with a constabulary under the control of the Home Secretary. It was the first metropolitan public service and by far the most enduring: 'the Met' keeps its original geographical basis to the present day, and its controversial direct control by the Home Secretary, (though that is under review at the time of writing). In 1833 the Registrar-General introduced a different definition of 'Greater London' for statistical purposes (1831 population: 1 776 556). Covering parishes within the 8-mile radius of St Paul's Cathedral, it was an extension of the Bills of Mortality, an early seventeenth-century monitoring system of London and its hinterland established to give the Court warning of epidemics (Fletcher 1844). The Registrar-General's definition was taken as the basis for a second London-wide public service, the Crown-appointed Metropolitan Commission of Sewers (1847).

Such *ad hoc* devices did not provide London with a municipal system to compare with provincial cities that had been reformed with modern boundaries in 1835–7. The City Corporation, always defensive of its ancient liberties, had fought off proposals by the Municipal Corporations Commissioners in 1837 to merge it with Westminster and the suburbs, and similar reform bills in 1839, 1856 and 1858. In 1835 the Corporation decided to sever its links with 600 acres (and 98 000 population) of Southwark on the south bank which had been incorporated as a City Ward since 1551, without voting rights. In the same spirit of withdrawal from wider London, the City resisted the imposition of the Metropolitan Police in 1829 (setting up its own police force for the Square Mile, which survives to this day) and the Metropolitan Commission of Sewers (again, establishing its own Medical Officer of Health in 1848).

The City's exemption from national reform was due partly to the political radicalism of a proud but diminishing community of independent small tradesmen, partly to a recognition by government that the Square Mile's concentration of money and markets made for special treatment. There was also the aspect which

Victorian cartoonists liked to caricature with the image of plump aldermen guzzling turtle soup, or – after Oliver Twist's adversary – the word 'Bumbledom' (Porter 1994: 244). With a declining resident population the City's ancient communal structures had lost civic meaning, leaving a well-endowed but rotten borough. With their ancient wealth, hereditary membership, chartered privileges, restrictive practices, anachronistic boundaries and ceremonial banquets, the Corporation and Livery Companies were a curiously resistant outcrop of the *ancien régime* at the epicentre of the modern market economy. Leading bankers and brokers, the Rothschilds, Barclays, Barings and their like, generally had little to do with the civic side of the Square Mile, but its encrusted institutional shell did ensure a high quality of local services for those inside, and it added an intangible dimension of ritual separation to the evolving relationship between an imperial government and the financial markets on which it depended (Kynaston 1994).

Whatever the underlying causes, the City's stance was decisive for the continuing debate about London's government (Briggs 1963; Davis 1988; Young and Garside 1982). It ensured that the rest of London would remain unreformed under a miscellany of authorities based on the old ecclesiastical parishes whose governing bodies, the vestries, were either self-elective or politically inert. A Royal Commission on the City of London, established in 1852, endorsed the localist perspective of London as a cluster of diverse civic entities, which should come together to provide joint services as the occasion demanded. This philosophy provided the basis in 1855 for an institutional reform very different from that applied to provincial cities: under the Metropolis Management Act, London's street improvements, drainage, paving, cleansing and lighting would be the responsibility of an upper-tier authority, the Metropolitan Board of Works, indirectly elected by the localities. Its geographical coverage was extensive, being based on the 120 square mile area which derived from the Bills of Mortality: but once again, there was a hole in the middle for several functions over which the City Corporation reserved exclusive powers.

So, at the mid-century, London's institutions were set in a pattern of diversity and difference. Young and Garside (1982: 20) quote the comment of the *Spectator* magazine in 1849 that London 'has ceased to be a unity . . . It is more a constellation or cluster of cities, each having its separate district and conditions of existence – physical, moral and political'. The debate about London government was a counterpoint between this motif and an alternative image of metropolitan unity. The great unifier was transport, and at mid-century London's transport revolution was only just about to begin.

THE TRANSPORT REVOLUTION

Familiar landmarks in the 1852 Great Exhibition maps of London are the railway stations, with all their connotations of travel and arrival. London Bridge Station (1836) was the newly created gateway to Kent and the Channel ports, Waterloo

(1848) to Southampton and the south coast, Paddington (1838) to Bristol and the West Country, Euston (1837) to Birmingham and the North West, King's Cross (1852) to the East Midlands and Yorkshire, Bishopsgate (1847) and Fenchurch Street (1841) to East Anglia.

While the very first railway lines in the 1830s were local, short-distance links from Greenwich and Blackwall, most effort in the railway mania of the 1840s went into long-distance transport. The wide spacing of the London railway termini, around a circumference of some 11 miles, represented a compromise between the property interests of the ground landlords and the desire of the new railway companies to arrive and depart from the heart of town, as stagecoaches had done. Resistance was weakest to the east and south of London, where residents were poor, landownership was more fragmented, and the lie of the ground allowed lines to be brought in overhead on brick viaducts, avoiding the expense and difficulty of closing off rights of way. The Blackwall Railway passed close by the Tower of London to within a few hundred yards of the Bank of England; the South Eastern Railway reached across the Thames to place its station at Charing Cross, the point conventionally regarded as the geographical dead centre of London. But railways entering from the north could get no closer to the City than the lee of Islington Hill, where Euston, King's Cross and St Pancras Stations lined up along the northern edge of the Bedford estate. Brunel's Great Western Line could penetrate only to Paddington, more than 2 miles from Charing Cross and almost 4 from the Bank (Sheppard 1971; Olsen 1982).

The speed of rail travel contrasted with the extreme congestion and inconvenience of travel between termini or to final destinations. Repeated calls for action to bring the lines together into a grand central terminus – a *Hauptbahnhof* – were (characteristically for London) frustrated by commercial rivalry and the absence of a central municipal authority. More by fortune than design, it had a beneficial consequence of stimulating, in 1863, the next phase in London's railway development, the creation of the underground railway system (Simmons 1973). The Metropolitan Railway began as a cut-and-cover tunnel joining far-flung Paddington to Farringdon Street on the north-eastern corner of the Square Mile. It was so hugely successful, carrying 9 million passengers within twelve months of its opening in 1863, that the District Railway at once opened a parallel line to the south, linking Hammersmith to the City by way of Victoria and Charing Cross stations. Twenty years later the two companies combined into the Circle Line. The Cities of London and Westminster were symbolically wedded in a loop of comfortable, frequent railway trains which transformed distance and accessibility within the central area. The circle made a frame for links extending outwards in all directions. The process began in 1890 with the first electrified underground line, from Bank to Stockwell, subsequently extended to Clapham Common and Morden. In 1900 the Central Railway opened its deep-tunnelled 'Twopenny Tube' from Bank through the heart of the West End all along the north of Hyde Park to Shepherd's Bush, and the next 7 years took the Hampstead Line out from Charing Cross to Golders Green.

Meanwhile, the surface railways had opened up their tracks and their termini for local stopping trains with suburban destinations, and were switching to electric traction. The southern railway companies took the lead: having less hinterland, shorter main lines and comparatively little freight traffic, their profits were more dependent on commuter travel, and they had more scope for suburbanisation in the relatively underdeveloped sector beyond Southwark and Lambeth. Surface railways also opened up the less fashionable and more polluted sector to the north-east of the City. In the early 1860s the Great Eastern Railway Company wanted to move its terminus at Bishopsgate a little closer towards the Square Mile, at Liverpool Street. The project involved the displacement of many hundreds of poor residents at a time of growing concern about the problem of housing and homelessness. Parliament did not require the company to rehouse the evacuees but it did impose a condition obliging it to run daily trains from the suburbs at cheap workmens' fares (a twopenny return). A similar obligation had been imposed on the London Chatham & Dover Company in 1860 and was extended to all lines under the Cheap Trains Act of 1883. The Great Eastern truly built its business on mass transit, fuelling suburbanisation with ten times its statutory requirement of workmen's trains (Simmons 1973).

In the 1870s, while the suburban railway network continued to grow, competitors began to lay street tracks for horse-drawn trams. Electric traction was introduced in 1901 and by 1905 London had 28 tram routes in service, with densest coverage in the new London south of the river. With their frequent stops and cheap fares, trams gave a strong stimulus to the development of local sub-economies, creating a pattern of shopping and services along radial corridors which was to become one of the most distinctive features of London's morphology. Each improvement in the infrastructure reinforced the habit of travel and the volume of demand. In the last two decades of the nineteenth century the total number of trips more than trebled, from 256.4 million to 819.2 million (Green 1991: 12).

TO THE SUBURBS!

The fixed-rail public transport network – tram, rail and underground – more than doubled the mean radius of London from 3 miles in 1850 to 7 miles at the turn of the century. The physical effect is vividly clear in 21 successive editions of the large-scale map (6 inches to the mile) produced by the cartographer Edward Stanford of Charing Cross between 1862 and his death in 1904. As London spreads, its scale and density diminishes. Looking back 60 years from 1909, Walter Besant (1909: 5) calculated that 'continuous London' had multiplied by six, its population by two and a half.

Apart from those tentacles along the main roads, land development prior to 1850 had still been largely monopolised by the ring of large estates within walking or riding distance of town. Now it opened out to involve thousands of proprietors in the metropolitan region, building for the clerk, shopkeeper, teacher or artisan. A girdle of small terraces spread right around London, stretching southwards to meet the middle-class villas on the higher ground of Wimbledon, Sydenham and Lewisham, and eastwards in the immense hinterland of suburbia created by the Great Eastern Railway's fares policy: Tottenham, Edmonton, Wood Green, and Haringay on one side of the River Lea, Stratford, Walthamstow, Leyton and Leytonstone and Forest Gate on the other, and still further east across the River Roding, West Ham and East Ham, Plaistow and Barking. Railway and tramway suburbanisation produced outliers which reach from Ruislip (west) to Romford (east), and from Waltham Cross (north) to Croydon (south) leaving it for the twentieth century to paint in the gaps of a 600-square-mile metropolis. In the eighteenth century Pope's villa at Twickenham offered the archetype of suburban living: late nineteenth-century London gave the world its first taste of mass suburbia (Fishman 1987).

It was a push and pull process. The market was driven by intense economic and social pressures at the centre as living space was sliced away by railway building, river embanking, warehouse, office and factory development, and road improvement (Kellett 1969). The displacement of resident population, common to all cities, was most intense in London because of its nodal position in the railway network, and its status as the premier port and distribution centre for imports: as the national manufacturing economy expanded, so did the demand for goods-handling space. The squeeze on the London poor was worse because of those exclusive private enclaves of the great estates, impermeable (as they hoped) to the ecological process of invasion and succession. Olsen (1982) shows how the Bedford Estate north of Holborn struggled to maintain low occupation densities and high rents while in the neighbouring Northampton Estate in Clerkenwell, the ground landlord's elaborate covenants (see page 36 above) could not stop the building up of back gardens and the subdivision of dwellings as 'lodging house dry rot' set in. A landlord might regain the initiative by slum clearance and redevelopment of model tenements for 'respectable mechanics' (as in the Peabody Trust's dwellings for the Bedford Estate on Drury Lane) but this purging only worsened conditions beyond the estate boundaries.

So in the second half of the nineteenth century, as prosperity rose, the living conditions of the London poor deteriorated. The third of the population earning less than a pound a week was forced to crowd into residual spaces – back alleys, fringe zones, multioccupied old buildings, and the dead-ends between old estate boundaries and new infrastructure improvements (Stedman Jones 1971; Wohl 1977; Yelling 1986). Charles Booth's poverty investigation in the 1880s revealed the abject conditions of these districts where every house was 'filled up with families' and every back garden overbuilt with courts and slums.

Space standards in the new suburbs, by contrast, were relatively high. The average London terraced house was built to more generous proportions than its Manchester or Birmingham counterpart. Densities of only 25 persons to the acre contributed to the relative overall healthiness of the capital's population and its high rate of natural growth, particularly when compared with Paris (Lees 1973:

416). In a city rigidly regulated by class convention, a suburban address held out the promise of health and esteem to the clerk, the small tradesman, the artisan, and the shopkeeper (Olsen 1982). But the new suburbs lacked the mechanisms and expertise for social control deployed by managers of the great estates. The flux of social geography was relentless. The brothers Grossmith captured the strains of keeping it at bay in one of the funniest books in the English language, *Diary of a Nobody* (1892), chronicling Charles and Carrie Pooter's struggle to maintain the 'correct tone' in Brickfield Terrace, Holloway. 'Suburban respectability' in the words of H.J. Dyos (1961: 23) 'was largely a matter of the right address and possession of it was the source of an indefinable satisfaction which did not evaporate until the social structure of the suburb was unbalanced by the emigration of its top people and the immigration of a different breed of newcomers from some inner suburb. This social leapfrogging made the suburb one of the transit camps of modern society.'

London was the first city to discover the self-reinforcing nature of suburban growth. Each extension of the building frontier exerted a disequilibrating effect on districts within, stimulating further demand (Konvitz 1984). As demand pushed outwards, landowners and developers rushed in to meet it. Building land was cheap and plentiful, and investment capital available in abundance. Already by 1854 London had over 400 building societies. Large capitalists might look to shares, gilts or consols, but for security and 3% growth the savings of the mass of small investors were channelled by solicitors and trustees into property investment. Declining world commodity prices after 1875 released more real income to invest. Money flowed from all over Britain through the London law firms into suburban property speculation. Dyos and Reeder (1973: 378) liken it to the delta of a great river system, 'made fertile by deposits collected in distant places and carried along irreversibly by superior force'.

The new suburbs of outer London were different in kind from the model of estate development that had dominated for the previous century and a half. The great majority of firms operated in a very small way, working a freehold plot or block at a time. To stimulate the market, builders put variety into the detailing of doors, porches and window bays. Layouts were generally a monotonous elongated grid based on bye-law requirements (Figure 2.9). H.G. Wells grew up in the middle of 'this mercenary eruption' (above a crockery shop at 47 High Street, Bromley) and was at once its greatest chronicler and harshest critic (Briggs 1963):

> To most Londoners of my generation these rows of jerry built unalterable houses seemed to be as much in the nature of things as rain in September and it is only with the wisdom of retrospect that I realise the complete irrational scrambling planlessness of which all of us who had to live in London were the victims (Wells 1934: 275).

Not quite all. In the high-status inner suburbs to the west of London, the sequence of spacious classical terraces continued through Bayswater and Kensington in the

44
—

Figure 2.9 Home Sweet Home. *Town planners sought to replace London's 'obsolete' Victorian terraces with standardised mass housing. Instead, householders have extended their life by a process of piecemeal improvement which leaves no two dwellings identical – at least from the rear*

1860s to Earl's Court in the 1880s. Street trees – generally avenues of London planes – became a standard feature, competing for light and space with an increasingly ornamented terrace architecture (Figure 2.10). In reaction, wealthy taste shifted back to the Regency types of the freestanding villa and the semidetached house. Jonathan Carr's speculative development at Bedford Park, begun in 1875, was an early example of the new planned suburbia: a verdant scheme built around existing mature trees, its twin-gabled semidetached houses, without basements, set back in their own gardens. Taste for the house and garden developed most strongly along the Thames Valley to the west of London, where royal parklands, river pleasures, and fast suburban rail connections to Waterloo and the City laid the basis for a stockbroker belt of low-density suburbia. All around London, higher ground and oases of green spaces (the two often went together) attracted fringes of low-density middle-class housing. Protection of the spaces themselves became an active political issue in the 1860s as the suburban development wave threatened to engulf all that remained of the historic girdle of parks, woods and commons (Crowe 1987). As the century progressed, the geographical distribution of the professional and business classes shifted further and further out from the centre, scattering to railway suburbs or freestanding country residences such as Robin Hill in John Galsworthy's *Forsyte Saga* (1922) and Howards End in E.M. Forster's novel of that name (1910).

Figure 2.10 London Planes. Platanus acerifolia *was a favourite shade-tree in ancient Greece and Rome. Because its shiny leaves and self-renewing bark proved resilient to soot pollution it became the staple of eighteenth-century squares and nineteenth-century avenues. Here in Lotts Road, Chelsea, its shade dapples the eclectic bays, balconies, turrets, classical pilasters and gothic crockets of late Victorian terraces*

Galsworthy and Forster between them capture the balance of attitudes at the end of the century. The Forsytes are a bourgeois dynasty founded by a Dorset stonemason who comes to London as a builder early in Queen Victoria's reign and makes a small fortune which his sons compound in the City of London – in the tea trade, law, property, and stock investments. They live in an arc around Hyde Park, a few minutes' reach from their clubs in St James's. The ring of Westminster properties embodies the success of the Forsytes and the certainties of their world. Margaret Schlegel's London, in *Howards End*, offers no certainties:

> 'The house opposite has been taken by operatic people. Ducie Street's going down, it's my private opinion.'
> 'How sad! It's only a few years since they built those pretty houses.'
> 'Shows things are moving. Good for trade.'
> 'I hate this continual flux of London. It is an epitome of us at our worst – eternal formlessness: all the qualities, good, bad and indifferent, streaming away – streaming, streaming for ever. That's why I dread it so' (1910: 171).

UNIFICATION AT LAST

Dread was a dominant literary response to nineteenth-century London. The affection that Swift, Pope, Gray and Johnson felt for the eighteenth-century city or Verlaine, Baudelaire and Rimbaud for contemporary Paris finds few echoes in Victorian literature. Dickens loved to explore its streets and mine its characters, but his London was always a dark and turbulent setting for the human drama. William Morris's political radicalism was driven by revulsion with the dull regimentation of London streets and their hangdog occupants – 'joyless, hopeless, shameless, angerless, set in their stare' (words from *The Pilgrims of Hope* 1886). The literary cliché of London combined a bourgeois fear of the power of the masses with regret for arcadia dispoiled by sprawl and smoke-pall, as here in Roden Neal's *Lay of Civilisation* (1874):

> This huge black whirlpool of the city sucks
> And swallows, and encroaches evermore
> On vernal field, pure air and wholesome heaven –
> A vast dim province, ever under cloud,
> O'er whose immeasurable unloveliness
> His own foul breath broods sinister like Fate
> (cited by Strange 1973: 479).

In the last quarter of the century this dark literary perception of London combined with the moral appeal of social reformers and philanthropists exposing the abject living conditions of the poor. Andrew Mearns's pamphlet *The Bitter Cry of Outcast London* (1883) had a most powerful and immediate impact, leading directly to the first building of workers' housing by local authorities, and to measures to protect green spaces and open up squares and churchyards for Londoners. Above all, by pushing the 'social question' up the political agenda it reopened the issue of the interconnectedness of metropolitan life. The London economy depended on the casual labour of a inner-city population denied tolerable housing. The divisions of London government forced the poorest areas with the least services to pay the highest taxes:

> The glitter of the West end in the 1880s and '90s sharpened the sense of contrast with the East . . . The 'two worlds' of London, one dark and mysterious, the other dazzling and ostentatious, were of increased public interest just because late-Victorian London was being thought of more and more as a 'world city' (Briggs 1963: 326–8).

The issue of London reform had been shirked in 1835–7. Half a century later, exposures of corruption in the vestries and the Metropolitan Board of Works brought it to a head. In 1884 Parliament debated a London Government Bill which would have made the Corporation of London a directly elected council for the metropolis. It was bitterly opposed by City interests, including leading bankers and financiers of the Square Mile who usually kept their distance from Corporation matters (Kynaston 1994: 370). The next round of local government legislation, in 1888, established a system of elected county councils for the historic shires of England and Wales. This time London was included, in three short clauses which abolished the discredited Board of Works and put a directly elected County Council in its place, with a jurisdiction of 117 square miles, slightly larger than the Registrar-General's (i.e. Bills of Mortality) definition of the metropolis. The City Corporation was left untouched as an island of autonomy in the heart of the new County of London (Davis 1988; Young and Garside 1982).

At the moment of its designation, the LCC broadly matched the full extent of the continuous built-up area reaching west to Roehampton, east to Plumstead, north to Stoke Newington, and south to Upper Norwood. For the first time, the administrative boundary matched the urban reality. Contemporaries were vividly aware of the historical significance of this event. The new county was presented as the culmination of a centuries-long effort to align the legal and statistical definitions of London with the urban reality (Whale 1888). Laurence Gomme, the promising Board of Works officer who rose rapidly to become Clerk of the LCC in 1900, was also a folklorist and constitutional historian. For him, the LCC reincarnated the democratic spirit of the medieval charters, and traditions of citizenship as ancient as the Saxon and Roman origins of the city. The Corporation of London had betrayed this legacy. The living principle had passed to a larger and nobler London, 'the greatest self-governing local community in the world' (Gomme 1907: 394).

THE LAST SIX MILES

CHAPTER 3

THE LAST SIX MILES

The first elections to the London County Council attracted a good spread of candidates, with businessmen and professionals in equal number, various celebrities, and some representation of the peerage and the aristocracy of labour. Remarkably, 14 of the 137 new councillors were also members of parliament. The Progressives, a metropolitan coalition of Liberals and Fabian socialists, won political control and held it until 1907. Within the restraints of the tax base and the legal powers available, they gave London a taste of the active local government which had already transformed Birmingham, Manchester and Leeds. 'They worked with zeal, the most lively of them holding that a County Council "ought to be driven night and day like an Atlantic liner between New York and Liverpool"' (Briggs 1963: 350). The Fabian Sidney Webb urged his colleagues on to great schemes of municipal ownership and action. The LCC made an early start in council housing. Water, gas and electricity utilities proved too complex to municipalise, but they did purchase the various private tramway companies, electrifying them to create a single, modern transport network under collective ownership. John Burns, one of the council's few working-class members, had been a tram-driver and was keenly aware of the role of transport in civic unification (Winter 1993: 191). Parks, playgrounds, playing-fields, road improvements, technical training, paddle-steamer riverbuses and slum clearance were other areas of municipal progress under unified London government (Saint 1989).

There were, however, far more obstructions to civic unity in London than in the great provincial cities. The parochialism of the vestries was stimulated by the LCC's expansion of municipal action and the consequent rise in rates (property taxes) and redistributive transfers across the city. For all Laurence Gomme's appeal to ancient communal memory, there were more votes to be won in London from local than metropolitan interest. The Conservative Party, having failed to win control of the LCC, aligned itself with the localist cause. Under cover of the London Municipal Society it built an effective and durable political axis between the (nominally independent) Corporation of London and the grassroots Tories – tradesmen and small proprietors – who managed local affairs in the parochial vestries (Young 1975). In 1899 Lord Salisbury put this municipalist interest on a modern statutory footing in a further round of reform. The small-scale vestries and district boards were combined into 28 metropolitan boroughs deliberately intended to provide, with the City of London at their head, a political counterweight to the central LCC (Figure 3.1). His act scotched any hopes that the County Council would in due course amalgamate the historic Corporation of London into its contemporary jurisdiction. The 1899

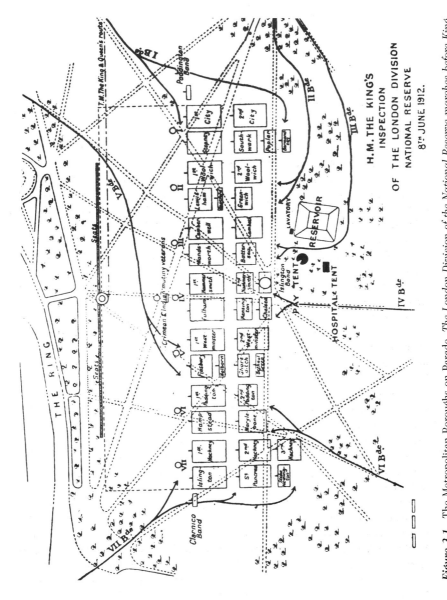

Figure 3.1 The Metropolitan Boroughs on Parade. *The London Division of the National Reserve marches before King George V at the Royal Review on 8 June 1912. Each borough raised at least one battalion, Hackney raised three*

two-tier settlement gave the City a new lease of life, creating a system of permanent ambiguity in the issue of who would speak and act for London (Davis 1988).

A second factor which undermined the territorial integrity of the LCC was suburbanisation. The areal limits of the County of London had seemed generously drawn, but the tide of building was already spilling over them in 1888 and the pace of growth was about to be accelerated by electrification of the tramways and railway lines, extension of the Underground, and the revolution in road transport, trends thoroughly documented and analysed in the eight volumes of the Royal Commission on London Traffic in 1903–5 (PP 1905).

Ignoring the Commission's recommendations for strategic intervention, the government left railway companies, the newly electrified tramways and the rapidly expanding fleets of motor buses – London already had 1000 by 1900 – to slog it out for market share (Simmons 1973). The railways' strategy was to lengthen their commuter networks. In five hectic years from 1900 to 1905 the entrepreneur Charles Tyson Yerkes brought an influx of US capital to electrify the District Railway and build the Bakerloo and Piccadilly Lines. Yerkes was also responsible for the boldly conceived Hampstead Line, which extended all the way under the Heath to open up a new development front beyond the rim of the London basin at Golders Green. Jackson (1974: 74) calculates that it raised land values from an agricultural value of £150–250 per acre to £10 000 per acre or £1000 per plot. To the east, where building land could be had for £500 per acre, the overground railway lines leading to Broad Street and Liverpool Street continued to feed the vigorous suburbanisation of south Essex. Builders and estate agents mobilised to meet the requirements of the London commuter, and from 1908 the Homeland Association published regular residential search guides on *Where to Live Round London*, answering the footloose householder's questions about train fares and frequencies, local rates, utilities, golf courses and schools.

In 1900–10 the LCC area began to show a net loss of population while the region beyond its boundary was growing by an annual 50 000. The County actively supported the dispersal trend. It extended the system of travel subsidies for suburban trains and trams, and as a pioneer of municipal landlordism from 1890 onwards it was a large-scale housebuilder on peripheral greenfield sites. LCC estates at Totterdown Fields in Tooting, and Old Oak at Wormwood Scrubs were within its boundaries but schemes in the south at Norbury in Croydon and up north at White Hart Lane in Tottenham were extraterritorial. Their location was only partly due to the price and difficulty of land assembly within the built-up area. It also reflected a powerful and lasting political reaction to the issue of overcrowding. LCC estates provided low-density cottage housing with gardens. With their grass verges and privet hedges, they were a distinctively English attempt to improve the lot of working-class households by transfer from an urban to a suburban environment (Swenarton 1981).

The alternative to cottages was flats. The turn of the century saw profitable development of French-style apartments for the middle classes in favourable locations near the river and open spaces such as Hyde Park and Battersea Park. Some of the early council schemes for the working classes were developed at high density in the five-storey tenement block form pioneered by philanthropic providers of 'model dwellings' such as the Peabody Trust, the Artisans' Dwellings Society, the Guinness Trust, the Four Per Cent Industrial Dwellings Co. and the East End Dwellings Company. The most striking scheme from an architectural point of view was the LCC's Boundary Estate built in 1897–1900 a little to the north of Bishopsgate. With its shops and services, polychromatic brickwork, and streets radiating from a central circus with park and bandstand, the estate is a superb piece of urban design, at a density of 200 people per acre. But the LCC for that very reason regarded it as a second-best solution suitable only for the minority of workers who needed to live near the centre, 'the quiet poor' as Booth (1903: 176) called them.

LCC housing philosophy had a pronounced anti-urban flavour. Parisian pleasure boulevards had no place in Progressive London. Alongside the utilitarian concern with overcrowding and public health ran a moralistic desire to protect the working class from the pernicious environments of pavement, pub and music-hall (Saint 1989: ch. 12). The more developed their civic consciousness, the more reformers used rhetoric 'which presumed the street to be a source, or *the* source, of urban ills' (Winter 1903: 153). The final volume of Charles Booth's *Survey of London*, published in 1903, argued for 'expansion' as the one and only cure to overcrowding, congestion, squalor, poverty, disease and degeneracy: first a physical, bricks and mortar expansion, then the administrative enlargement to embrace a population of eight or more millions as citizens of London:

> The further need, which includes everything else, is the mental expansion which will make full use of opportunities. We want to see London spreading itself over the Home Counties, not as an escape from evil left behind, but as a development of energy which will react for good over the whole area as it now exists, even in its blackest and most squalid centres (Booth 1903: 204).

These arguments carried broad appeal to temperance reformers, eugenicists, Imperialists, Ruskinites, proponents of Christian Civics, Progressives and Conservatives. Ebenezer Howard's scheme of self-financing Garden Cities, siphoning off London's population through a voluntary programme of mass colonisation, was only the most ambitious of the dispersal strategies. While Howard pursued his prototype Garden City 40 miles out of London at Letchworth, Henrietta Barnett was building Hampstead Garden Suburb besides Yerkes's Hampstead Line, and working-class cooperators with philanthropic support from the Great Western Railway were building their own Garden Villages at Hayes and Acton. Speculative builders soon caught on, prompting LCC bye-laws against using the names 'garden' and 'grove' other than for green, low-density schemes (Jackson 1974: 201).

So, the establishment of the first metropolitan government did not imply any institutional check upon London's process of suburbanisation: quite the opposite.

While the old Corporation clung reverently to its antique boundaries, the capital's new elites had an expansionist and dynamic vision of the city (Gomme 1907). H.G. Wells, the Fabian who so disliked the 'planlessness' of the suburban streets he grew up in, hailed the telephone and motorcar as agents of dispersal, low density, and delocalisation, 'a new and entirely different phase of human distribution': the epoch of the *urban region*, with London as its prototype (1901: 40).

THE LONG WEEKEND

The prophesied diaspora was renewed in earnest after the 1918 Armistice. The armaments industry vacated a score of large industrial sites in and around the edge of London, fully serviced and ripe for factory development. Wartime precedents of public estate development for munitions workers – London's largest was at Well Hall in Eltham – paved the way for council housing to be subsidised by government on a substantial scale, removing the financial difficulties which had impeded the LCC's prewar cottage estates. Public works relief for the unemployed in the aftermath of demobilisation was used by the Metropolitan Railway to extend its line from Wembley Park to Stanmore, and by the Underground Group (Yerkes's empire) to underwrite by £5 million the costs of extending the Hampstead Line's extension north to Edgware, and (in 1924) south to Morden. Unemployment relief also stimulated an ambitious programme of road construction, under the prewar statutory provisions of the Development & Road Improvement Act (1909). Rapid progress was made in implementing a series of radial highway schemes identified by the Greater London Arterial Road Conference 1912–16; New Cambridge Road (London to Cheshunt), Barnet Bypass (Hampstead to Hatfield), Watford Bypass (Elstree to Kings Langley), Western Avenue (West London to Uxbridge), the Great West Road (Chiswick to Hounslow), Staines Road (West Hounslow to Staines) and Chertsey Road (Twickenham to Chertsey). Other schemes launched in the 1920s were the North Circular Road (Finchley to Wembley), Eastern Avenue, Sidcup Bypass, Croydon Bypass, and Kingston Bypass. Built on cheap agricultural land, the roads were generously engineered as dual carriageways, 37 metres (120 feet) wide with bicycle lanes, planted verges and parallel sliproads for access and parking.

The Road Board had unwittingly laid runways for the take-off of British mass consumerism: frontage sites around London were the prime location for the new type of assembly industries using electric power and semi-skilled labour to produce convenience foods and electrical accessories for the suburban household, their white facades floodlit in vivid, permanent publicity (Smith 1933). Wembley Stadium is the most enduring symbol of the era (Figure 3.2). Built in reinforced concrete, it was the centrepiece of the 1924–5 British Empire Exhibition, a huge event with 15 miles of streets on an out-of-the-way 132-acre site well beyond the County boundary. Its displays included a Ford assembly line, an all-electric house,

Figure 3.2 Wembley Stadium. *The architecture of the British Raj in reinforced concrete. Redolent of footballing glories, the twin towers are to be preserved within a total redevelopment of the National Stadium by Sir Norman Foster*

model kitchens, neon lights, a Palace of Engineering – 'the largest concrete building in the world' – and a life-size sculpture of the Prince of Wales in New Zealand butter. Thinly attended despite these attractions, the exhibition site was sold off after losses of £1.5 million to become one of the main nuclei of the thriving West London factory belt (Weightman and Humphries 1984).

The London region's economic growth in the two decades after 1918 was exceptionally strong for reasons discussed more fully in Chapter 6. The world dominance of the manufacturing industries of the Midlands and the North had been broken. Countermagnets to London for most of the nineteenth century, they would now become net exporters of population to a new industrial heartland. In the words of a contemporary geographer 'a new inward flow of population met the older outward movement from the heart of London, and the two movements met in the "Outer Ring", that is in Greater London outside the bounds of London County. A million people were added to the population of the Outer Ring in the 10 years 1921–31 – as many as the whole population of Birmingham, England's second city' (Thornhill 1935: 101). By 1939 one in five of the population of Great Britain was a Londoner and half of them lived in 'those vast new wildernesses of glass and brick', as George Orwell described them, 'the new red cities of Greater London' (Green 1991: 24).

While factory development spread along main roads and river valleys, the interstices filled with a thick, even layer of suburbia. At first it was the London County Council which took the lead, redoubling its out-County building efforts under the council housing provisions of the 1919 Addison Act. Municipal production of housing for the workers was energetically scaled up. In LCC estate developments at Roehampton, Bellingham (Catford), Becontree, Watling, White City, Bromley (the Downham Estate) and Morden (the St Helier Estate), Arts and Crafts cottages and gardens were incongruously mass-produced by the tens of thousands. The quality of the individual dwellings was high, but in contrast to the closely parallel postwar housing drive in Dutch cities, the estates lacked shops, schools, social centres, churches, employment and soul. Coordination of housing with electric tramlines was patchy (Pollins 1964). The largest estate, far to the east at Becontree, was the worst provided (Home 1997). Financial constraints on the LCC and other providers of council housing led to a slackening of estate development and a return to flat building after 1930. At its peak year, 1927, the output of municipal developers had already been overtaken by the private sector.

The private enterprise housing boom exceeded all the expectations of the late Victorian dispersalists. Never before or since has the British building industry enjoyed such a favourable combination of cheap land, cheap labour, cheap money, plentiful transportation infrastructure and minimal planning control. An arrangement between developers and building societies (the 'builders' pool') extended the scope of owner-occupation to lower-middle-class householders who were on a weekly wage rather than a monthly salary. The system no longer required purchasers to make advance cash payments of 25%: 95% mortgage advances became normal (Thorns 1972). The London speculative building market was a seedbed for many leading names of the twentieth-century construction industry: Richard Costain, a Liverpool builder, entered in the mid-1920s with Selsdon Garden Village (Croydon) and the Elm Park estate (Hornchurch); John Laing & Sons of Carlisle, an established civil engineering contractor, turned to speculative building in 1929 with estates at Colindale, Sudbury, Golders Green and Woodford; Frank Taylor (Taylor Woodrow) came south from Blackpool in 1930 to build the Grange Park Estate in Hayes, and within five years was one of the largest volume builders in suburban London. Other small-scale builders who expanded on the back of the boom were Wates, Wimpey, Henry Boot, Comben & Wakeling and Gleeson (Jackson 1974).

In terms of design, the benchmark for suburban housing estates was set by the municipal sector's pitched-roof brick cottages, set back behind front gardens at densities of twelve to the acre (Figure 3.3). Speculative builders, working to tight margins in a highly competitive market, had to match the state sector in the provision of gardens while adding such tokens of private ownership as sunburst gates, stained-glass hall windows, hung tiles, and gables with half-timbering (actually creosoted floorboards): a distinctive mix, as Arthur Edwards (1981: 127) puts it, of 'elaboration and meanness'. Developers evoked country living with their street names – Roseleigh, The Dell, Willowside, Fernbank – as landscape features, trees and hedges were grubbed out and terrain levelled. Only at the top end of the speculative market (elevated outer locations like Ham, Keston or Barnet) were mature trees incorporated into estate layout. Clear-site development and hard surfacing was often a regulatory requirement of small suburban councils concerned to minimise maintenance costs. New schemes looked all the more barren when councils began to take motorisation into account, pushing the line of new building further back from the road to protect drivers' sightlines (Edwards 1981: 108).

The rawness of this new 'outer London' was mitigated by the quantity of earlier development within the 14-mile radius. The main road corridors had their ribbons of coaching inns, smithies, shops and villas. London's countryside was peppered with the conspicuous consumption of merchants, jobbers, nabobs, and adventurers from Tudor times onwards. Some country houses were preserved by suburban local authorities as museums or public buildings, and many pleasure grounds became municipal parks. Outer London was well endowed with open land – commons, woodland or heath – surviving either through popular struggle or through philanthropic action. One beneficial effect of the threat of abolition in the 1870s had been to prompt the City Corporation into an uncharacteristic display of public-spiritedness on behalf of open spaces for the enjoyment of Londoners. It acquired West Ham Park in 1873, the 6000 acres of Epping Forest in 1878, Burnham Beeches in 1880, Coulsdon Commons in 1883, Highgate Wood and Queen's Park, Kilburn, in 1888 and West Wickham Common in 1892 (Crowe 1987).

Another feature distinguishing London's suburban sprawl from Chicago's or indeed Manchester's was the density of ancient settlements whose parish churches, alms houses, grammar schools and inns provided a sense of place (Jenkins 1981:

58

Figure 3.3 Suburbia. *Ringing the changes on Arts and Crafts, Tudor and Queen Anne, a developer could offer these semidetached homes for a freehold price of less than £1000*

45). The existing nuclei expanded with new shopping parades, often in a distinctive herringbone brick, the trademark of Edward Lotery, a retail developer who ensured his centres' success by bringing the multiple stores – Woolworths, Marks & Spencer, Boots, Home & Colonial, Timothy White's, Sainsbury's – into suburban high streets (Jenkins 1986: 116).

Local government tried to keep pace with the newly created geography of suburbia. During the 1930s the frenzy of speculative housebuilding was matched by the construction of handsome civic complexes for the newly chartered municipal councils. The town halls of Dagenham, Wandsworth, Wembley, Hendon and Walthamstow bravely compensated for awkward out-of-centre locations with imposing external elevations and marbled interiors. Their magnificence was a reminder that London's new suburbs could already match many freestanding cities in size and wealth, and were staking their claim to the unitary County Borough status already enjoyed by East Ham, West Ham and Croydon.

Suburbia proved its appeal by its rate of growth. More than anywhere else, it was here that the British discovered the hedonism of Robert Graves and Alan Hodge's *Long Weekend* (1941). The most popular guide to the capital, to judge by its frequency in second-hand bookshops, was Harold Clunn's *The Face of London*. First published in 1932 and continually revised and reissued for the next three decades, it took a comfortably optimistic view of the transformations on the outskirts:

The suburbs of London can justly claim to be a hundred years ahead of those of the majority of the capital cities of the world in respect of their town-planning, roads, sanitary appointments and other kindred blessings of modern civilisation. Those of Paris are commonplace by comparison, with inferior sanitation and narrow main roads still paved with atrocious granite blocks . . . With all its shortcomings London is undoubtedly the most magnificent city in the world and a victory of civilisation, for the larger it grows the more attractive it seems to become (Clunn 1932: 17).

Not long before, Clunn's genial optimism about suburban growth would have corresponded with the wide consensus of experts, reformers and intellectuals. But by 1939, educated opinion had swung strongly, even virulently, against it. Suburbanisation, hailed by Charles Booth as a mental expansion or development of energy, was now viewed by reformers as a pollution.

These sentiments were reinforced by the rise of rural protectionism as a political force (Sheail 1981). If London had doubled in physical extent, its shadow effect had increased tenfold. Continuous suburbia stretching east to Rainham, south to Caterham, west to Uxbridge and north to Enfield was still inside a framework of ribbon development which had existed for a century or more, but the tentacles of the 'Octopus', as Clough Williams-Ellis (1928) called it, reached deep into the English countryside. London's attractive hinterland had been colonised since at least the 1870s by well-to-do commuters or retirees. Now came the exurbanites, as Londoners in the mass acquired mobility, spending power and leisure time. Throughout the Home Counties the long weekend left its imprint in kiosks, cafés, billboards, holiday camps, filling stations and roundabouts with 'roadhouse' inns. Land was cheap because of the agricultural depression, bringing the chance of a seaside bungalow or a country shack within reach of thousands of ordinary families: for them a taste of arcadia, but a scandal for the guardians of 'unspoiled' landscape (Hardy and Ward 1984).

Greenfield development predominated in 1919–39. Correspondingly little investment went into renewal of the urban fabric. The stock of pre-twentieth-century housing tended to decline into a vast gloomy backwater as upwardly mobile Londoners drifted to the new suburbs. Most of those left behind in the older urban districts were tenants of private landlords whose attitude towards management and maintenance had been adversely affected by the imposition of rent control during the First World War. Little affection was felt for the miles upon miles of terraced housing, with their deteriorating paintwork and unreliable plumbing. The LCC and other councils carried out some localised clearance of slum housing, but public expenditure constraints precluded large-scale urban renewal (Yelling 1992). In London, as in other British cities, the Victorian street pattern of inner residential districts remained unchanged in 1939.

The same was true of the central commercial and shopping area. The City of London had replaced four fifths of its buildings in 1855–1905, but only one fifth of its stock was renewed in the subsequent four decades. Apart from a handful of steel-framed buildings the City in 1939 was essentially as it had been at the death of Queen Victoria (CoL 1951: 178). More change had occurred in the West End, where the superior commercial power of the dollar cut through an archaic property sector dominated by old families and trusts (Whitehouse 1964). US developers and architects – 'Yankee megalomaniacs' G.K. Chesterton called them (in Adcock 1935) – dominated London's largest real estate projects. The Aldwych (Figure 3.4) was an LCC road improvement with an antiquarian name chosen by Sir Laurence Gomme when 'Connecticut Avenue' and 'Broadway' were deemed too sensitive (Winter 1993: 212). At Bush House, its monumental centrepiece, the advent of American marketing and media power was symbolised in 1922 by J. Walter Thompson's installation of a basement sound studio to record commercials for Radio Luxembourg. When ICI, Britain's chemical giant, built a pair of office blocks on the Embankment opposite Lambeth Palace, the chairman asked Chase National Bank to headhunt a salesman in Manhattan. They recruited Malcom McKenzie, a true-to-type US realtor weighing 17 stone who smoked six cigars a day and introduced American valuation and preletting techniques into a series of highly profitable West End schemes (Jenkins 1986). Even if not American-owned, West End hotels and department stores were often fitted out by New York design teams. The Grosvenor Hotel, built by the Duke of Westminster on the site of his London home, even opened a booking office on Fifth Avenue to attract custom (Weightman and Humphries 1984).

Around the turn of the century artists, poets and musicians had shaken off that habitual English anti-urbanism to rejoice in the bustle of London, its new electric street lighting, its imperial pomp and circumstance, its cockney colour. That mood had vanished completely since the First World War. Intellectuals generally detested the brash, American commercialism of central London, the dinginess and decay of the inner ring, the petty-bourgeois individualism of the suburbs, the spoilt country-side beyond. Their sense of urban alienation was aggravated by the increasing difficulty of earning a living except through commercial art. Across the political spectrum from T.S. Eliot to W.H. Auden the literary image of the metropolis was tawdry and sterile (Hynes 1976; Williams 1973). Gloom was deepened by the appalling predictions from psychiatrists and military men of the mass slaughter and panic that would be caused by city bombing in a future war (Titmuss 1950: 15); pessimism was deepest in London, prime target for air raids under the strategic theory of the 'knockout blow' (Ziegler 1995: 8).

So experts and opinion-formers shared none of Harold Clunn's cheerfulness about the changing face of London. In 1938–9 a dystopian, negative view was presented by almost all the witnesses to the Royal Commission under Sir Montague Barlow charged with examining the causes and consequences of the recent spectacular growth of the capital. In the report and minutes of evidence (PP 1940) we can see Victorian reform themes such as the idea of decentralisation to garden cities gathering new strength from a mix of ideas peculiar to the 1930s: the impact of architectural modernism, with its image of cool, white cubist buildings set in green landscape; the revival of eugenics, prompted by evidence of the decline of fertility in a consumerist, suburbanite society; the idea of 'planning' as an

Figure 3.4 Bush House, Aldwych. *The focal point of Kingsway, the LCC's most ambitious essay in Haussmanism. 'Bush' was the American developer Irving T. Bush who developed the site in stages between 1913 and 1931*

alternative to the blind muddle of the market economies; the elegaic nationalism of rural protectionists; Labour Party concern over London's disproportionate share of new employment; and a grim foreboding of aerial bombardment once the 'long weekend' ended.

WAR AND RECONSTRUCTION

Air raid sirens sounded all over London within half an hour of Neville Chamberlain's broadcast announcing the outbreak of the Second World War on 3 September 1939. The shelters stood prepared, the gas masks had been issued, and a million and half people (including 600 000 schoolchildren) were already evacuated or on their way out of the capital. Air raid precautions had been discussed and planned for a decade beforehand, and evacuation plans had already been put into action for nursery and disabled children during the Munich crisis twelve months earlier. Evacuation was one of the few topics on which Metropolitan Boroughs and adjacent local authorities were willing to work with the London County Council and the LCC with central government. It was regarded as a certainty that war would involve heavy bombing of civilian areas and that London would be the prime target of aerial attack. A network of observers was already in place to monitor civilian morale. Unlike almost everything in London's previous history, the Blitz was foreseen and planned for. In this respect and others, the Second World War was a turning-point in the history of London.

No bombers arrived on 3 September or for months afterwards. Heavy bombardment began a year later. The autumn raids on the East End involved 160 bombers on average, rising to a maximum of 410 planes on the night of 15 October 1940. From November 1940 the Luftwaffe began to attack provincial targets, beginning with Coventry. The London blitz continued intermittently throughout the next four years, ending in the summer of 1944 with the random menace of V1 flying bombs and some 500 of the violently destructive V2 rocket missiles during the last winter of the war.

At a Civil Defence luncheon at County Hall in the summer of 1941 Winston Churchill described London as a prehistoric monster into whose armoured hide a shower of arrows could be shot in vain (Ziegler 1995: 180). It was a good metaphor for the blitz. Prewar experts on air raid precautions had envisaged scenes of total administrative breakdown and civilian panic. In fact, the most striking feature in the many good accounts by historians and novelists was the normality of London life in the Blitz. The capital was vast and dispersed enough to absorb the destruction. In a city of 8 million people the casualties over five years totalled 29 890 deaths and 50 507 serious injuries. Ruined buildings were cleared, streets were kept open, railway tracks made good. London was no Hamburg (37 000 deaths), Tokyo (100 000) or Dresden (135 000). Graham Greene set the scene in his novel *The Ministry of Fear* (1943: 87): 'Knightsbridge and Sloane Street were not at war, but Chelsea was, and Battersea was on the front line . . . an odd front line that twisted like the track of a hurricane and left patches of peace.' In the East End, Poplar High Street was almost intact but behind it stretched one of the most extensive areas of devastation in London. In the City of London, the main financial district around the Bank of England sustained only slight damage, but the warehousing districts west of Aldermanbury were obliterated (Figure 3.5). Most of London's street network remained undamaged, with its bus and trolley-bus lines, its postal deliveries and milkfloats. All that was needed for reconstruction was to allow redevelopment of the gap sites – which, by the way, had been the object of a lively speculative activity throughout the war years.

But there would be no return to business as usual. The impact of the Blitz was as much psychological as physical. It shifted perceptions of London, spreading that sense of dissatisfaction already so prevalent among intellectuals, experts and reformers (Robson 1941). The patchwork of local authorities in outer London had performed poorly in air raid precautions. Margaret Cole observed of a failure of civil defence in West Ham: 'It was more than bricks and mortar that collapsed . . . it was a local ordering of society that was found hopelessly wanting, as weak and badly constructed as the single-brick walls which fell down at the blast' (Ziegler 1995: 119). Because of its amorphousness, London offered a peculiarly potent image of the old complacency and muddle. It was commonly said that the Luftwaffe had not destroyed enough. Too much had been left standing (Purdom 1945). 'When Hitler has finished bombing our cities' wrote Herbert Read 'let the demolition squads complete the good work' (in Gutkind 1943: 326). The London *Evening Standard* yearned for 'clean, wholesome, well-directed sticks of dynamite' (Ziegler 1995: 153):

> Before the Blitz Londoners took their dingy streets as a matter of fact, an unavoidable act of fate. But when whole streets were cleared away during one night it opened their eyes. They understood that houses were not built for eternity. They might be demolished (Rasmussen 1948: 428).

Just as in Vichy France and Nazi Germany, urban streets, pavements and buildings became charged with political symbolism. A new postwar order called for a new setting (Diefendorf 1990).

Against Winston Churchill's wishes, the image of planning for a new London became a significant propaganda motif for the Army Bureau of Current Affairs and the Home Morale Emergency Committee (Mack and Humphries 1985). With or without official sponsorship, the rebuilding of the capital prompted hundreds of pamphlets and meetings. It captured the imagination of a generation of Londoners whom war had cut loose from the old patterns of living (Porter 1994: 342). The Royal Academy's exhibition *London Replanned* in November 1942 was packed with visitors. Great crowds went to County Hall for the launch of the *County of London Plan*. Both it and the *Greater London Plan* of 1945 were lavishly produced and sold widely, and Penguin produced a bestselling summary of the County plan with

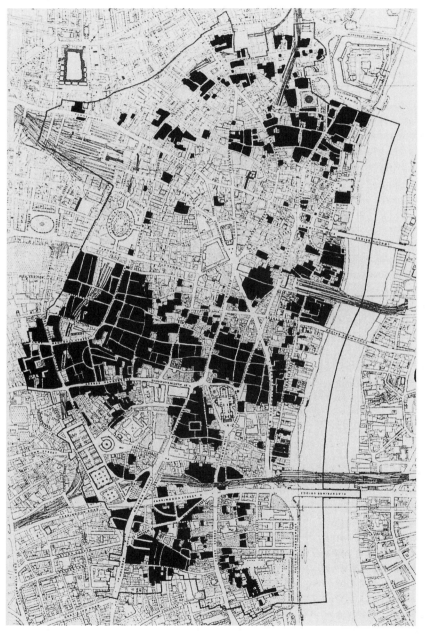

Figure 3.5 Blitz in the City. The main devastation in the Square Mile was concentrated in warehousing, publishing and workshop areas stretching from the Barbican to Blackfriars. The adjacent financial office district around the Bank had been largely rebuilt in steel frame architecture during the interwar period. Source: CoL (1951: 149) by kind permission of the Corporation of London

illustrations by Gordon Cullen and text by E.J. Carter and Erno Goldfinger (1945) which promised to end the old 'violent competitive passion' and give London 'order and efficiency and beauty and spaciousness'.

THE GRAND DESIGN

After the Great Fire in 1666 the reconstruction schemes of Christopher Wren, John Evelyn, Valentine Knight and Robert Hooke (Figures 2.5, 3.6) had offered variations on the themes of geometrical order, enlarged block size, public squares, and a riverside esplanade (Porter 1996b). There was no such common ground after the Blitz: rival plans differed on fundamentals (Foley 1963). The Modern Architecture Research Group (MARS) took Le Corbusier as their model and called for a clean sweep, creating a modernist landscape of towering 'residential units' in open parkland (Fry 1944). Sir Edwin Lutyens, commissioned by the Royal Academy, proposed great axial vistas lined with frontages in the Imperial classical manner (RAPC 1942). The Corporation of London's City Engineer put forward a conservative rebuilding scheme based on development practice. The contrasting visions of modernists, traditionalists and pragmatists set a frame for the central contribution of Sir Patrick Abercrombie, a synthesis of all three elements.

Abercrombie had a distinguished interwar career as a regional planner, was a founding officer of the Council for the Preservation of Rural England in 1926, and sat on the Barlow Commission. He and his team were what Lord Reith called 'men with wings to their minds', responding to the unique opportunity for bold, civic vision on the largest scale. He worked first with J.H. Forshaw, the Architect of London County Council, to produce a *County of London Plan* (Forshaw and Abercrombie 1943), then with the Technical Committee of the Standing Conference on London Regional Planning for the *Greater London Plan* (Abercrombie 1944). Both were handsomely published in folio, on good paper, with full-colour maps and illustrations. Despite the constraints of wartime book production the volumes could stand comparison with Daniel Burnham's sumptuous Chicago plan of 1909. In his intellectual history of twentieth-century planning, *Cities of Tomorrow* (1988), Peter Hall shows the extent of Abercrombie's debt to American theories of city planning, and particularly the work of the Regional Planning Association of America. In the unique context of the era of Beveridgism and the postwar Labour victory of 1945, he achieved for London what Lewis Mumford and his circle had dreamed for New York, an official plan with an holistic philosophy and a regional scope which treated neighbourhoods, districts, metropolis and region as an organic whole. The key to the design, both in New York and London, was the use of landscape to define urban form. In London – a circular inland city – it took the form of a containing green belt.

London already had a green belt of a sort. In 1935, when the interwar housing boom was at its height, the London County Council had allocated the substantial sum of £2 million from county funds to protect threatened landscape, whether by

Figure 3.6 Warning of 1666. *As speculators dream of the postwar housing boom, Sir Christopher Wren reminds Londoners of the opportunity lost after the Great Fire. One of the powerful images created by Oswald Barrett ('Batt') for C.B. Purdom's polemical* How Should We Rebuild London? *(1945). By kind permission of J.M. Dent & Sons, now Orion Publishing*

outright purchase or by compensating landowners for agreeing not to build. Within two years 30 000 acres of countryside were covered by preservation orders, and a further 10 000 were added when the LCC promoted private legislation – the Green Belt Act 1938 – allowing it to extend grants to local councils (Sheail 1981). These heroic efforts, masterminded by Herbert Morrison, had taken growth management as far as it could go in the context of a free land market. Yet they could safeguard only narrow sectors of protected landscape against a background of speculative building activity. Sir Raymond Unwin, in his prewar advisory role to local planning authorities in the London region, had argued that London needed a more radical form of planning to safeguard farmland and give planners discretion in selecting the sites for building. In his concept of the 'open background', Unwin evoked Ebenezer Howard's image of a town with fixed limits, girdled with fields, gardens and orchards. In 1939 the Barlow Commission – with Sir Patrick Abercrombie as a member, and Ebenezer Howard's disciple F.J. Osborn as expert witness and back-door lobbyist – seized on this vision and argued that government must make the green belt a practical possibility if it wanted to redress the fundamental geographical disequilibrium between the London region and the rest of Britain. The Green Belt proposals of the *Greater London Plan* were the direct outcome (Abercrombie 1945: 11). There should be no more sprawl. Future growth must take the form of compact urban units against a green rural background. To the Dane Steen Eiler Rasmussen (1948: 425) that simple policy response to London's immense interwar growth – 'we must stop this' – seemed an example of English pragmatism at its best (Figure 3.7).

If the green belt defined the outer skin of the metropolis, highways were to provide its 'stiffening structure'. For decades, engineers (a profession with a marked colonial and military bias) had been frustrated by the apparent impossibility of achieving improvements to the capital's road network (Ashworth 1954: 218). Plans for an arterial system of freeways with multilevel intersections segregated by speed had been devised as early as 1903–5 in detailed submissions by technical witnesses to the Royal Commission on London Traffic (Winter 1993: 193). An impressive start had been made in the 1920s with outer London's dual carriageways. However, they ran through farmland and involved relatively little demolition, whereas any extension into the metropolis was inhibited by compensation costs. Professor William Robson of the London School of Economics, visiting Moscow with the leading Mancunians Sir Ernest and Lady Simon, contrasted slow progress in London with the Mossoviet's ability to root up obstructive houses and trees: the Moscow City Architect was amazed that Regent Street had been rebuilt to John Nash's original width 'instead of being made three times as wide as it would have been under socialism' (Simon et al. 1937: 211). Shortly before the war the engineer Sir Charles Bressey had carried out a complete survey of the capital's arterial road system, and – in conjunction with the architect Sir Edwin Lutyens – set out a 30-year plan to complete the trajectory of high-speed arterials into central London, with orbitals or 'loopways' linking them for the benefit of through-traffic (Bressey and Lutyens 1938; Forshaw and Abercrombie 1943: ch. 4).

Figure 3.7 'We Must Stop This'. *London's interwar extremities remain intact, with fields beyond*

Abercrombie's starting point – following Bressey – was that these arterial routes should not be boulevards, but grade-separated, limited access, multilane motorways on the Italian or German model (Hart 1976: ch. 3). Whereas Bressey could be criticised for approaching urban road-building from a narrow engineering perspective, Abercrombie's genius turned the 'canalisation' effect of motorways into a positive social benefit. He was clearly influenced by the thinking of the Metropolitan Police Commissioner for Traffic, Sir Alker Tripp, a forceful advocate of traffic segregation in the interests of road safety (Hass-Klau 1990). Solving the problem of urban motor traffic by replacing streets with heavily engineered highways, the philosophy which was to become so drearily familiar in postwar years, was by no means uncontroversial in the early 1940s. Experiments such as the 'Play Streets' pioneered in Salford and introduced to the capital under the

London Traffic Act 1934 had shown that substantial safety improvements could be achieved at a fraction of the cost by speed restrictions, pedestrian-priority crossings and traffic management within the existing street network. But Tripp's books *Road Traffic and its Control* (1938) and *Town Planning and Road Traffic* (1942) argued categorically that building new roads was preferable to regulating old ones: 'Nothing should ever be done by means of legal restrictions which it is practicable to effect by layout; this principle must be regarded as an axiom of traffic science' (Tripp 1942: 21). That was to be the philosophy of the postwar plans for London.

Haussmann's insertion of boulevards into nineteenth-century Paris had been a surgical act – a *percement* – which left intact the surrounding urban tissue. Tripp's principles of circulation required a physical separation of local access from distributor roads, and distributor roads from the arterial system: districts would need to be redeveloped entire (Tetlow and Goss 1968: ch. 3). Clear-felling was regarded with equanimity or anticipation. Experts were agreed that the existing street pattern was 'outworn' and building obsolescence was assumed to occur after a maximum 60-year life. Sir Charles Bressey put it simply to a meeting of London architects, 'Sir Edwin Lutyens and I have driven round innumerable portions of London, and found very few that were not in need of demolition' (Boumphrey 1940: 162). Any buildings of value could – as in America and Russia – be put on rollers and moved backwards to a new street line (Forshaw and Abercrombie 1943: 59–60). Besides, many of the major roads would be encased in landscape. The London plans pioneered the application of the American parkway principle to urban areas. Green highway corridors would extend the benefits of open space while removing the opportunity for frontage development of the sort which had spoiled interwar arterial roads for commuters and long-distance traffic. Like miniature green belts, the highway barriers between one district and the next would define community units as cells within the larger organism of London (Foley 1963; Hart 1976; Hall 1988). Never has the medicine of urban motorways been served more sweetly.

In 1945 the LCC Town Planning Committee, chaired by Lewis Silkin, endorsed the design principles of the Abercrombie plan, though not the specific targets for overspill and redevelopment densities, which remained controversial. Silkin announced that the council would pursue seven tasks in reconstruction: it would construct a series of ring roads; establish density zones; relocate industry in relation to residential areas; create new industrial estates; increase the amount of open space; create balanced communities each comprising several neighbourhood units; and preserve buildings of architectural and historic importance (Young and Garside 1982: ch. 8; Saint 1989: ch. 12).

SEIZING THE MOMENT

Sir Patrick Abercrombie's Personal Foreword to the *Greater London Plan* urged the need for courage 'to seize the moment when it arrives and make a resolute start'

(Abercrombie 1945: vi). Even before the end of the war and the return of a Labour government in 1945, government had already demonstrated commitment to a radical rather than a remedial approach to the reconstruction of London. It legislated in 1944 to give local councils powers to assemble and clear extensive areas for redevelopment without incurring punitive liability for compensation. Originally intended to deal with bomb damage, its scope was extended (against Treasury opposition) to allow districts with streets and buildings regarded as obsolete to be 'laid out afresh and redeveloped as a whole'.

The symbolic test case of the new philosophy was the City of London. Whenever reconstruction was discussed some reference would be made to the precedent of the Great Fire and the betrayal of Wren's plan by individual rapaciousness and City self-interest (Purdom 1945; Figure 3.8). Stung by these criticisms, the Corporation of London devoted an entire appendix of its reconstruction plan (CoL 1944) to setting the record straight on its handling of Sir Christopher Wren's proposals 270 years previously. The modern Corporation faced many of the same problems as it had after the seventeenth-century catastrophe: the Great Fire had levelled three-quarters of the Square Mile (437 acres), the Blitz a third (225 acres), though with a smaller proportional loss of floorspace – about a quarter, or 25 million square feet – because the major damage was in the Barbican and Moorgate districts of smaller, older offices and warehouses while larger steel-framed offices of the core financial district survived intact. As in 1667, speculators were active, there was impatience for development, and a fear the City might lose it to the West End (Marriott 1967: 45). The image of St Paul's Cathedral intact in the flames of the Blitz was as eloquent a symbol of reconstruction as the ruined cathedral of Coventry.

The *County of London Plan* had excluded the Square Mile – that 'minute kernel' within the 'nut' of the LCC, surrounded in turn by the 'husk' of Greater London. The reconstruction ethos of Barlow, Abercrombie and Silkin did not extend to the City Engineer, whose reconstruction plan of 1944 was deliberately conservative. Apart from road widenings to allow through-traffic to be carried around the edge of the central business district, the plan left intact the topography of City streets, with their expensive underground infrastructure and their historic associations – many being 'world-wide or household names to some branch of commerce, professions or industry'. The plan's respect for urban morphology was matched by a care for its outstanding contribution to the skyline of London, the flotilla of the spires and towers around the great dome of St Paul's. It was assumed that new building would keep to the 100-foot height limit defined by the London Building Acts. Modern office space would be accommodated – as in the 1930s – by steel-framed buildings clad in Portland stone, rising from the pavement to the cornice line, with internal lightwells and courtyards to bring light into the centres of the blocks.

The City explicitly distanced itself from the fashionable preference for clean-sweep planning, whether in the Beaux-Arts tradition of Sir Edwin Lutyens or the pastoral modernism of Sir Patrick Abercrombie:

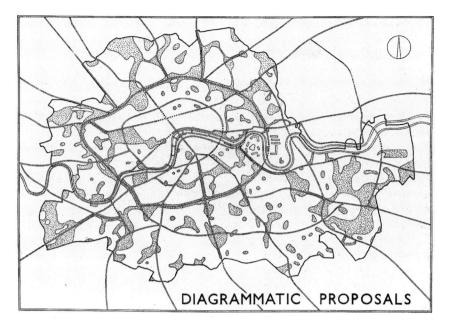

DIAGRAMMATIC PROPOSALS

Figure 3.8 County of London Plan 1943. *The black and white summary of the key highway and open space proposals shows Abercrombie's intention to divide up London into discrete neighbourhoods and precincts. The original maps conveyed this cellular vision in ravishing colour evocative of a microscope slide (Forshaw and Abercrombie 1943: 46)*

> We suggest the conservation wherever possible of features which are of traditional and archeological significance and add to the architectural dignity of the City. Can it seriously be though that we, proud to have had a part in promoting its welfare, are unconscious of the romance and history which the very street names breathe? . . . Whatever the surface destruction, the City can in no circumstances be regarded as virgin land, upon a blank plan which the pencil of a planner . . . can freely or fancifully travel (CoL 1944: 2).

The plan caused an immediate furore. Its proposals to permit rebuilding on existing street lines contradicted the Minister's preference for modernist 'open planning'. It offered architects no prospect of escape from the confines of the building facade on the corridor street. It made no acknowledgement of the Barlow Commission's concerns over congestion, and was considered incompatible with the Abercrombie plans (Purdom 1945: 148). William Holford, within the government's technical team, made a damning appraisal of the plan for the eyes of the Minister then helped to draft a highly critical assessment by the Royal Fine Art Commission chiding the Corporation of London to keep pace with 'the cultural as well as the utilitarian standards of the time' (RFAC 1945; Cherry and Penny 1986).

It is rare for a Conservative Minister of the Crown to challenge the Corporation of London, but Anthony Greenwood did so. The Corporation, he said, had lost a great opportunity in 1666 and must not lose this greater one. The City should be 'visibly the capital of a world-wide community of great nations', a result 'unlikely to be achieved by the Plan now presented' which seemed to be 'dominated by the desire to avoid the purchase of land and interfere as little as possible with existing ownership'. William Holford and the architect Charles Holden were drafted in to prepare an entirely new plan, which became the prototype for town-centre planning in postwar Britain. The old-fashioned regulation of the building frontage, cornice and height control which had served so well since 1667 was replaced by new rules controlling the ratio of building floorspace to site (the plot ratio) and the access of daylight through windows. The deliberate intention was to break up the corridor street and produce a varied geometry of building shapes, letting in light and air, and offering scope for modern architects to make their own contribution to the London skyline (CoL 1951; Esher 1983). To lead the way, the main blitz-damaged areas around the Tower of London, St Paul's and the Barbican were designated for compulsory purchase and comprehensive redevelopment, and entrusted to designers from the team of left-wing modernists in the LCC architects' department. It seemed that the walls of the City had fallen at last.

While this vital drama was being acted out within the Square Mile plans for the larger reconstruction of London proceeded apace. The political context was ideal. London had one of the UK's highest swings to Labour in the 1945 general election. The politicians who had been the strongest protagonists of planning within the London County Council now held cabinet office. Lewis Silkin, former chairman of the LCC Housing Committee, became Minister of Town and Country Planning. He promoted the legislation to turn the Abercrombie plans into reality. The New Towns Act 1946 made provision to rehouse populations displaced by comprehensive redevelopment. The 1947 Town and Country Act nationalised the right to develop land and set up the system of flexible regulation or development control which forms the basis of British planning to this day. Of course, these were national enactments, affecting every part of the country. But the policy process had been largely dominated by the capital. These legislative remedies would never have reached the statute book with all-party support were it not for that vision of London – the archetypal scattered city – contained, unified, and made new.

FESTIVAL OF BRITAIN

CHAPTER 4

CITY IN A RING

CHAPTER 4
CITY IN A RING

Philip Ziegler (1995) ends his fine history of the London blitz with an echo of 1666: the promises held out to the people of London in the reconstruction plans were not honoured. So too argue the social historian Roy Porter (1994) and geographer Peter Hall (1994). Fifty years on, Hall had succeeded Sir Patrick Abercrombie both to the chair of town planning at University College and the role of London's pre-eminent strategist. Much of his research over the years has revolved around the encounter between the planners' vision of reconstruction in the mid-twentieth century and the great forces of postwar change that were beyond their reckoning: the decline of manufacturing industry; the transport revolution; counterurbanisation; the rise in owner-occupation and household fission; Commonwealth immigration; tertiarisation and globalisation. Many of these themes are picked up in the next three chapters, which deal in turn with the government, economy and changing population of modern London. Here our concern is with the physical fabric of buildings, streets, spaces and townscape. Looking back on the past fifty years it is hard to say which is greater, the change or the continuity. London combines elements of a wholeheartedly modernist city like Rotterdam and a preserved urban masterpiece like Paris. Because growth has been arrested by a green belt, the physical extent has altered little in half a century: new lines have been inserted into Harry Beck's tube diagram but its scope and scale remain unchanged. And despite the war and the passage of years, the layout in the *A-Z of London* when Phyllis Pearsall died in 1996 is substantially the same as in the first edition she trundled to W.H. Smith in a wheelbarrow in 1936. The promise to stop London's growth has been honoured, making it a 'city in a ring' in a new sense, but that radical remodelling never left the drawing board. In this sense the analogy between the 1660s and the 1940s is correct. London resisted the grand design.

In a more paradoxical way, though, the vision of reconstruction was fulfilled. What marked out the Abercrombie plans from all the other designs of the 1940s was their sense of the metropolis as a huge cluster of living residential communities. They included memorable coloured maps of the community mosaic (Abercrombie 1945: 111; Forshaw and Abercrombie 1945: 21, 28) – legacy, as we saw in the previous chapters, of the capital's early suburbanisation and late development of municipal institutions. The first postwar plan of the London County Council reaffirmed the objective 'to recognise and develop the existing system of communities' (LCC 1951: 1). They remain recognisable half a century later thanks only to the collapse of the original well-meant strategy to 'emphasise identity' through segregation and single-use zoning. Great town planner though he was,

Abercrombie's design contained a lethal cocktail of the old paternal reformism (disperse the poor) and the new rationalism of the modern movement ('neighbour-hood theory'). It sought to eliminate the life and variety of the streets and parcel London into a series of self-contained new-built enclaves. This chapter shows how, more by fortune than design, reconstruction plans were frustrated and the curious street network kept intact, together with most of the surviving prewar housing stock and the spider-shaped pattern of shops and services based on early ribbon development along approach roads.

There is another parallel with 1666 here. If the process of change in modern London owes little to overall design, it has all the same been closely regulated. The London Building Acts and the estate management practices of ground landlords have their parallel in the use of planning and environmental regulation by local authorities in modern London. We are not concerned in this chapter with the mechanisms of regulation (well described in Simmie 1994) but with the results of this largely invisible hand, shaping the world in which Londoners live and work, and – to argue a revisionist case – shaping it, overall, for the better.

ROAD-BUILDING

The key idea of the Abercrombie plan was to lay out the spatial structure of London afresh inside the spokes and rings of a comprehensive arterial road system. It was an ambitious spider's web with multiple concentric 'A', 'B' and 'C' ring-roads running through the built-up area, and an outer 'D' orbital in the green belt. The last of these roads was completed in 1986 as the M25 motorway. The others died a slow political death.

First, in the context of extreme financial austerity and materials shortages which took hold in 1945, housing was given absolute priority over roads. Throughout 1946–50 there were disputes between the ministries of planning and transport and between Labour and Conservative groups in County Hall over the financial responsibility for safeguarding the alignments (Munby in Senior 1966: 158). In 1950, the LCC made its first specific proposals to implement the innermost 'A' Ring, a motor equivalent of the Circle Line linking the main-line railway stations. The government declined to support the £120 million project: on Keynesian principles, it should be reserved as a countercyclical public works measure. Then in the mid-1950s Sir Ernest Marples, an energetic Minister of Transport with his own civil engineering company, launched a national programme of trunk motorways. City authorities in Glasgow, Newcastle, Sheffield, Liverpool, Manchester and Birmingham responded, using planning powers to speed the linkage of their city centres to the motorway net. London did not. Within its relatively narrow boundaries the London County Council had other political priorities than to tie the knot of the national motorway network. It seemed that the new highways converging on the capital would be left dangling into a conventional street system (Hart 1976: 105–10).

Arterial roads – or rather the lack of them – were a dominant consideration for the government in the 1963 reform (described in the next chapter) which abolished the London County Council and replaced it with a larger and more powerful Greater London Council (GLC). Part III 25 (3) of the London Government Act (1963) required the GLC to lay down 'considerations of general policy with respect to the use of land in the various parts of Greater London *including in particular guidance as to the future road system*'. The council was created expressly to get the primary road network built. Within twelve hours of its launch on 1 April 1965 it announced plans for a £450 million Urban Motorway Box – Abercrombie's 'B' Ring – 35 miles long and eight lanes wide, linking the radial roads into London at a distance of 4–6 miles from the centre.

Over the next four years the council's highway engineers elaborated a complete scheme of freeways, largely following Abercrombie's alignments but replacing his landscaped parkways with the harsher, high-capacity extensions of a modern motorway system. To support the 400-mile Primary Road Network of three concentric rings and thirteen radial expressways, 1000 miles of existing roads were to be widened and upgraded into a Secondary Network. When the entire project was unveiled in 1967 its total cost was estimated at £2 billion. The Primary Network alone would take 6200 acres and displace 100 000 population. The GLC engineers worked closely over the design and specification with the Department of Transport, who were separately engaged on the Abercrombie 'D' Ring (the modern M25), but they undertook no consultation with the London boroughs who would be dealing with the environmental and social shock waves. The uncouth 2-mile stretch of the A40(M) Westway from Paddington to White City, developed unilaterally in the 1960s by the Ministry of Transport on one of Abercrombie's route lines, gave a practical demonstration of what the rest of London could expect.

Intended like John Burns's tramway lines as an affirmation of the new-found unity of London, the Ringway scheme became a political timebomb in the lap of the metropolitan government. The road alignments published in the *Greater London Development Plan* of 1969 prompted 22 000 objections and put the council on the defensive throughout a two-year public enquiry. Vehement opposition from boroughs, individuals, amenity and community groups (including the growing population of opinion-formers resident in the threatened inner suburbs) encouraged the London Labour Party to change its line and delete the Primary Road Network from the plan when it regained control of County Hall in April 1973 (Hart 1976: 158–75).

Abandonment of the scheme which had been its *raison d'être* posed the question for what purpose the metropolitan council existed (to which the eventual answer was to be abolition; see next chapter) but it was a vital moment in London's history. Other British towns and cities pressed ahead with inner ring and radial roads which in Edward Relph's metaphor (1987: 160) cut across the urban grain like igneous intrusions in sedimentary rocks, leaving a track of blight and severance to either side. Central areas were confirmed as places to drive and to park in, and mixed-use streets on the lines of approach were cleared, widened or bypassed in favour of traffic roads. London alone was left in possession of an intact conventional street network. The Westway and the Blackwall Tunnel approach road are (until the completion of a highly controversial extension of the M11 into the East End) the only motorways within the 6-mile radius of Charing Cross. Other scattered fragments of road improvement – such as the monstrous overscaled flyover blighting the end of the Old Kent Road and adjacent portions of the Secondary Network (Figure 4.1) – only highlight what has been avoided. Having survived the double onslaught of the 1944 and 1969 plans the high streets into town from all directions continue to perform as they have since Tudor times as mixed corridors for shopping, business and pleasure. Notorious among traffic engineers as the 'most inefficient roads in Britain', they are the rudiments and grammar of London knowledge.

COMPREHENSIVE REDEVELOPMENT

One of the paradoxes of the London blitz was the relatively limited extent of long-term damage to the building stock. The swathe of building damage caused by high-explosive bombs in the last year of the war had been tackled with splendid energy by Ernest Bevin who recruited more than 45 000 building workers from the provinces for emergency repair work. Billeted in hostels, they repaired more than 800 000 houses over the harsh winter of 1944–5 (Ziegler 1995: 304). In districts such as Stepney and Poplar in the East End, which had taken the brunt of the blitz, four out of five households still lived in conventional terraced houses. The new lease of life for the older stock was accompanied by a marked improvement in the levels of overcrowding. During the 1940s, the population of the LCC area had dropped by 600 000 or 18%. Despite the shortfall of dwellings, evacuation and mobilisation had a permanent effect on living patterns, and districts such as Stepney never regained their high prewar density levels.

Back in 1938 the Bermondsey general practitioner Dr Westlake had argued passionately in evidence to the Barlow Commission that the community's best interest would be to improve the nineteenth-century stock of single-family terraced houses, with their backyards and chicken coops, instead of clearing them for municipal tenements. The case against demolition might have been all the stronger after wartime destruction, but the spirit of the times was firmly for the clean-sweep approach. Removal of streets and the elimination of private ownership were two sides of a coin, the task usually described as 'undoing the damage of the Industrial Revolution'. A community that complained was sternly told that reconstruction 'was in no sense a task of preservation' (Moye 1979). The LCC's official development plan reprinted Lewis Silkin's seven ground rules of 1945 (page 69 above), adding an eighth for emphasis – the commitment to *comprehensively redevelop* areas considered 'obsolete' (LCC 1951). Beginning slowly with the largest

Figure 4.1 Heygate Estate, SE17. *Southwark Council monstrously applies the Alker Tripp principles of traffic canalisation, pedestrian segregation, and a mastic of landscaping*

tracts of blitz damage in Bermondsey, Stepney, Poplar and the Square Mile, its programme gathered pace until by 1963 it was proceeding with the clearance and redevelopment of almost 1000 hectares, while the Metropolitan Boroughs pursued their own slum-clearance programmes in parallel.

Like a haircut which has got out of control (a little schnoop here and a little schnoop there), councils found that the more they demolished, the more needed to go. According to the LCC, the initial rationale of war damage had been overtaken by other motives for clearance: streets were condemned to meet engineers' rising requirements of space for public utility vehicles and car-parking; or as part of the great reordering of the street pattern around the anticipated new urban highways; or to provide the large sites needed for a mechanised building industry (LCC 1960).

Industrialised building erected by tower cranes represented an important shift in the design of redevelopment areas. The subsidy structure had been altered in the mid-1950s to favour higher densities of public housing, beginning in the untypical context of the Square Mile with the design of Britain's most dramatic high-rise council estate, the Barbican Comprehensive Development Area (Figure 4.2). Wimpey, Laing, Costain, Taylor Woodrow, Wates and other creators of interwar private suburbia had been locked into large-scale public contract work during the Second World War (Powell 1980; Smyth 1985: 92). Their corporatist connections

Figure 4.2 The Barbican Towers. *Initiated in 1955 at government prompting, the City Corporation's Corbusian scheme by Chamberlain, Powell and Bon was the prototype for 20 years of high-density mass housing in Britain. The City's Smithfield Meat Market stands in the foreground*

with government now secured a stream of large-volume housing contracts based on municipal land assembly (Dunleavy 1981). Politicians looked for mass solutions to the problem of numbers on their waiting lists, though even at high densities of redevelopment they found it difficult to achieve a net gain in the number of units on land previously occupied by terraced housing. Higher yields could have been achieved by redevelopment of lower-density suburban sites, but those were difficult to acquire, even for an enlarged Greater London Council (Young and Garside 1982).

The ideologies of local government professionals also became a significant influence on the face of London. Just after the war, the architects had wrested control over housing design from the valuer's department of the LCC and put London on the map as one of the world's leading centres of progressive public architecture. Taylor (1973) and Esher (1983) trace the evolution of the County Hall style. The first redevelopments, in the Lansbury neighbourhood in the East End of London were a light and graceful architecture of stock bricks and pastel stucco. The tower blocks of the Alton West estate at Roehampton of 1955–8 marked a shift towards a more abrasive Corbusian style which grew denser and more aggressive during the 1960s and 1970s. The contradictions of modernist mass housing – Peter Hall's 'City of Towers' (1988: ch. 7) – were nowhere more acute than in London, centre of stylistic experiment and glossy-paper journalism, source of public patronage, and home to so many of the fashionable architects who, as Nicholas Taylor put it, 'sit all day at their drawing boards in County Hall designing harsh piazzas for Battersea and Bermondsey and then at 4.51 p.m. sharp descend to the tube train, roaring out under the forgotten development areas for which they are responsible, until they come to the surface at their own cosy creeper-hung suburban cottages in Hampstead and Wimbledon' (1973: 19) A gas explosion and partial collapse of a system-built block in east London triggered a national policy shift away from towers to horizontal blocks, but the high density remained, and the estate-based approach with all its consequences: eradication of the street network, removal of industrial and service activies, and the replacement of multiple ownership by municipal monopoly.

The last point was perhaps the most telling. Postwar planning placed local authorities in a role of large-scale estate-management for which they were administratively not well equipped. Land acquisition and clearance always progressed faster than rebuilding, leaving empty pavements and void sites. Corrugated iron sheets became 'the character armour of the council' in the words of a Lambeth graffitist captured by McKean (1977: 20). Labour's aversion to small business was unhelpful to a metropolitan economy based on small-scale entrepreneurship; its institutional links to public service unions favoured conservative working practices and an indifference to consumer preferences. Municipal monopoly drove away the young and ambitious blue-collar workers who found upward mobility and a chance to own their own homes outside London: their out-migration was actively encouraged by the LCC and its successor, the GLC, in the interests of 'overspill'. Blight was reinforced by the steep decline of goods-handling and manufacturing described below in Chapter 6. Postwar nationalisations had consolidated some of the largest urban landholdings in the hands of statutory gas, water, coal and rail boards who felt no commercial urgency about disposing of land surplus to their shrinking operational requirements. In the borough of Tower Hamlets, to the east of the City, a Thames Television investigation in 1980 identified 590 acres of vacant land, nine tenths of it owned by public bodies, and 30 miles of corrugated iron fencing (Nabarro and Richards 1980).

In the first decades of the welfare state, local state monopoly had been a taken-for-granted side effect of environmental improvement. It took time to grasp its implications. In the 1970s the journalist Simon Jenkins's 'Living in London' feature in the *Evening Standard* trained a sharp critical eye on the deteriorating environment of the new council estates and the miscellaneous landholdings acquired for roads, parks, housing and other purposes. His book *Landlords to London* (1975) looked at local councils from an unaccustomed angle, as heirs to the tradition of great estates which laid out, built and managed the initial suburban extensions of modern London, and defined its urban character. Jenkins tracked the long rise and decline of the private estates, and the steep recent rise of public ownership through negotiated or compulsory purchases under a widening range of statutes. The local government sector had grown into London's largest landlord, but its estate was marked by monotony and blight, particularly in inner London: 'boarded up shops and broken windows have become the hallmarks of public ownership' (Jenkins 1975: 278). In those pre-Thatcher days officials and academics generally assumed paternalistically that the growth of council owner-ship was benign. But that is not how it was seen at the grass roots. Day 128(!) of the public inquiry into the Greater London Development Plan in July 1971 heard some robust views on these unspoken issues from Tower Hamlets residents. Why, they asked, did the planning debate revolve interminably around the quantitative aspect of population numbers, densities and distributions, instead of addressing the real problem, the process of municipalisation that was turning inner London boroughs into 'one massive housing estate' and 'making the place uninhabitable'? (Figure 4.3). 'Of all the things done to London in this century' wrote Ian Nairn in 1966 'the softly-spoken this-is-good-for-you castration of the East End is the saddest' (1966: 161).

MODERNISING THE CENTRAL AREA

Blitz damage around central London provided the opportunity to give London a taste of one of the classic visions of modernism, the multilayered city, with pedestrians and vehicles moving freely on different levels instead of being confined together within the walls of a street canyon. Pedestrian decks were first applied on the doorstep of County Hall in the 1953 master model for the redevelopment of the

Figure 4.3 The Aylesbury Estate. '*Proudly proclaimed as the largest system built housing blocks in Europe . . . the contrast with London's long and honourable tradition of "client-oriented" housing, typified by the neighbouring terraced housing in other streets in Southwark, could not be greater' (Jenkins 1975: 264)*

South Bank site vacated by the 1951 Festival of Britain. Its designer, Percy Johnson-Marshall, submitted a scheme to the 1958 International Competition for the Replanning of Central Berlin to show how an entire city centre could be reconstructed in the form of megastructures with podium decks interconnected by walkways and bridges (Johnson-Marshall 1966: 116). His collaborator in this project was Colin Buchanan, an engineer-planner who had begun professional life as a young assistant civil engineer reporting on the road conditions at the sites of serious accidents in the pedestrian carnage of the 1930s, and became a leading expert on urban road design (Hass-Klau 1990: 160). Buchanan followed Tripp in arguing that separation of pedestrians from road traffic should be the first aim of urban reconstruction, but in keeping with the technological optimism of the 1960s he preferred vertical decks to horizontal precincts. In 1960 he became urban road planning adviser to the Ministry of Transport and produced a report on *Traffic in Towns* (1963) which made his name a household word, popularising ideas which had been previously been confined to the minority, Corbusian wing of the architectural avant-garde (Esher 1983).

The report challenged readers to think afresh about the juxtaposition of human beings and moving mechanical objects in the conventional urban street: it offered a radical vision of a modernised urban world in which traffic would flow without obstruction, and pedestrians move without danger. Artificial decks would provide a new ground level from which 'buildings would rise in a pattern related to but not dictated by the traffic below. On the deck it would be possible to recreate in an even better form the things that have delighted man for generations in towns – the snug, close varied atmosphere, the narrow alleys, the contrasting open square, the effect of light and shade, and the fountains and the sculpture' (Buchanan 1963: 46).

London was the testing ground for these ideas. The first opportunities came in those blitzed parts of the City by the Tower of London, to the north of St Paul's, and the extensive tract of Moorgate and the Barbican to the north of the Guildhall. Having assembled these sites in municipal ownership, postwar planners could play with layout, unlike their predecessors after the Great Fire. With LCC architects at the helm, the historic street patterns of Tower Hill and the Paternoster Square area by St Paul's were replaced by monolithic redevelopments in the podium and tower format. In the Moorgate Barbican area, redeveloped in stages from 1955 to 1975, a network of walkways allowed the pedestrian to range freely along more than 2 miles of walkways through residential flats, an arts complex, the Museum of London and office towers; it is one of the most complete modernist megastructures in Europe (CoL 1959; Hebbert 1992a; Esher 1983).

While the Barbican was still a huge building site the LCC announced its intention to apply the principle of multilevel redevelopment as widely as possible in the central area (LCC 1960). The implied preference for large-scale schemes which would burst conventional plot boundaries and span the street was wonderfully timely for the property industry, booming after the deregulation and lifting of the postwar charge on development profit. The supply of blitz sites had long since dried up, and with rising values it was growing harder for developers to consolidate the large plots they needed for modern office blocks and retail units – it took more than a decade of patient, secretive dealing to assemble some of London's prime sites (Marriott 1967; Whitehouse 1964).

Comprehensive multilevel redevelopment offered another fruitful basis for partnership between private money and public land assembly. Engineers would get their traffic flow, developers their floorspace, and politicians their landmarks. Schemes blossomed at Victoria, Piccadilly Circus, Covent Garden. Unassuming Uxbridge, out in the suburbs of Middlesex, announced its intention to pursue a 20-year plan of modernisation culminating in a multilevel town centre with complete pedestrian–vehicle segregation. With the City Corporation in the lead, local authorities began to impose walkways in the planning consents for individual buildings, requiring developers to provide decks, staircases and abutments for connecting bridges in expectation that the flow of pedestrian traffic would eventually shift upwards by 20 feet from the pavements to the new walkway system. The City Architect announced plans for a 32-mile 'Pedway' network within the Square Mile: stretches of it still exist as public rights of way (Figure 4.4), and the proposed extensions to the West End can still be traced in isolated fragments of podium and

Figure 4.4 Modernisation Plans Aborted. *All over central London attempts were made in the 1960s and early 1970s to replace conventional streets with vertically segregated decks and walkways. The defeat of comprehensve development at Covent Garden was a turning point which left many fragments of walkway literally hanging in mid-air, for example here at the back of the Guildhall, epicentre of the City's 32-mile 'Pedway' system*

tower development up Tottenham Court Road and along Euston Road (Hebbert 1992a). London pedestrians, who once had priority on the roads, were penned off them by metal railings, forced up ramps and onto bridges, or pushed down into murky subways, a humiliation described by E.R. Wethersett, heir to Harold Clunn's great tradition of London perambulations, as 'Safety with Indignity' (Clunn 1970: 11).

LONDON PRIDE

Disillusion with the planners' strategy of modernisation took political root in the period 1965–75. It was a slow process. Attitudes of quiescence, apathy and deference to expertise were deeply engrained in Londoners, as the American political scientist Stephen Elkin observed with surprise in his book *Politics and Land Use Planning; the London Experience* (1974). He did notice, though, an upturn in grassroots activity. In 1958 there had only been 18 amenity societies in the whole of London. By 1978 there were more than 100 established groups and scores more groups formed on an *ad hoc* basis to fight unpopular proposals (Aldous 1980). The Civic Trust, formed in 1955 by Duncan Sandys MP, provided an umbrella organisation and support for local action. An important early victory for it was the abandonment in 1960 of a scheme by the developer Jack Cotton for office towers and a pedestrian deck across Piccadilly Circus. Ten years later planners and developers brought back another scheme for a split-level redevelopment of the Circus to stronger opposition and a more conclusive defeat. The Greater London Development Plan, intended to promote 'strategic' thinking, had given a spur to local political activism – John Gyford (in Simmie 1994: 81) calls it an 'insurrec-tion'. The new political forces which caused Labour to drop the motorway system in 1972 also halted Conservative Westminster's Piccadilly redevelopment in 1973 and encouraged a Conservative minister in 1974 to block the GLC's scheme for comprehensive redevelopment of Covent Garden – a fragment of the intended concrete deck with underground car-parking which was to have blanketed the area can still be seen at the top of Drury Lane. 'Almost all the planning files dealing with London at the Department of the Environment were adorned with a special flash signifying that they were politically sensitive' (Jenkins 1975: 255).

Simon Jenkins, perambulating London for his *Evening Standard* column, felt that the mid-1960s had been a watershed in its collective psychology. The cultural renaissance of the 'swinging city' was attracting international notice, and many visitors stayed. Comparing their situation with New Yorkers, Londoners were becoming more appreciative of their taken-for-granted life style of streets, houses, gardens, parks and pubs. The 'mood of London' encountered by agents of change became increasingly sceptical and challenging as owner-occupation spread steadily through the stock of older family housing and the politically radicalised 1960s generation sent its activists into working-class estates and communities (Glass

1973). Local communities could no longer be seen, as Abercrombie had seen them, as so many supine cases awaiting surgery. Falling residential densities and rising standards of living were shifting the perception, still so strong only 20 years before, of London as a blot on the face of Britain, 'dulled by such extensive drabness, monotony, ignorance and wretchedness that one is overcome by distress' (Purdom 1945: 8).

GREEN RENAISSANCE

The drabness had not been imaginary. As Ira Gershwin wrote in 1936, 'A foggy day in London town/Had me low/And had me down'. Until the 1960s London's atmosphere was almost always hazed. Moist winter days brought frequent fogs as moisture droplets formed around the pall of smoke particles which lodged permanently over the city, shifted slightly eastward of the built-up area by the prevailing west wind. In 1957–8 Chandler mapped the long ridge of intense smoke pollution curving down from Stoke Newington through Hackney and Poplar across the Thames to Deptford. Carbon, ash and dust rained on Poplar at a rate of 450 tons per square mile per year, and most of London received over 200 tons (Coppock and Prince 1964). Each winter, lung-related illness peaked at times of heavy smog, taking 4000 lives in the notorious pea-soupers of 1952. In the last major smog, ten years later, 340 died (Howe 1972). Air pollution masked architectural detail and levelled the colour of buildings to a bleak grey, and stunted the growth of trees and shrubs. The only tree which could grow in quantity was the London plane because it shed its polluted bark as well as its leaves (Fitter 1945).

Air pollution explained the intense desire of 1940s reformers to open up the urban fabric, create green spaces and replace outworn soot-stained buildings with the whitewashed towers of modernism. But the simpler and more effective remedy was to control the pollution at source – 84% of smoke was caused by coal burning in domestic grates. The introduction of smoke control zones under the Clean Air Act 1957 eliminated the problem. Civil servants monitored the progressive improvement from panoramic photographs of the horizon taken by a camera in the cross above the dome of St Paul's. Year by year the heights of Hampstead grew clearer to view. (The insidious growth of motor pollutants – carbon monoxide, nitrogen oxide, hydrocarbons – for the moment went unnoticed: Clout and Wood 1986: 92–100.)

The city was becoming greener as well as cleaner. As recently as 1945 the editors of the Collins *New Naturalist* series had bleakly described their new volume, *London's Natural History* by R.S.R Fitter (1945), as a chronicle of 'the progressive biological sterilisation of London'. But the biodiversity of the city would soon be on the turn as a result of deindustrialisation and tougher environmental regulation. Hollis (in Clout and Wood 1986) has traced the contributions of sewage treatment, effluent controls and industrial change to the recovery of the Thames since the 1950s. Then it was deoxygenated and black with scum. Today it runs clean enough for salmon to rise, brown shrimps thrive downstream of Battersea and prawns below Greenwich, and sea trout, roach and flounder are found along the length of the tidal Thames (Wheeler 1979). Cormorants, gannets, shelduck, pochard, terns and kingfishers come to the heart of London.

A parallel process of recolonisation and species diversity occurred on land, most startlingly in the blitzed sites in the heart of the City, then more generally along railway embankments, in disused waterworks, and railsidings (Burton 1974). On the human side, the new grassroots politicisation produced an upsurge in environmental interest, wildlife trusts, city farms, community gardens, waterway groups and green activism. Max Nicholson, a founding father of modern environmentalism, reminds us that in 1689 London had given the world its first natural history society – the Temple Coffee House Botanic Club – staking the claim for knowledgeable amateurs to study flora and fauna alongside professional scientists (Nicholson 1987: 89). Alongside his seminal role in the protection of the global commons, Nicholson was an amateur in this great tradition, travelling around on the top deck of London buses to count starling roosts in the 1930s, and 40 years later initiating the William Curtis Ecological Park, an experimental inner-city site for nature conservation and education right beside Tower Bridge (Nicholson-Lord 1987). Built upon such practical activism, the city's green renaissance – as David Goode calls it – showed itself increasingly effective as a force in urban politics.

A significant case was the Gunnersbury Triangle, a geometrical thicket with no special ecological interest formed by junctions on the District and North London railway lines. Developers had earmarked it for warehousing, but objectors pursued its defence in a public inquiry:

> The crucial factor was its value to local people which was well demonstrated when two hundred residents packed the town hall and argued forcibly that this was the only place where they had contact with the natural world in their neighbourhood. The inquiry inspector decided in favour of nature conservation largely because of this strength of feeling (Goode 1990: 6).

One of the important achievements of the Greater London Council was to reinforce green initiatives throughout the capital and systematise the standing of nature conservation in land use decisions (Goode 1986). Though London never had a systematic ecological survey or strategy to rival that of German cities, its characteristic philosophy of community linkage was to pay unexpected dividends when the metropolitan government was abolished in 1986. The green strategy might have disintegrated. Instead, through channels of voluntary joint action, notably the London Ecology Unit, it survived so well that the London boroughs now have 1183 sites scheduled (with an implication of permanent protection) in their statutory plans, a level and density of nature conservation unmatched in any other British city.

THE PROTECTIVE WEB

Londoners' solicitude for the habitats of moths and newts reflected the already-mentioned growth of collective concern with their own living environments. Both needed a philosophy of conservation. The basic planning system had not been designed to preserve London in aspic – quite the contrary – but it did supply the necessary mechanisms (Figure 4.5). The Town and Country Planning Act 1944 had given the Minister power to compile a national list of buildings of special architectural or historic interest, and the 1947 Act provided teeth, setting out the statutory procedures and allowing owners no right of appeal. Grant aid for building repair became available for the first time in 1953 – the government had been thinking primarily of the problem of decaying country houses, but much of the demand came from urban conservation. In the 1960s political support for conservation was boosted sharply by scandalous demolitions of the giant Doric arch which frowned over the entry to Euston Station, and the fabulously ornate cast iron Coal Exchange on Lower Thames Street. The list of casualties was long (Hobhouse 1971) and of buildings under threat even longer (Booker and Green 1973). Though bulldozers were at work throughout the land, London seemed particularly vulnerable because of its high land values and the degree to which its character lay in urban ensembles of buildings that might not justify individual listing. It was to meet this problem that Duncan Sandys, as a London MP, moved the private member's bill which became the Civic Amenities Act 1967. A vital instrument in the conservation cause, it extended protection to whole areas of historic interest. London's first such zone was drawn around the Royal Naval College, Greenwich in 1968. By 1974 there were 257 conservation areas. Today there are 800 designated areas, and 35 000 individually listed buildings.

It can be seen at a glance that the map of conservation areas (Figure 4.5) covers all surviving eighteenth-century London and its satellite villages and many Victorian suburbs. What it does not show is the more extensive web of protection woven around more recent and ordinary residential areas through other kinds of planning control. These little-understood mechanisms are distinctive to London and have proved surprisingly resilient through the institutional upheavals described in the next chapter. There is, first, a general presumption in the capital against any change which replaces dwellings with non-residential land and buildings; second, a use of quantitative density controls – unusual in the UK – to regulate new building and protect the amenity of existing areas; third, a unique collar of control drawn around the Central Activities Zone (CAZ) of the City and West End, to shield adjacent residential districts or Community Areas from the pressures of hotel and business development.

Appealing to the original Abercrombie principle of community protection, the CAZ policy was developed by the City of Westminster to demarcate the residential character (and, it must be said, the Conservative-voting electorate) of eighteenth-century streets under pressure for conversion into embassies, offices and hotels.

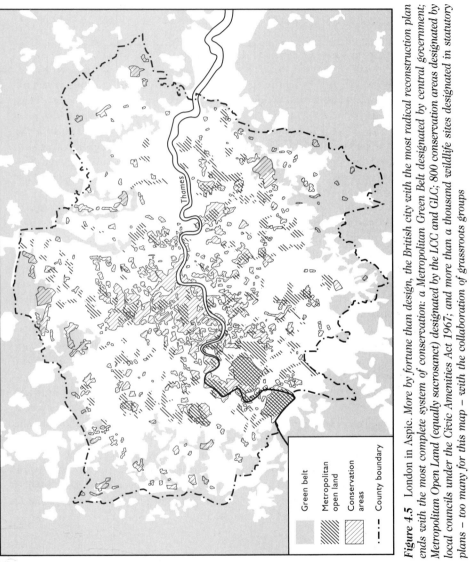

Figure 4.5 London in Aspic. More by fortune than design, the British city with the most radical reconstruction plan ends with the most complete system of conservation: a Metropolitan Green Belt designated by central government; Metropolitan Open Land (equally sacrosanct) designated by the LCC and GLC; 800 conservation areas designated by local councils under the Civic Amenities Act 1967; and more than a thousand wildlife sites designated in statutory plans – too many for this map – with the collaboration of grassroots groups

Green belt

Metropolitan
open land

Conservation
areas

County boundary

Thames

Table 4.1 *Age of Dwelling Stock (1983 estimate (%))*

	Pre-1890	1891–1918	1919–44	1945–70	Post-1970	All (thousands)
London	18.2	17.5	27.2	22.0	15.1	2 959
GB	14.1	12.6	19.1	31.4	22.8	23 470

Source: DoE (1994) *Housing & Construction Statistics 1983–1993*.

Subsequently adopted by all the councils of the inner periphery, it was formalised by the GLC into an *enceinte* of 16 Community Areas around central London. Being a bottom-up policy it managed to survive the abolition of the metropolitan council without difficulty and it remains in place today as a non-negotiable element of the statutory planning system. The Coin Street project of low-density affordable housing on the South Bank at Waterloo is its most striking advertisement. The international heart of London has become a 'city in a ring' in a new sense (GLC 1985a; Nicholson 1988).

Taken together, these policies create an expectation of stability in London which contrasts utterly with the perpetual motion described in Roman Cybriwsky's companion volume on Tokyo (1991: ch. 7). The age profile of London's housing stock has stabilised and is significantly older than that of the country as a whole – 63% prewar against England's 46%. While new units continue to be added at a cracking rate of 17 000 dwellings a year, the attrition of older dwellings is minuscule (Table 4.1). Policies to protect the residential component may be regressive if they do not make it affordable and accessible to lower-income residents. For decades, gentrification and displacement have been a dominant concern in studies of London's intensely competitive housing market. The squeeze on tenants and new owner-occupiers is real and critical (Whitehead in Halsey, Jowell and Taylor 1995). But Ruth Glass's foreboding (1973: 426) that Inner London – the old LCC area – would be 'gentrified with a vengeance and be almost exclusively reserved for selected higher-class strata' was not fulfilled. The physical mixing of tenures within neighbourhoods, the security of council housing, the survival of philanthropic landlordism, and the inventiveness of the private rental sector (legal and otherwise) sustain a degree of social mix in even the wealthiest parts of west Inner London – a point well shown by comparisons with New York (Fainstein, Gordon and Harloe 1991: ch. 7). The 'village' metaphor applied so often to London's neighbourhoods is not just a conceit of property writers or tourist guides: it captures a real quality of social and tenure mix unique in urban Britain.

TWO HUNDRED CENTRES

Urban villages are also supposed to be clusters of local services, shops and pubs, with those qualities, increasingly elusive at the end of the century, of vitality and viability. Insofar as London's local centres retain these qualities, which they do, it is due again to unobtrusive processes of regulation. Each local authority maps its town, district and local centres, defines primary and secondary frontages, and steers activities to them so far as its planning powers will allow (Hebbert 1991). The cumulative effect is clearly reflected in London's pattern of shopping provision (Figure 4.6). Outside the world-class retail districts of the West End and Knightsbridge, boroughs have tended to concentrate comparison shopping in one main centre, often the civic hub, and convenience shopping in local and district satellites. National rankings by the retail data specialists Experian Goad show the strong position of the larger centres in outer London. The vitality of Kingston and Bromley – measured by the number and type of units, and the level of occupancy – ranks them above giant out-of-town malls such as the Gateshead Metro Centre or Sheffield's Meadowhall Centre, and Croydon ranks only just below them. With the West End of London, they form the pinnacle of a protected hierarchy of more than 200 centres extending down to the scatter of local parades. Of course, London has not been completely immune from the trends of modern retailing which cut across the concept of shopping centres as central places. Only 32 of London's 'centres' are out-of-centre malls or retail parks, and the first and largest – the Brent Cross mall near Hendon in north-west London – was deliberately planted by planners in the early 1970s to fill a gap in the pattern of suburban town centres. But it is the exception to prove the rule. With its predominance of small scale over large-scale retailing, the profile of shopping given in Table 4.2 has a distinctively old-fashioned feel: further confirmation, perhaps, of the village ethos.

Table 4.2 also strikingly reveals the unique vitality of London's street markets. Historically, because of its weak local government, London had proportionately few markets established by statute or franchise – only 13 in the entire 600 square miles of the metropolitan area – but compensatingly large numbers of informal traders. They enjoyed surprising rapid growth in the first half of the twentieth century, when the number of licensed stalls in the LCC area more than doubled, refuting the idea that open-air shopping was a by-product of poverty (Benedetta and Moholy-Nagy 1936). Officialdom was concerned with the issue of obstructions to traffic, and the policy in postwar years was to relocate traders off the highway (LCC 1951: 104). An early example which still flourishes is the Market Square in the Lansbury Estate, Poplar, developed as a showcase for the 1951 Festival of Britain. Other markets transplanted in comprehensive development schemes (such as the nearby Watney Street market) fared less well.

But street trading benefited from the policy shift back towards preservation of the street system and encouragement of existing mixed-use shopping centres. Accurate measurement is difficult: the data in Table 4.2 are incomplete (not all boroughs provide returns) and they include various forms of licensed outdoor traders other than street pitches, but the 23 000 recorded in 1994–5 must by any measure have more than doubled the 8300 pitches measured in a Wye College study twenty years earlier (Kirk, Ellis and Medland 1972). Demand for pitches

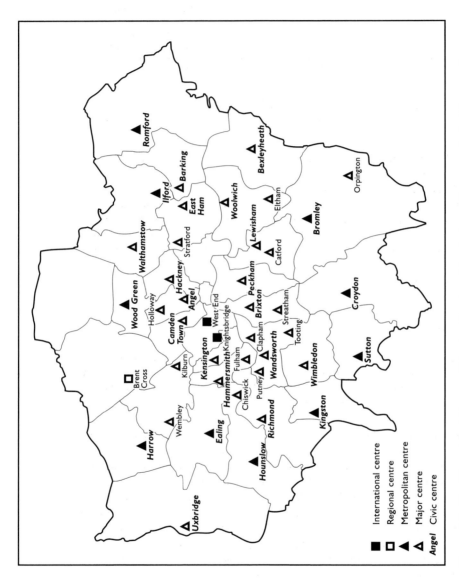

Figure 4.6 The Hierarchy of Centres. This classification of London's retail centres, devised by consultants on behalf of the London Boroughs, was adopted as part of government's strategic plan for the capital (GoL 1996). A hybrid, it combines empirical measurement (ranking centres by turnover and numbers of multiple stores) with a policy aim of borough councils to protect their retail flagships. In many cases, italicised on the map, these coincide with the main civic centre

International centre
Regional centre
Metropolitan centre
Major centre
Angel Civic centre

Table 4.2 *Size Distribution of Retail Units in London and the Rest of England, 1995 (units per 10 000 population)*

	Large-scale retail units	Small-scale retail units	Services and repairs to goods and property	Market, mobile and temporary units
London	7.7	130.4	49.0	32.9
Other metropolitan areas	8.9	93.7	35.9	8.9
Non-metropolitan England	9.3	125.5	52.0	14.4

Source: original tabulation based on CIPFA (1996) *Trading Standards Statistics 1994–5 Actuals*. London: CIPFA Statistical Information Service.

remains buoyant, especially in ethnic areas where they provide a flexible entry into retailing for minorities.

A vibrant example is High Street, Walthamstow, Europe's longest market with one and half miles of stalls, where one trader in five is black. Another is the Whitechapel Road market, now strongly Bangladeshi, which lines the pavement opposite the porticoed facade of the London Hospital, spilling out onto the highway and narrowing to one lane the the main arterial road eastward out of London in a way that would astound Sir Alker Tripp. It demonstrates the complete subversion of London's grand design.

DRAWING THE RING

One element of the design was implemented and remains to be considered as a conclusion to the chapter: without it, none of the rest would have occurred. The ideal of a fixed, determinate urban edge had been a recurrent theme in London history since Tudor times. For the past 50 years, the line has been drawn, and it has held.

The freeze on building activity around London began at the outbreak of the Second World War. Plans for the capital's defence envisaged a hardening of the outer edge of 1939 with a giant ring of of tank traps, deep trenches and pillboxes. They were never completed, but a different sort of hardening did occur as a result of the *Greater London Plan 1944*. At first, development of agricultural land beyond the prewar suburban boundary was effectively limited by building licences and materials shortages. The green belt was truly put to the test after the return of the Conservatives in 1951 and the start of the great private building boom of the 1950s. For a moment it seemed that the defence line would crumple under the outward surge of bricks and mortar, but Duncan Sandys (again!) in his then role of Minister reponsible for town and country planning issued a strongly worded circular confirming the status of green belts as national policy. Local planning authorities were invited to prepare detailed maps for approval. The shire counties around

London responded rapidly, and by 1961 the boundary lines of the metropolitan green belt had been drawn (Thomas 1970). They have remained fixed ever since, with only two short hints of relaxation, both under Conservative governments.

In 1972, as a specific response to house price inflation – which it attributed to overtight rationing of building land – the government asked local authorities to release 2000 acres of green belt to the builders. Ten years later, with prices rising again and a free-market régime in power, developers pressed for a more fundamental deregulation. The government responded with a draft circular which overtly reaffirmed support for the green belt but in fact – when taken in conjunction with another draft circular on land for housing – implied a fundamental loosening of control in favour of market demand. It summoned up a powerful coalition of political opponents under the leadership of the Council for the Protection of Rural England, including the Civic Trust, local government associations and the National Farmer's Union. Cross-party opposition from backbench Tory MPs and peers, and vocal public opinion, forced the Secretary of State to retreat (Elson 1986: ch. 10), an incident marked by several commentators as a momentus turning point in the history of Thatcherism (Ward 1994: 256). It was an important and timely outcome, because the policy was about to be put to its hardest test with the completion of the M25 orbital motorway in 1986. The motorway was the largest public development to encroach on the belt, taking 5000 acres of land directly, and reinforcing development pressure in towns and villages throughout the inner fringe. Speculative money surged into options to purchase sites if planning permission could be won, particularly around the prime locations where the M25 intersected radial roads into London. But the line held firm. The only M25 intersections to be released for development were at Grays, Thurrock and Dartford, on opposite banks of the Thames in the depressed corridor to the east of London, where major out-of town shopping centres were built on the site of derelict mineral workings. For the rest, the orbital motorway still runs through countryside so 'unspoilt' that a Norwich coach company introduced a new style of London excursion trip, not visiting the city but driving round its green perimeter and home again.

The attractiveness of London's countryside is as great a policy achievement as the permanence of the stop-line. It was not easy to make the green belt a zone of recreation and beauty as the government intended (MHLG 1962). The lesser prewar belt created by Herbert Morrison's LCC involved direct public acquisition and management of beauty spots and stretches of countryside around London. These holdings, with Crown land, National Trust estates and Forestry Commission sites (mapped by Thomas 1970), remained a significant presence in the hugely expanded modern green belt. But most of it was privately owned and subject to market forces. In terms of landscape quality, the basic problems of agricultural change (loss of hedgerows) have been compounded by effects of urban proximity (horticulture) and by continuing speculative hope, however remote, that development might be resumed. Richard Munton's (1983) meticulous research into land ownership and management in London's hinterland showed that the green belt reduced but could not eliminate the characteristic rural–urban fringe ecology of short leases, interim land uses, and deliberate neglect (see also Land Use Consultants 1993). Empirical research offered an unflattering view of tipped rubbish, denuded hedgerows, diseased and dying elm trees, and unkempt fields inaccessible to public enjoyment, or overgrazed by riding stables. Davidson and Wibberley (1977) showed the imbalance between the negative aspect of green belt policy – stopping development – and the lack of positive policies to manage the countryside.

By slow degrees the imbalance was corrected. Gradually, the encompassing landscape is being reworked to express its permanence as a planted boundary. Paradoxically perhaps, the process was stimulated by local government reorganisation – discussed in the next chapter – which brought several thousand acres of green belt inside the administrative boundary of the capital, including (in clockwise order) the valley of the River Cray, Chislehurst Commons, Hayes Common, Keston Common, the rolling country from Biggin Hill to the Darenth valley, the commons south of Croydon, Hounslow Heath and Ruislip Common, Bushey Heath, the heights of Mill Hill, Enfield Chase, Hainault Forest and the open country south of Hornchurch. As urban authorities, the boroughs and the metropolitan council were inclined to take an active stance towards access and recreation within their green outer perimeter. Extensive programmes of treeplanting, hedgelaying, coppicing, and footpath signage and maintenance were launched with grant-aid from the Countryside Commission. Another national body, the Forestry Commission, became involved in the 1990s in developing 'community forests' to multiply tree cover on the two barest stretches of green belt, on the flat gravels of Rainham beyond the East End of London, and the northern uplands of Shenley. The cumulative effect of planting programmes can already be seen from the heights around the London basin.

The concept of London's green belt as a resource for the active enjoyment of Londoners is most imaginatively expressed in the London Outer Orbital Path or LOOP, a 150-mile 'round London footpath' in 24 sections linked to public transport connections. The first sections, launched in 1996, run along the downs to the south of Croydon and the northern heights of Elstree, Cockfosters and Barnet. Each has its own pocket guide, with information boards along the way. Conceived by the London Walking Forum and implemented through complex partnerships of local authorities and funding bodies, LOOP neatly expresses the image of London as a city in a green ring, where a bus or train ride will lead to 'the best of the English countryside'.

London's artificial boundary is an extraordinary geographical phenomenon, particularly when it abuts the last line of speculative semidetached housing where bricklayers laid down their trowels in September 1939 (Figure 4.7). What has it meant for Londoners, for the cost of housing, for patterns of living and working, for the British economy? Vigorous controversy surrounds all these questions.

What is sure is that putting an impermeable barrier of agricultural land around a dynamic city has two effects. The first is centrifugal, the dispersal of activity systems to the further side of the green belt, a process definitively analysed in Peter

Figure 4.7 Containment. 'When the Green Belt came into force in 1938, the outward swell of building stopped dead, two fields away . . . There is a terrifying forty miles of solid brickwork behind those demure-looking semis half a mile away. You feel as Canute might have on the beach, but unexpectedly successful' (Nairn 1966: 176)

Hall's monumental PEP study *The Containment of Urban England* (1973) and in his subsequent work on the regional dynamics of south-east England. In the 1960s and 1970s the leapfrog effect could be seen clearly in the industrial estates and the housing estates of towns like Reading, Colchester and Luton; in the 1980s and 1990s the frontier of high economic and demographic growth was shifted further by the completion of the M25 and electrification of radial railway lines (Hall 1989).

The impacts of London's growth in and beyond the south-east have been well studied. Less well understood are the centripetal effects of containment. By no means all footloose activity leapfrogs outwards: some is deflected or refracted back into the city. The belt broke the spell of suburbanisation, and the long historical association between upward and outward mobility. It was a neat historical symmetry that London, the first world city to experience untrammelled suburban growth, should become the first to turn the process into reverse, pioneering the ideas of growth management and densification which would be so widely pursued in the developed world at the century's end. Possession of a green belt encouraged new forms of living, most notably a revival of the urban flat, first in the suburbs (Whitehand 1992) then in inner London (Hamnett and Randolph 1986; Hamnett 1990). Arguably – it is difficult to prove – containment contributed to the shifts of mood and policy described in this chapter, to the social changes discussed in Chapter 6, and the economic regeneration described in Chapters 7 and 8. These relations are speculative and under-researched. We are on surer ground when it comes to the effect of the green belt on political geography – the topic of the next chapter.

CHAPTER 5

ALBION AWAKES

CHAPTER 5

ALBION AWAKES

City form and government are interconnected – each affects the other. London grew up with the physical character and the political habits of a collection of townships. Late nineteenth-century reform created the typical modern big-city pattern of a large core authority amid a dispersing sprawl of suburban jurisdictions. Mid-twentieth-century legislation, in reaction, stopped the sprawl with a green belt. In defining a new physical entity it laid an eventual basis for political identity. If the old geography of dispersal encouraged a political culture of localism and particularism, the new geography of containment had the potential to create a more inclusive concept of citizenship. One of the great themes in the history of modern London, and the topic of the present chapter, is the struggle to reconcile those two traditions. It has taken the system of London government through two radical reforms, and a third is in progress. This history of institutional experiment just might have a happy ending. More by fortune than design, London at the end of the twentieth century may stand closer than ever before to finding a pattern of government that expresses both its unity and its diversity.

The story begins with the postwar reconstruction in the mid-twentieth century, when London for the first time in its history was subjected to an overall plan. The very word 'planning' implied new structures of control as well as new ways of living. The more radical the plan, the greater the implicit shift for government. Le Corbusier's English disciple Arthur Korn, chairman of the MARS group, looked to Stalin as an example of the leadership qualities required by London's planners (Korn 1953: 88–95). Wiser commentators such as William Robson who recognised the evils of Stalinist town planning might still envy Mossoviet's centralisation of power (in Simon et al. 1937). Robson was a key figure in the campaign to modernise London government. Professor of Public Administration at the London School of Economics, he was a favourite disciple of the Webbs and a true practical Fabian, campaigning with equal vigour for London to be remade physically and institutionally.

Robson's *Government and Misgovernment of London*, published in 1939 just before the outbreak of war, was a withering critique of the status quo, a catalogue of administrative confusion, political indecision and (a favourite word in the Robson vocabulary) 'obsolescence'. Though the previous year he had contributed to a celebratory volume for the first half-century of the London County Council, the basic argument of *Government and Misgovernment* was that the LCC could not rest on its laurels: it was time for a fresh round of reorganisation, based on modern realities rather than the requirements of metropolitan management in the 1880s.

Robson also vigorously attacked the failure of the 1888 reform to deal with the City Corporation, with its medieval boundaries and indefensible constitution. In strong prose he pointed out the absurdity of a situation where the democratic LCC was denied the ceremonial trappings of London municipal pride (the Lord Mayoralty, the Guildhall), while the oligarchic City was allowed to perform metropolitan tasks such as the provision of wholesale and retail markets, bridges, parks and public health in the Port of London. Robson saw the City's survival as the key to all the wider problems of misgovernment in the London region. He was amazed at the ability, in mid-twentieth century, of the Livery Companies and the Corporation to disarm potential critics and charm senior officers of government and the law through the primitive alurements of lavish hospitality. 'It is not necessary to suggest that these festive occasions were deliberately devised to curry favour in high places in order to appreciate the subtle result of their cumulative effect over a very long span of years' (Robson 1939: 41).

The outbreak of war immediately after the publication of *Government and Misgovernment* confirmed many of Robson's criticisms of administrative short-comings of London local government. His proposed remedy – a unified admin-istration for the metropolis as a whole – suddenly became politically practicable. For purposes of civil defence administration the government appointed Regional Commissioners with emergency powers of direction over local authorities in the capital. At the end of the war reformers hoped that the wide-area administrative structure would be given a democratic mandate to implement the *Greater London Plan* (Sharp 1969; Young and Garside 1982). The idea was considered but rejected by the incoming Labour government in 1945.

The existing arrangements suited Labour well. It had controlled the LCC since 1934, and the demographics of the core were in its favour. Herbert Morrison, the leader, had built up a formidably effective Labour machine, concentrating power in a small elite of senior politicians and officers (Donoughue and Jones 1973). County Hall, 'headquarters of the greatest municipality in the world', looked across the river to the Palace of Westminster (Morrison 1935): the parliamentary layout and procedure of its council chamber expressed a long-held image of itself as a state in miniature rather than a municipal council (Briggs 1963). It had become Labour's greatest political stronghold. The idea of regional enlargement to the scale of 'Greater London' – favoured by William Robson – might be administratively logical but it held no political appeal for Labour: Isaac Hayward continued to run the LCC in the fortress-statelet tradition of Herbert Morrison from 1947 until its abolition in 1965 (Mason in Saint 1989: ch. 14).

Meanwhile the Conservative Party was shifting from its traditional position of hostility to London-wide government (Jones in Saint 1989; Young 1975). The London Municipal Society, the Conservative front organisation in the metropolitan arena (see page 50 above), was the traditional champion of borough rights and local identity against the centralising bureaucracy of County Hall. Having lost control of the LCC in 1934, the Tories saw their political base eroded by outmigration of business and professional classes, and by Herbert Morrison's aggressive use of housing policy to 'build the Tories out of London'. In 1952 Enoch Powell took the directorship of the LMS. With radical insight, he argued that the right's best prospect for breaking Labour's grip on the capital would be within a new and enlarged authority for Greater London, a metropolitan council of the type proposed by William Robson in *Government and Misgovernment* (Young and Garside 1982).

During the 1950s the case for change was revived by practical problems of planning, road-building, traffic management, housing construction, and the overspill of population and employment from areas of blitzed or slum building under redevelopment. None of these policies were suited to an administrative geography based on late nineteenth-century boundaries. Besides, the economy was strong, standards of living were rising, and the first property boom was under way: business was frustrated by the slow pace of decision making and the diffusion of responsibility. Local authorities managed to collaborate successfully over cemeteries and crematoria but their attempts at joint provision of economic infrastructure – drainage, waste disposal, transport, roads – were littered with failure (Rhodes 1970; Smallwood 1965).

With the issue of London government reorganisation already on the political agenda, action was triggered by a series of applications from suburban district councils – particularly in the County of Middlesex – for unitary status. West Ham and East Ham were County Boroughs in their own right; large wealthy districts such as Harrow, Enfield and Walthamstow sought the same status. The demands from suburban municipalities could not be shelved indefinitely. They could perhaps be harnessed to break Labour's grip on the core.

THE HERBERT COMMISSION

In 1957 the government announced the appointment of a Royal Commission on Local Goverment in Greater London under the chairmanship of Sir Edwin Herbert, a city solicitor with extensive business interests. The six other members included Sir Charles Morris, Vice-Chancellor of the University of Leeds; Paul Cadbury of the progressive Quaker chocolate dynasty; and W.J.M. Mackenzie, Professor of Government at Manchester University. The Commissioners were given a review area of 721 square miles – the 1829 Metropolitan Police District, broadly matching the modern conurbation within the green belt – plus the Square Mile of the Corporation of London, which for the first time was to be incorporated into the review process.

The area under consideration contained a sixth of the total population of the United Kingdom and a third of its ratable value (the property tax base). Its local government structures comprised 16 *ad hoc* public bodies running police, transport, utilities and health, and 117 elected councils: the City of London at the centre of the web, around it the 28 metropolitan boroughs and the London

County Council (3.5 million residents), to the west the County of Middlesex, fully built-up with 2.25 million population, and elsewhere parts of the shire counties of Kent, Surrey, Hertfordshire and Essex. The suburban boroughs of Croydon, East Ham and West Ham were (as we have seen) counties in their own right. The metropolis embraced 42 additional non-county boroughs, 28 urban districts, three rural districts, and six parish councils.

A much larger review area would have been needed to capture the functional metropolitan region which had developed around the outer edge of the green belt, diffused and extended in inverse relation to the compactness of development inside the inner boundary. The prevailing view among intellectuals was that any new system of London government should be based on the functional and not the physical metropolis. For Derek Senior, who wrote on planning, local government and gardening for *The Guardian* and who was to play a prominent part in later debates about local government organisation in Britain, a distinction between townsmen and countrymen was just nostalgic English sentimentalism: 'nothing is so irrelevant to the structure of the urban region as continuous built-upness' (Senior 1966: 18). This view was well entrenched among academic experts. The Herbert Commission wrote to every university in England and Wales, and received two substantial responses from the Centre for Urban Studies, linked to University College London, and from William Robson of LSE and his Greater London Group, who undertook special research with the aid of a grant from the Nuffield Foundation. The experts were divided on most issues except the need to base reform on a larger geographical area.

Herbert received the evidence from 'the Academic World' with great courtesy and respect but decisively rejected the argument that a physical metropolis was somehow less important than its penumbra of activity systems and travel-to-work areas. The Royal Commission report – a brilliant piece of writing, largely the work of Herbert himself – was emphatic that the boundary that mattered was 'the one where the built-up area gives place to the surrounding countryside, that is to say, the inner edge of the green belt' (Figure 5.1). The commissioners formed their opinion over a remarkable research process which involved informal visits to 79 local authority areas over 88 days – not just to town halls but also to housing schemes, open spaces, schools, swimming pools, refuse destructors. They found 'an entity which is so closely knit, so interdependent, so deeply influenced by the central area and so largely built up, that it truly makes up the London of today' (PP 1960: 226–7).

Advanced in the face of expert opinion, this view of London was new and radical. It marked the first political recognition of the structural importance of the green belt. Challenging all the cherished divisions of political allegiance and social status between inner and outer London, LCC and shire counties, core and suburbs, the Herbert Report presented a vision of the entire metropolis as a single entity deserving effective self-government.

The Royal Commission was conscious of its historic responsibility as the first body since 1834 to review London as a whole, including the City. Like Sir Laurence

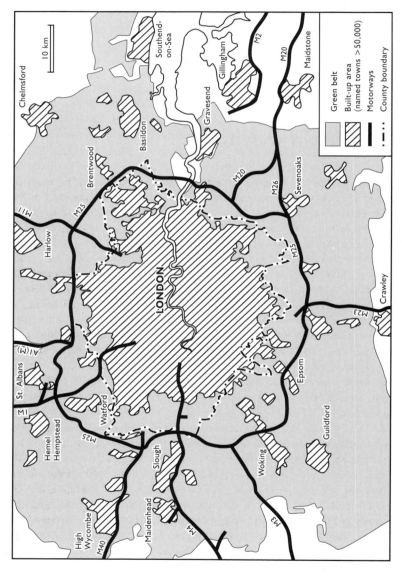

Figure 5.1 City in a Ring (2). *The Herbert Commission saw London inside the green belt as a single territorial community. Thirty years ago it was wishful thinking. Today it is political fact*

> ### *Visions of Albion*
>
> I behold London, a Human awful wonder of God!
> He says: 'Return, Albion, return! I give myself for thee.
> My Streets are my Ideas of Imagination.
> Awake Albion, awake! and let us awake up together.
> My Houses are Thoughts: my Inhabitants, Affections,
> The children of thoughts walking within my blood-vessels,
> . . . .
> So spoke London, immortal guardian! I heard in Lambeth's shades.
> In Felpham I heard and saw the Visions of Albion.
> I write in South Molton Street what I both see and hear
> In regions of Humanity, in London's opening streets.
>
> William Blake, *Jerusalem* II, cited in PP (1960: 4)

Gomme 50 years earlier, its members saw democracy as a living principle needing new forms of expression to match a city's geographical growth (Gomme 1907: 394). They used poetry – William Blake's mystical waking call to Albion – to make the case for reform. 'The Royal Commission on Local Government in Greater London had its vision of a New Jerusalem which, with all its faults, represented no less than the vision of the old Jerusalem as it was praised in the Psalms – "a city that is at unity in itself"' (Smallwood 1965: 313). Lecturing on the theme of metropolitan government to a Manchester audience, Professor W.J.M. Mackenzie used the same phrase from Psalm 122 in the King James Bible translation which was even more appropriate to the London case: 'a city that is compact together'.

It was one thing to have the vision, another to turn it into legislation. The Herbert Commission faced problems common to all metropolitan reform: how to balance area-wide and local representation; how far to respect tradition; how much power and what functions to entrust to the central authority; and what, in the case of a capital city, to leave to central government (Self 1982; Rusk 1993; Sharpe 1995).

The Herbert Commission reviewed four types of solution (PP 1960: 182). The first, on the model of the Metropolitan Police, was to entrust responsibility for London to central government ministers: but that was administratively impractical and constitutionally undesirable. The second solution, on the model of the London Transport Board, was to appoint *ad hoc* bodies for specific London-wide tasks: but Herbert saw fatal objections of democratic accountability, and the inappropriateness of single-function solutions to the interlinked problems of metropolitan governance. 'What is needed is some means of considering them as a whole and dealing with them. It is no solution to separate them still further by giving each to some specially designed *ad hoc* body' (PP 1960: 188). The third solution, to rely on cooperation and joint working between local authorities in Greater London, was dismissed on the evidence that such arrangements had already been tried and failed. Herbert opted for a scaled-up version of the two-tier system operating within the County of London since 1889. There should be an overarching council for strategic functions and external representation, and a primary system of municipalities for functions relating to local areas, both directly elected. The bold simplicity of the blueprint had a strong international impact (Rowat 1980; Barlow 1991).

The Herbert Commission's solution would merge the divided worlds of the Labour-controlled London County Council area and the predominantly Conservative interwar suburbia. In their initial evidence to the Royal Commission none of the outer local authorities responded with any enthusiasm to Herbert's holistic vision of metropolis. Inner London was equally opposed, with the exception of Hampstead and some riverside boroughs. LCC witnesses, to the exasperation of the Royal Commission, refused to acknowledge any need for change or even to see that there could be any definition of 'London' other than that of the 1888 LCC boundaries. The gist of the local authority evidence was that existing structures worked, and wider problems could be handled through voluntary cooperation (Rhodes 1970). The commissioners disagreed, offering in evidence the cases of some eight years of indecision over the replacement of an unsafe swingbridge over the entrance to Limehouse Basin, and the fifteen year lead time to build the Hammersmith flyover. In the case of the Hammersmith Road 'the present machinery is so confused that it is difficult even to put down on paper a description of what it is, let alone how it works' (PP 1960: 323–7).

'Awake Albion, Awake!': the Herbert report invoked William Blake's radicalism for a new vision of London. With it came the promise of a new sort of London-wide authority, intelligent and light of touch. Unlike the paternalistic, service-providing LCC, it would deal only with strategic issues. The primary work of government would be entrusted to boroughs. Much of the evidence heard by the Commissioners had to do with the frictions and delays of the two-tier arrangements already operating everywhere in the review area apart from the four islands of unitary all-purpose government in the City, Croydon, West and East Ham. Herbert's recommendations on size and function were inspired mainly by the need for clear and distinct lines of responsibility, with no 'papering over the cracks' by delegation of powers from one level to another. Where powers had to be shared, as in planning and education, they tried to define separate roles as a basis for cooperation. In view of the subsequent history of metropolitan governance in London it is worth recalling the Royal Commission's emphatic assertion that: 'Above all we hope to get away from the conception of superior and inferior or upper tier and lower tier. We cannot emphasise too strongly that our proposed redistribution of functions is not on the basis of upper and lower, superior and inferior, but on the basis of wider and narrower' (PP 1960: 198). Dealings between the boroughs and the Council for Greater London were to be based on the subsidiarity principle: 'the primary unit of local government in the Greater London Area should be the borough, and the borough should perform all local authority functions except those which can only be effectively performed over the wider area of Greater London or which could be better performed over that wider area' (PP 1960: 192).

These arguments made a real impact, shifting attitudes even during the course of the Commission's proceedings. Councils who had initially opposed any change came round to support it – a good example of the policy-shaping role of an independent commission. The only unyielding opponents were in the outer suburbs of suburban Surrey, gateway to the stockbroker belt, and in Labour-controlled County Hall, where the concept of a Greater London Council still seemed just a Conservative plot to break up Labour's greatest municipal stronghold (Smallwood 1965).

With unusual speed, the government announced its acceptance of the recommendations of the Royal Commission and its intention to bring London government into line with the physical boundaries of the metropolis. The government accepted Herbert's central premise that the built-up tract within the green belt should have a civic identity. 'All of its citizens are "Londoners", not only those who live within the City and the 28 metropolitan boroughs. Greater London is their city and all are involved on what happens to it' (MHLG 1961). The bill went through Parliament in 1962. Lobbying in the House of Lords by the Surrey districts of Ewell and Epsom led to boundary adjustments on the south-west fringes of London, but few other concessions were made. Sir Keith Joseph, as Minister for Housing and Local Government, had the following to say at the second reading of the London Government Bill on 10 December 1962:

> No one existing authority has any responsibility for considering the needs of Greater London as a whole. Yet Greater London is, in a very real sense, a single city. Admittedly it embraces many places of distinctive character which attract strong loyalties. Nevertheless, the whole of the great urban area, which spreads out to and is contained by the green belt, is one metropolis. It owes its existence to the unique position of London in the economic, industrial and political life of the country. The great and diverse activities of the capital affect the character of the whole area. Every man, woman and child who lives there is concerned in its prosperity and is affected by the way in which it is governed . . . The Bill will ensure that there is a body directly elected by the people of London charged with responsibilities for watching over the whole physical environment in the interests of London as a whole and having powers and resources to match its responsibilities.

This episode abounded in political irony. The green belt which Herbert Morrison had fought to establish (see page 67 above) had dug the grave of his beloved LCC. But that was not all. The Labour Party shared Conservative Central Office's belief that an elected council for London within the green belt would be Tory-controlled. Labour MPs opposed it at every stage, hard put though they were to find convincing arguments for the status quo. The London Government Act became law in 1963 and the first GLC elections were held in April 1964. Instantly, both parties realised that they had made a great electoral miscalculation (Young and Garside 1982: 295). Instead of placing London under permanent Tory control, the new system – as Table 5.2 later shows – delivered a much more interesting equilibrium, comparable to that of the country at large. In the political climate of spring 1964, with public opinion in strong reaction to 13 years of Tory government, it delivered 36 seats to the Conservatives, 64 to Labour. Half of the newly elected GLC Labour councillors, including all the key committee chairmen, were LCC veterans. Newly elected members arriving to the first meetings of the new authority were surprised to find a going concern with its customs and practices ready-made. The 1963 Act had not destroyed the political leadership, the departmental structure, the senior officers, the quasi-parliamentary procedures, the routines and the mentality of the old LCC, it had extended their geographical jurisdiction by 10 miles. Apprehension gave way to triumphalism.

THE MAKING OF THE BOROUGHS

The Herbert Commission combined a strong sense of historical destiny with a ruthless drive for reform. They took the typical view of the first postwar decades that modern functions required modern and uniform structures. The miscellaneous clutter of units which confronted them in the review area ranged from the metropolitan Borough of Holborn (406 acres and 21 300 population) to the County Borough of Croydon (12 700 acres and 249 000 population). The commission recommended a rationalisation into units of at least 100 000 population, the threshold specified in the Local Government Act 1958 beyond which a borough could claim a *prima facie* entitlement to be upgraded to a county borough and take responsibility for the full range of local government services. They offered a provisional scheme of division into 52 boroughs. The government of the day decided in favour of fewer, larger units with a minimum population of 200 000 so as to attract a better calibre of councillor and achieve greater efficiencies in service provision. 'Larger units would mean more work for each authority in all the personal services and so make specialisation in staff and institutions more efficient and economical. In addition larger units would be stronger in resources and so better able to secure the major development which many boroughs now need' (MHLG 1961: 3).

The irregularities of the pre-1960 local government system were administratively untidy but they had a logic of their own that matched the structure of living and working communities in London, of high streets and local newspapers, telephone exchanges, stations and bus destinations. The hundred or more town halls with their polished brass handrails and scrubbed steps defined the civic geography of the capital. Even today, large-scale maps of London are more likely to carry the names of the old units than their 30-year-old replacements. In their evidence to the Royal Comission, areas such as Bethnal Green, Camberwell, Chelsea, Deptford, Finsbury, Fulham, Greenwich and Leyton argued the importance of the local town halls as a focus of civic activity, and first point of contact for public enquiries of all kinds:

The Leyton Town Hall is a Town Hall in every sense. Not only is it the centre of the municipal administration but for years it has been the meeting place of numerous local associations and societies, trade union meetings, school speech days, whist drives, dances, concerts, plays – all the facets of a town's life can be found in the Town Hall at one time or another (*Minutes of Evidence* Vol. III, 257–8).

The commissioners were unimpressed by what they regarded as backward-looking parochialism:

We have been forced to recognise that many of the representations made to us are emotional rather than rational. We have heard in constant use phrases such as 'local interest', 'local feeling', 'remoteness from a county town' and so on. We have often been told that a service would become more 'personal' if it were administered solely from the Town Hall, or that 'chaos' would result if certain changes were made. We do not doubt that these phrases have some basis in fact, but they are so highly charged with emotion that they are relevant to our inquiry only after the most careful analysis . . . Evidence of opinion from a local authority (as distinct from their factual evidence) only becomes of real value to us when its objectivity and consequent cogency have been tested (PP 1960: 47).

This cool scepticism slipped when it came to the City of London, the smallest unit in population and area, and the least defensible on rational grounds. The Square Mile had been included in the Royal Commission's review area and could have been reformed: William Robson, of course, argued cogently for it. But Herbert ruled out any change – and this was explicitly a definite and not a provisional recommendation – on the grounds that the City Corporation's wealth, its antiquity, its part in the national history, its dignity, its traditions and its historical ceremonial, 'with the patina of centuries upon it', made it an institution of national importance. Herbert hoped that the City could give historical lustre to the new system of local government, but provided no mechanism for breaking its perennial isolation from the rest of municipal London. Options to retain the Lord Mayor for ceremonial purposes only, or combine the offices of the Lord Mayor and the Chairman of the GLC, were considered and rejected. In sharp contrast to the root and branch reorganisation applied to the rest of London, the City was felt to be untouchable – its position 'owes much to its peculiar constitution and area and all these things are really inseparable from one another. If one is to be preserved all must be' (PP 1960: 237). Understandably dissatisfied with this logic, MPs made several attempts in the passage of the 1963 London Government Bill to create a single borough for the whole central area of the City and Westminster, or at least to establish a single jurisdiction for town planning purposes. All were defeated and the old salamander of the Square Mile survived intact, once again.

The only other local government unit to escape reorganisation was Harrow, a municipality of 12 600 acres created in the 1930s for an area of modern suburbia around the old nucleus of the school and village on Harrow Hill. Elsewhere, the government's 'big is beautiful' philosophy meant abolition or merger for all. London

became the testbed for the general reorganisation of local government in the next decade, with the same emphasis on size and efficiency at the expense of identity. The enforced merger of neighbours was equally acrimonious whether they were matched pairs such as East Ham and West Ham, Barking and Dagenham, Bromley and Beckenham, or misalliances such as cockney Romford and genteel Hornchurch, respectable Hornsey and scruffy Tottenham, industrial Wembley and tree-lined Willesden. To keep at arm's length from the controversy the government employed the town clerks of Plymouth, Cheltenham, Oxford and South Shields to make final decisions. Their map reflected administrative convenience but had no defensible logic in terms of community structure (Rhodes 1970; Davis 1988: ch. 9).

Choosing names for the new boroughs was equally controversial. Where one authority was clearly dominant it effectively incorporated its neighbours: Finsbury disappeared into Islington, Battersea into Wandsworth, Erith into Bexley, Penge into Bromley, and Barnes and Twickenham into Richmond-upon-Thames. Mergers of equally sized authorities were more problematic. After violent rows Hornchurch and Romford, the ill-matched newly-weds on London's easternmost extremity, agreed to compromise on 'Havering' from the medieval manor of Havering-atte-Bower. Similar geographical or historical substitutes were used in Brent, Hillingdon, Redbridge, Merton, Tower Hamlets, and Waltham Forest. 'Newham' was a simple enough answer to the problem of the two proud county boroughs of East Ham and West Ham. Many councils refused to be renamed and fought to preserve their old identity in the new structure (Rhodes 1970). The Minister Sir Keith Joseph banned the compound names common in suburban areas – Chislehurst & Sidcup, Heston & Isleworth, Merton & Morden. In deference to its influential residents he made an exception for the Royal Borough of Kensington & Chelsea, but insisted that the mergers of Dagenham (population 114 000) and Barking (75 000), Fulham (113 000) and Hammersmith (109 000), should be called simply 'Barking' and 'Hammersmith'. (He underestimated the persistence of local patriotism: by 1980 both decisions had been reversed.)

The driving purpose behind all the travails of reorganisation was the Herbert Commission's aim, confirmed by the London Government Act, to make a uniform system of primary, all-purpose local governments. And in this, it succeeded remarkably well. The boroughs took over most local and personal services, with the major exception of education in the former LCC area, which passed to an indirectly elected Inner London Education Authority. Boroughs accounted for around two thirds of local government expenditure in London. As intended, the reorganisation helped to attract a new calibre of officer into local public service, with a rising proportion of graduates. The London boroughs pioneered many aspects of modern local government practice including corporate management, chief executives and neighbourhood decentralisation. They were, for better or worse, the prototypes on which the entire national system of local government was remodelled in 1974–5, and they set in train the ultimate spread of the unitary model to most of England (in population terms) and all of Scotland and Wales in 1986–96.

In contrast to their predecessors and Victorian precursors, the 1965 London Boroughs appealed more to the principle of functional efficiency than to democratic representativeness (Davis 1989: 257). They were substantially larger than intended by Herbert – 16 of them exceeded the upper limit of 250 000 and several others were close to it – submerging established patterns of local loyalty and sense of place. For the majority of Londoners the new town halls were less accessible than the old. Artificial at first, the boroughs are now more than three decades old, with active corporate images – free 'newspapers' for all residents were another innovation pioneered here. They have become imprinted on the locality structure of London through the so-called 'public choice' effect, reflecting the cumulative effect of tax and service reputations upon residential mobility. Besides, they have ingrained themselves into London geography through town planning and transport powers, incrementally manipulating shopping and service hierarchies to their advantage, which is why – see page 92 above – modern London's central place system shows a clear 'borough effect', isomorphic with the division into 33 units (Hebbert 1991).

COUNTY HALL

The key to the Herbert Commission's vision of metropolitan unification was to be found in the 12 000 rooms and 12 miles of corridors of County Hall, the palatial seat of London government beside Westminster Bridge (Figure 5.2). It was to house a truly strategic authority, less involved in local service provision than the LCC, but more able to reclaim from central government ministries some of the powers of control, supervision, direction and sanction accumulated in the hands of central government ministers since 1944. The subsidiarity principle (as we would now call it) implied a reallocation of functions at every scale, redressing, as Herbert put it, the balance of power equally between Whitehall and County Hall, County Hall and Town Hall (PP 1960: 184).

The 1963 London Government Act, however, transferred no powers from central government, and it left numerous functions shared between the GLC and the boroughs, including parks and open spaces, highways and traffic management, licensing, emergency planning, museums and culture, sports and recreation, and historic buildings. The most difficult splits were housing, planning and roads. On housing the GLC inherited a substantial stock of council houses and flats from the London County Council, legacy of its prolific role as a world pioneer in municipal provision of working-class housing. Building and running council estates was not part of the strategic role conceived by Herbert, but for administrative continuity the stock was transferred to the GLC on the understanding that it would be shed to the local ownership and management of the boroughs. For planning, the 1963 Act produced an awkward division of labour, making the 33 boroughs planning authorities in their own right and giving the GLC no power to approve or refuse

Figure 5.2 County Hall. *The seat of the LCC and then the GLC, County Hall was designed by Ralph Knott, built between 1908 and 1922, and sold off with great difficulty after Mrs Thatcher's abolition of London-wide government. A basement aquarium was opened on the day this photograph was taken*

their plans. The Minister was left holding the ring. The transport provision left central government responsible for main roads while involving the GLC in the local detail of consents and approvals for traffic management schemes. From day one, the GLC found itself squeezed between central government, on the one hand, and the 33 London boroughs on the other (Rhodes 1970; Young 1984; Young and Garside 1982).

Intergovernmental friction could be expected when political control varied across the three levels, but the real damage may have been done in the earliest, formative years of the council, when Labour had returned to power in Westminster, controlled the GLC with 64 seats to the Conservatives' 36, and held 20 of the 33 new London boroughs. Labour's hegemony, so unexpected by the designers and opponents of the London Government Bill, allowed a carry-over of organisation and attitudes from the LCC days. County Hall contained the largest and best-paid professional teams of architects, surveyors, valuers, planners, highway engineers and service professionals in the country. Instead of scaling down to a strategic, 'staff' agency role, the executive functions of the old LCC were scaled up to cover the GLC's enhanced geographical area. At its peak the gargantuan bureaucracy of County Hall had a payroll of 25 000. The old upper-tier mentality still affected GLC dealings with the new London boroughs, though they were, on average, twice the size of the old metropolitan boroughs, had many more powers and felt themselves to be the primary units. Lastly, the GLC's modernising ethos set it on a collision course with the emerging grassroots movements for environmental and community protection.

In the previous chapter we saw the GLC alienate the boroughs by unilateral and controversial road proposals. Other policies followed the same pattern of ineffective high-handedness. The new plan for London was based on a 'metropolitan structure' of broadly alternating land-use zones – 'settlement areas', 'work areas', 'metropolitan open land' – punctuated by a circle of six secondary centres: to the north, Ealing, Wood Green and Ilford, to the south, Lewisham, Croydon and Kingston. County Hall planners intended these subcentres to be major transport and shopping nodes, providing a focus for deconcentration of employment from the congested central area, as in Shinjuku and Shiboya (Tokyo), or La Defense and St Denis (Paris). The deconcentration strategy failed in Lewisham and Ilford because GLC planners were working, as the American political scientist Hank Savitch observed, in a very different political environment from their Parisian counterparts. Policy could not be imposed monolithically by a political-technocratic elite, but had to be broken into pieces and negotiated with the boroughs (Savitch 1988: ch. 8). They refused to accept a hierarchy of primary and secondary centres that would favour some and hold back others. The panel enquiry agreed, criticising the 'metropolitan structure' as over-intrusive. So the final version of the GLDP provided for 28 strategic centres, almost one per borough, instead of the six originally intended. The plan's 40 'preferred locations for offices' and 43 'preferred locations for industry' showed the same tendency to dilution and equal shares. Outer London has inherited many nondescript and poorly located buildings from a suburban office boom of the 1960s (Whitehouse 1964) because the GLC proved less adept at regulating them than its predecessor the LCC (Daniels 1975).

In its strategic plan, the GLC identified 54 large-scale redevelopment sites or 'action areas' where it proposed to take the lead in land assembly and redevelopment. Action areas that corresponded to local priorities went ahead – the town centres of Kingston and Ilford, for example, were equipped with ringroads which reinforced the 'borough effect' of retail and service centralisation. But the majority remained inactive, among them those prominent schemes for comprehensive redevelopment at Victoria and Piccadilly, opposed by the City of Westminster, and key sites in Docklands which would eventually be plucked altogether from local authority control.

Housing policy followed a similar pattern. Soon after the creation of the GLC, an important study of London's housing problems was undertaken by the Milner Holland Committee. It documented the severity of homelessness and overcrowding in inner London, contrasting the inner densities of 200 persons per acre with the 20 per acre in suburban boroughs (PP 1965). The policy effect was unfortunate. The Labour government of 1964–70 decided to make the GLC the flagship of its national housing programme. The council launched a major drive to equalise housing opportunities by buying land in the suburbs for the construction of council estates – a controversial enough policy even in the LCC cottage-and-garden era, but doubly so in the architectural context of 1960s brutalism. Schemes such as the massive Kidbroke Park estate south of Blackheath or the cluster of tower blocks rising high above the tiled roofs of semidetached interwar suburbia beside Woodford tube station did not encourage suburban cooperation.

The GLC Housing Committee found itself blocked by outer London boroughs, forcing already densely developed inner boroughs to provide the sites for most of its output of 85 000 housing units in 1965–85: so the strategic imbalance identified by Milner Holland was reinforced, not reduced. Besides, County Hall acquired a poor reputation for the remoteness and inaccessibility of its housing management: playing the role of landlord to a dispersed stock of 240 000 rental dwellings had been no part of the Herbert Commission's vision for London government.

The GLC retained its international celebrity as a successful experiment in metropolitan government. Its big technical departments received a stream of overseas visitors and were seen as the pinnacles of their professions, offering salaries up to 30% higher than those of the boroughs. But behind the facade was a sense of unease at the GLC's inability to establish for itself a settled position in the hierarchy of government comparable to its predecessor, the LCC (Deakin 1983). The logic of circumstances tended to deflect it from an intended strategic or 'staff' role within the metropolitan region, onto a miscellaneous set of activities under its direct control. In its early years it could offset the difficulties of road-building and urban renewal within London by energetically pursuing the LCC strategy of population dispersal, subsidising the migration of blue-collar families and manu-facturing companies from inner London to distant New Towns and Expanded Towns; it seemed easier to create housing and jobs on the greenfield sites around Thetford, Honiton, Plymouth and Andover than on its own territory. But from 1970 onwards the evidence of employment and demographic decline led to a reluctant abandonment of dispersal policy, forcing the GLC to redefine its role on the internal frontier of the inner city. The derelict London Docklands should have been its great opportunity to show leadership in urban regeneration. Instead – with the boroughs, the Department of the Environment, and the new wave of grassroots community groups all in competition for control – it became the most prominent example of policy deadlock.

Perhaps all this was unfair. The GLC did initiate important capital projects for tidal defence (the Thames Barrier and associated floodworks, opened in 1981) and for waste disposal and recycling. It maintained and developed all the activities for which the LCC had built a reputation for high-quality service provision: historic buildings conservation, museums, parks, traffic control, fire and ambulance provi-sion, adult education, metropolitan research and intelligence, scientific labora-tories. Function for function, the GLC fulfilled many of the expectations of its designers: but it was singularly unsuccessful in building a sense of community within its boundaries. That, as Herbert realised, was the key.

In 1977 when the Conservatives regained control of County Hall they commissioned a respected Yorkshire politician, Sir Frank Marshall, to undertake a review. Marshall went back to the original spirit of the Herbert report in a set of recommendations that would cut GLC bureaucracy, transfer service-delivery to boroughs, and shift strategic responsibilities for road, rail, police, and health from Whitehall to County Hall. His most innovative idea was to give the GLC a degree of control over the allocation to boroughs of the central financial grant for housing investment and general purposes (Marshall 1978; Self 1982). Marshall's blueprint for the London-wide authority was radical and remains relevant 20 years later. Its only concrete outcome, however, was a decision by the GLC to begin a gradual disengagement from landlordism. The rest was a dead letter, unappealling to ministers and borough leaders, and unsupported by any clear political demand on the part of Londoners for a strong, strategic body.

Soon afterwards Mrs Thatcher became prime minister, committed to deregulation, private ownership, monetarism, de-unionisation, and the free play of market forces. Big-spending metropolitan councils under Labour control were part of the problem that Thatcherism set out to solve. In the 1982 GLC elections the Conservatives lost County Hall to Labour, and an internal coup swung the Council to the left. Its leader, Ken Livingstone, shifted from Labour's traditional male, trades unionist constituency into a populist rainbow coalition of community and tenant groups, womens' movements, gays, lesbians, blacks and rights organisations. Instead of narrowing onto the core of London-wide functions defined by Herbert or Marshall, the Council expanded its policy range with units and committees covering the spectrum of issue-based politics, winning a popularity that had eluded its predecessors. It launched local economic initiatives against unemployment. Its cheap fares policy subsidised users of the bus and underground network, boosting ridership. Like no GLC leader before, Livingstone used the wealth of County Hall and its location beside Westminster Bridge as a political platform to challenge and tease the government, and the centre-left parliamentary leadership of his own party. He supported IRA hunger strikers. As monetary controls tightened and unemployment rose in the early 1980s, the six-figure total of London's jobless was displayed in huge figures along the cornice of County Hall. During the miners' strike of 1984 thousands of trades-unionist demonstrators were received and refreshed at County Hall. Most important of all, the GLC was flagship to the flotilla of local authorities controlled by (depending on your position) the 'New Left' or 'loony left'. New career structures developed as activists rotated between grant-aided voluntary groups, councillor seats and officer posts, awaiting the fall of Thatcher and their chance to form the cadres for the next government of the left.

The political electricity between Westminster and County Hall was abruptly shortcircuited in 1983 by a personal decision of Mrs Thatcher: the GLC was to be abolished on 31 March 1986, along with the parallel authorities created in 1974 for the metropolitan areas of Birmingham, Leeds, Liverpool, Manchester, Newcastle and Sheffield. The decision, widely regarded as an act of political spite, appeared in the general election manifesto out of the blue. It made an extraordinary contrast with the circumstances of the GLC's creation, the 3-year deliberations of the Herbert Commission, the judicious compilation of data and sifting of evidence, the public hearings and careful search for consensus. A senior civil servant observed, 'the present government does not proceed from analysis to conclusion but from commitment to action' (Flynn, Leach and Vielba 1985: 1). Sympathisers wondered how it could be done, when the trend in London's competitors – New York, Tokyo, Paris, Frankfurt – was reinforcing the powers and status of city governments. It seemed inconceivable to most observers that the 33 boroughs could run London satisfactorily by themselves, given their chronic divisiveness, bitterly aggravated by the abolition bill itself (Labour boroughs broke away from the Conservative-controlled London Boroughs Association to form their own Association of London Authorities, splitting the entire system in two). The GLC had many critics, but outright abolition of London-wide local government was right off the normal political agenda and in almost any other European country would have been unconstitutional.

The GLC put up a vigorous fight for survival, campaigning for the hearts and minds of Londoners with billboard advertising, and lobbying intensively through the committee stage and in the House of Lords. Several Conservative MPs and peers joined the arguments that abolition would divide services that were properly indivisible, and that it was a denial of Londoners' democratic rights of accountability and representation. Moderates searched desparately for compromises that would retain some form of London-wide governance on another basis, appointed, indirectly elected or accountable to Parliament. But Thatcherism was at its zenith, and compromise was out.

THE SPLIT-UP

Mrs Thatcher's decapitation of the tax-and-spend socialist administration across the river was impetuous and authoritarian, but it had its logics. On the one hand, it reverted to the old localist ideology of London Conservatism, and the image of the capital – familiar to Mrs Thatcher as a suburban London MP – as a cluster of distinct communities around the ancient City (Young 1984). On the other, it expressed the ideological force of neo-conservatism, its willingness to uproot the institutional legacy of the postwar years, and its image of a metropolis managed pluralistically, through contract and competition between multiple agencies (Bish 1971; ASI 1989). The government typecast metropolitan councils as leftovers from the 1960s vogue for strategic planning; their abolition would remove a source of administrative duplication and political conflict, save money, and provide a more simple and convenient system for the general public (PP 1983). Ministers reiterated that the GLC 'had no role'. The main tasks for which it had been created – public strategy, policy coordination, and (top of Herbert's list of functions to be performed by the metropolitan council) research and intelligence – were irrelevant within a New Right agenda based on functional separation, agency competition, and the application of market disciplines to the sphere of governance. Government had dropped the word 'planning', and the substance too: it was to take a genuinely hands-off approach to fundamental decisions such as rail connections to Docklands, and the route and terminal of the Channel Tunnel link. Its own strategy for the capital was a mere fourteen pages long with no diagrams or maps (DoE 1989). As we see below, there was some softening of this hard neo-liberal orthodoxy in later years, but the idea of a entrusting any single body with the oversight of London's growth and development remained taboo throughout the Conservative era.

The neo-liberal vision included a clear philosophy of local government, based on a public choice model of unitary authorities, each with its own tax–service mix, competing to satisfy the preferences of the consumer–resident (Bish and Ostrom 1973). The central plank of the government's strategy for London was the transfer of resources and functions from the GLC to the London Boroughs. Just as London's two-tier system had pioneered the previous round of local government reorganisation, so its 1986 reduction to 33 unitary councils was intended to show the way for the rest of Britain (Leach 1985). Certain boroughs, particularly the City of Westminster and Wandsworth, stood out as pioneers of the management practices and market ethos of the 'local right' (Beresford 1987). Others, particularly Lambeth and Brent, were defiant 'new left' strongholds whose service standards made a poor advertisement for Labour. The polarisation was aggravated when Labour boroughs committed to non-cooperation broke away from the Conservative-dominated London Boroughs Association to form their own bloc, the Association of London Authorities.

In this context of bitter division, opponents of abolition predicted administrative chaos and a breakdown of essential services (Wheen 1985). With the 1981 Brixton race riot fresh in the memory, there was no need to spell out the meaning of references to the streets of London as a 'tinderbox' or 'powderkeg'. The government remained suavely confident, in the knowledge of its two-thirds parliamentary majority, the presence of sympathetic friends in the (nominally independent) Corporation of London, its political nexus with the majority bloc of Tory boroughs, and the fact that so many of the main elements of the capital's administration – police, health, urban renewal, transport – were already under central control. It had made no precise promises about cost savings from abolition and having won the political battle was relaxed about the financial dimension of reorganisation. The 1985 Act gave it wide room for manoeuvre through newly acquired powers of appointment, supervision, direction and control (Hebbert and Travers 1988).

Starting from its premise that the GLC had no role, the government kept aloof from the difficult practicalities of abolition. These were handled at arm's length by a short-life quango, the London Residuary Body (LRB), set up with four employees in October 1985 to tidy up the technicalities of GLC debts, pension obligations and legal liabilities, and dispose of outstanding assets. Under the chairmanship of a former leader of suburban Sutton, Sir Godfrey Taylor, the residuary body assumed a much larger role, minimising the disruption, rebuilding a basis of consensus, and taking the sting out of GLC abolition. It collaborated closely (to the government's surprise) with the senior management team responsible for the GLC's campaign against the Local Government Act 1985. Once the parliamentary battle was lost it worked strenuously to ensure a seamless provision of services for Londoners and continuity of employment for as many as possible of the County Hall's 21 000 staff – 7000 uniformed firefighters, 5500 professionals and technicians, 4500 manual workers, 3000 clerical staff, 1600 administrators and managers, and 290 apprentices. Some functions were to be financed on an agency basis by the 33 boroughs, others were redefined as part of LRB's core business. On the eve of abolition the government gave it all the unsolved problems: Hampstead Heath, Covent Garden, Thamesmead (the GLC's 1700-acre new town on the Erith marshes), London's traffic lights, transport and travel surveys, County Hall's thirteen scientific laboratories, uncompleted road schemes (Hebbert and Edge 1994).

On 1 April 1986 the great majority of staff returned as normal to their desks and workbenches. County Hall clubs and societies continued to meet as though the cataclysm had not occurred. Several hundred politically appointed officers, funded by Labour boroughs, departed to form the nucleus of a 'GLC-in-exile' in readiness for the 1987 election. With the same deadline in mind, Mrs Thatcher pressed to have County Hall emptied and sold to a private buyer within twelve months, symbolising the irreversible break-up of London-wide government. However, court challenges and planning complications slowed the relocation process. Because of its size and status as a listed building (SoL 1991), the magnificent civic headquarters designed by Ralph Knott for the London County Council in 1907–8 were not easily disposable 80 years later. The LRB allowed the GLC administration to stay put within its old walls until new homes could be found for each function, whether under joint committees of the boroughs, by sale to the private sector, or as a freestanding agency. It could afford to ease the liquidation process with generous financial settlements as its property team (all former GLC officers) unloaded the former council's vast portfolio of shops, office blocks, hotels, factories, open land and housing onto the booming London property market of the late 1980s. In all, it distributed proceeds of more than £700 million to the London Boroughs (Hebbert and Edge 1994).

County Hall remained unsold as the LRB drew to the end of its its statutory 5-year lifespan. The government gave it a new lease of life to handle the abolition of the Inner London Education Authority in 1990. Taking on 1000 ILEA employees, it repeated the same process of liquidation for the education authority's portfolio of 260 properties, its 300 trust funds, its school transport fleet, museums and adult education colleges. The last former GLC staff left County Hall in 1991. LRB eventually made a sale in 1993 and 1994. The riverside buildings went to Shirayama, a provincial Japanese hotel company which holds the McDonald's hamburger franchise in Osaka. On the tenth anniversary of GLC abolition, the premises were still empty. The entrepreneur Richard Branson had a brief involvement, unfurling a banner with the words FAMILY FUN PLACE across the pilastered facade. Eventually an aquarium was developed in the basement and work started on a hotel conversion in the upper storeys. Meanwhile the back buildings of County Hall were being sold to property developers for subdivision into luxury flats. *'Marble Entrances – State of the Art Security – Fitted Carpets complemented with oak veneer flooring – Private Health & Leisure Complex . . . Houses of Parliament 346 Metres'*: the lurid publicity brochures gave no clue of the property's civic origins.

To many Londoners the problems over the disposal of County Hall symbolised a deeper malaise. 'Crisis' and 'decline' were the theme of London literature in the decade after 1986 (Thornley 1992). For the social historian Roy Porter, London's era of greatness began in 1570 with the opening of Sir Thomas Gresham's Royal Exchange on Cornhill, and ended in 1986 with Mrs Thatcher's closure of County Hall. His wonderful *London – a Social History*, published in 1994, exactly captured a Spenglerian sense of despair at a sudden, precipitate process of decline: London, he wrote was 'on a downward spiral of infrastructural and human problems that will prove hard to halt' (Porter 1994: 3).

At first sight, this perception of a city in terminal decline seemed curiously inconsistent with the facts. The hard data of crime and mortality rates showed a steady improvement in London's position with respect to other British cities. Many of the city's problems – congestion, the building boom, new infrastructure being put into the streets – reflected economic success. Variations in public services owed more to national policy trends than to particular frictions of balkanisation (Travers et al. 1991). In fact the competitive, polycentric milieu of London local government seemed to be more hospitable to initiative and innovation than its monolithic predecessor. Managers of specialist units, no longer required to implement policy, could concentrate on developing services under the lighter touch of joint committees (Table 5.1). The London Ecology Unit took its expertise into consultancy in Chile and China. The research and intelligence function, which had rather mouldered within the GLC, became a freestanding London Research Centre. The style and content of its work shifted from data gathering and dry statistical reportage to an active engagement with the intelligence needs of user communities. Really for the first time it became the widely connected, top-quality unit for which the Herbert Commission called in 1960 (PP 1960: 198–200). The strategic planners, so much criticised in the GLC years for their institutional isolation, now operated on a shoestring under a joint committee of the London boroughs, and used partnership mechanisms to commission an extraordinarily valuable stream of policy studies – on globalisation, labour markets, industry, minerals, transport, housing, open space, the green belt, town centres, urban environmental quality (see references in LPAC 1994) – which would have a longer shelf life than the bland background material of the *Greater London Development Plan*.

The most fascinating effect of the split-up into 33 governments was to be seen in the Square Mile. Despite internal misgivings within the Court of Common

Table 5.1 *Joint Bodies with London Borough Membership 1986–98*

Statutory committees
Concessionary Fares Scheme
Coroners' Courts Committees
LB Childrens' Regional Planning Committee
London Ambulance Service
London Boroughs Grants Committee
London Fire & Civil Defence Authority
London Planning Advisory Committee
London Research Centre
London Waste Regulation Authority
Waste Disposal Authorities (× 4)

Voluntary bodies
Docklands Consultative Committee
Docklands Transport Steering Group
Employers' Secretariat for Local Authority Services
Greater London Enterprise
Home Loans Portfolio
London Area Mobility Scheme
London Boroughs Disability Committee
London Boroughs Emergency Planning Committee
London Canals Committee
London Committee on Accessible Transport
London Ecology Committee
London Recycling Forum
London River Association
London Road Safety Committee
London Strategic Planning Unit
London Welfare Benefits
Waste Disposal Authorities (× 12)

Council, the Corporation emerged from its shell to take a lead role within the new order. It took over most of the work of representing London overseas and receiving important international visitors to the capital, parading the panoply of the Mansion House and the Guildhall – lace, beaver hats, gowns, swords – in a way that would have astonished Sir Lawrence Gomme or Professor William Robson, for all the world as though they embodied a living municipal tradition. At a practical level, the Corporation worked closely with the London Residuary Body to ensure continuity of services after GLC abolition, taking on (for example) London's traffic lights, the metropolitan archives, and Hampstead Heath. Taking its seat in the various new joint committees of the London boroughs, it used its curious status – venerable, immensely rich, a political eunuch – to broker between the ideological blocs of boroughs controlled by Labour and by the Conservatives. Equally important was its ability to mediate between the boroughs and the capital's nine Training and Enterprise Councils, patronage bodies responsible for manpower development and business services. Hitherto invisible within the London local government system, the City became an ubiquitous networker. Happenings that would have seemed wildly incongruous ten years before became commonplace. The City's heraldic shield appeared alongside the emblems of its northern neighbours, the Labour-controlled boroughs of Hackney and Islington, in colourful publicity brochures for 'The Heart of London', a hitherto unknown entity blessed with 'a population greater than Zurich, more graduates than Oxford and Cambridge combined, [and] more artists and artisans than Paris'. The Guildhall opened its doors to provide a forum for discussions about architecture, the environment, the global economy, the Underground system, the condition of London's plane trees. The Corporation joined with the *Evening Standard* to sponsor a historic series of debates under the auspices of the Architecture Foundation, providing Tony Blair MP with his platform to launch the Labour Party's manifesto plans for London (Labour Party 1996). Michael Cassidy, a solicitor who chaired the Corporation's pivotal Policy & Resources Committee, became the first City councilman within historical memory to acquire a London-wide political reputation. Without his statesmanship the Corporation might not have shaken off its introversion, and London's tissue of collaboration and partnership would have looked much weaker – rather as it did to the Herbert Commission.

Analysis of the Local Government Act 1985 and subsidiary orders showed that the decentralising transfers to boroughs were offset by a functional centralisation, 'with Whitehall departments obtaining a vast amount of extra powers over London, estimated as from 40 to 123 in total, to initiate, to guide, to control, to direct, to monitor, to approve, to be consulted, and in default to execute' (Hebbert and Travers 1988: 7). The first effect of the sharply increased involvement of civil servants and departmental ministers in the government of the capital was paralytic. Problems which an omnibus authority like the GLC had in principle been able to see in the round were now segmented between national departments of state. Because of the Thatcherite aversion to 'planning' it was impolitic to raise questions about the interconnectedness of ministerial actions. The problem was especially acute in the London Docklands, with its uniquely high concentrations of public investment. The Canadian brothers who built Canary Wharf found that they had to establish an office round the corner from No. 10 Downing Street and lobby the prime minister in person to synchronise the infrastructure elements of their project (see Chapter 8 below). The Canary Wharf development team, mostly North American, was astonished at the government's policy indifference, the diffusion of responsibility and the communication gaps that existed within and between the Departments of the Environment and Transport. The non-arrival of a high-speed rail connection from Folkestone to London was equally astonishing to French partners in the Channel Tunnel project.

The 1990s saw a gradual relaxation of the hands-off doctrine. First, a minister was appointed with special responsibility for the coordination of transport in the London Docklands. Then the 1991 Road Traffic Act made provision for the appointment of a 'Traffic Director' with powers to control parking and coordinate traffic improvements along key routes into and through the capital. After the fall of Margaret Thatcher and much publicity of London's problems in the 1992 general election campaign, the returning Conservative government set up a ministerial subcommittee for London of ten junior ministers, chaired by the Secretary of State for the Environment, with a remit 'to coordinate the Government's policies on London'. Next, in November 1993, the regional bureaucracies of the Departments of Employment, Environment, Trade & Industry and Transport were combined into a single Government Office for London (GoL), under a Grade 2 Deputy Secretary. Though parallel reorganisations were occurring in other English regions, civil servants had a far greater involvement in the day-to-day running of London than of any other part of the United Kingdom, except Northern Ireland. Relocated on the riverside in a tower block by Vauxhall Bridge, GoL was in some senses a reinvention of the integrated bureaucracy for London that had been dismantled in the abolition of the GLC. When it was launched the Secretary of State, John Gummer, took the unusual step of assembling civil servants responsible for London in the Royal Horticultural Society's Hall in Vincent Square for a pep-talk. His theme was the need for 'holistic' thinking, a very different message from the dry *laissez-faire* of his predecessors. The distance travelled could be measured by comparing the government's first derisory planning framework for London (DoE 1989) with its successor the *Strategic Guidance for London Planning Authorities* (GoL 1996), a strategy with substance, even vision, reflecting the role played as policy adviser in its initial preparation by none other than Peter Hall.

By the mid-1990s the focusing of central government's role in London mirrored the collaboration that was being acheived by the boroughs. These curious mechanisms of governance had their limitations – particularly in coordinating local aspects of provision such as cycle-ways across borough boundaries – but the overall profile of public services was not disadvantageous. Because of the direct involvement of ministers in the capitals' affairs, Londoners did well from the share-out of the expenditure cake. Scottish newspapers, particularly *Scotland on Sunday*, developed an appetite for expenditure statistics which showed Londoners to be the UK's most pampered region; it was a factor in the growing demand for political devolution north of the border. Suggestions that the capital's competitive edge had been blunted by its lack of an overall government were not borne out by the city's economic performance in the 1990s (see next chapter). By the criteria of tax burden, investment rates and migration trends, London had the appearance of a well-governed city.

Why, then, did public opinion remain deeply dissatisfied? Why did the *Evening Standard* debates on *London in the 21st Century* – 'truly remarkable events' as Tony Blair said in his own contribution – draw crowds of over 16 000 to Central Hall, Westminster, to discuss the future of their city? The answer was not to be found in performance indicators or output measures but in the minds and hearts of Londoners. Albion had woken up.

A Voice for London

Back in 1983, Kenneth Baker MP was moved by Mrs Thatcher from the Department of Education to the Environment front-bench team to drive the abolition legislation through Parliament. In his political autobiography he recalled his difficulty, in a televised debate with the GLC leader Ken Livingstone, in answering the argument that London needed an elected authority since every other capital city had one. He found that it was a topic on which Mrs Thatcher would brook no opposition: 'I really *won't* have the Lords saying that London is so significant that Londoners should have a voice for London' (Baker 1993: 102–4). Senior politicians from all political parties tried patiently to find a compromise. Towards the end of the parliamentary struggle in March 1985, an amendment was proposed which conceded the case for GLC abolition but retained an overarching structure by making the London Residuary Body (page 117 above) into a permanent London-wide authority democratically accountable to the boroughs. In the debate of 27 March 1985, supporters echoed the original logic of the Herbert Commission, based upon constitutional first principles. There was a case for a democratically elected county-wide body wherever a substantial body of services had to be administered on a county-wide basis. For a capital city which corresponded with a built-up metropolitan area, the case was overwhelming. Indeed, Conservative ministers had made it cogently only 20 years earlier when they set up the GLC.

The front bench and its supporters responded with arguments that will have a familiar ring to anyone who has followed the story so far. 'No one,' said Sir Geoffrey Finsberg (MP for Hampstead and Highgate) 'has ever satisfactorily defined what London is. What I am trying to say is that in the end the average Londoner is far more concerned and interested in his own borough council than in a vast amorphous body'. Echoing these arguments, the Secretary of State, Patrick Jenkin, and the Minister Kenneth Baker both invoked the academic authority of the political scientist Ken Young, 'principal historian of our municipality'. Baker had the final word:

> If one considers the history of London . . . it will be noted that over the decades and centuries there has not been one body, one institution, that has spoken for London . . . There has never been one voice for London in our history. It is one of the unique features of the development of our great capital city that it is an amalgamation of different communities, villages, cultures and ethnic groups. They have all added to the identity that makes up the unique – *It being half past ten o'clock, MR SPEAKER proceeded . . . to put forth the Question already proposed . . . The House Divided: Ayes 193, Noes 335.*

So Mrs Thatcher had her way.

However, this was a Pyrrhic victory. The effect of the 1985 system was precisely the opposite of that indicated by Jenkin and Baker. Involving local elites for the first time in metropolitan service provision, it nurtured their sense of common

124

Making the Case for GLC Abolition

– the boundary question

Mr Patrick Jenkin (Secretary of State for the Environment): Is it not clear, after
21 years' experience of the GLC, that the Greater London Area is an artificial
basis for planning and policy? Is it not clear that London, the capital city of
the nation, is the focus for government, business, commerce, shopping, the
arts, the theatre and many other services appropriate to such a city and that
its influence stretches far beyond the outer boundaries of the GLC area?
Mr Tony Banks: Let us have a bigger GLC then.
Mr Jenkin: Is it not clear that all the major planning and transport decisions fall
inevitably not to the GLC but to the Government and to the House?
Hon. Members: Oh!
Mr Jenkin: I invite the Opposition to consider this. Where does London begin
and end?
Hon. Members: In Marsham Street!*

– the issue of democracy

Sir Ian Gilmour: It is astonishing – this is a serious matter that touches not only
the government of London but deep springs of Conservative philosophy –
that the Government cannot answer the fundamental criticism that, instead
of their local authority legislation decentralising services, it is centralising
them. We must know what is so unique about London that it is not allowed to
have a directly elected authority.
Mr Patrick Jenkin (Secretary of State for the Environment): The London
Boroughs Association . . . could achieve greater importance and this could
represent what my right honourable friend is seeking in his rather emotional
arguments.
Sir Ian Gilmour: It is not an emotional argument at all. It is a fundamental
argument. The idea that a quango or an association such as the LBA could be
a substitute for a properly directly elected authority is extraordinary.

* Office towers, since demolished, housing the Department of the Environment.
Parliamentary Debates, House of Commons, 27 March 1985

---

purpose. Without a metropolitan council to react against, the separatist impulse of
the suburbs diminished. With the passage of years and a change of generations their
incorporation in 1963 was no longer a source of resentment. An unconscious and
unobserved shift in political geography was taking place. The old distinctions
between 'Inner', 'Outer' and 'Greater' London continued to be used by statisticians
but for everyday purposes the whole county within its green belt had become
London, and the overwhelming majority of its people identified themselves to
opinion pollsters as *Londoners* (Hebbert 1995). The problem was, as residents of
Croydon or Harrow they had representatives and a democratic vote: as Londoners
they were disenfranchised.

Table 5.2 *Political Outcomes of London Borough Elections 1964–94*

Numbers of Boroughs controlled by	1964	1968	1971	1974	1978	1982	1986	1990	1994
Conservatives	9	28	8	12	17	16	11	12	5
Labour	20	3	21	18	14	11	15	14	17
Liberal Democrats	0	0	0	0	0	0	2	3	3
No overall control	3	1	3	2	1	5	4	3	7
	32	32	32	32	32	32	32	32	32

The democratic deficit was heightened by shifts in political control at borough level. London politics were better balanced than other metropolitan areas, with a spread that broadly reflected opinion in the country at large. The Tories had the upper hand in the boroughs at the time of GLC abolition, but electoral disillusion steadily eroded their local base. In the London borough election of 1994 they lost control of large tracts of outer London. Croydon, Ealing and Enfield went to Labour, Kingston to the Liberal-Democrats, and in Barnet, Bexley, Harrow and Redbridge no party had an overall majority (Table 5.2). This result, the worst ever for the Conservatives in London, allowed the London boroughs to reunify into a single association, healing the split which had existed since GLC abolition between two blocs, a Labour-controlled Association of London Authorities and a Conservative-dominated London Boroughs Association. At its launch on 1 April 1995 the newly reunited Association of London Government described itself as the 'Democratic Voice of London'. Its secretary was John McDonnell, former deputy leader of the GLC.

With this political arithmetic no Conservative government would concede to the demand for an elected voice for London: however, the issue of representation refused to go away. Indeed it was raised most insistently by the business lobby: in the competitive environment of the globalised economy, who would represent the capital in international gatherings? Who would receive overseas visitors? Who would bid for European funds, and solicit inward investment? Who would initiate a London bid for the year 2000 Olympic Games? (Answer, nobody: two rival bids based on Wembley and the Royal Docks cancelled each other out.) Property professionals, selling space in London, were vocal on the need for a capital's need for a 'voice' in the specific sense of an agency to deal with inward investment (Travers et al. 1991).

A Conservative government had only two options. It could employ its extensive patronage network of appointed bodies. London was often represented by the London Docklands Development Corporation: for example, at the 1992 Seville International Exposition it sponsored the VIP suite in the British Pavilion. However, there were limits to the usefulness of an agency tied to the promotion of just one sector of London. In the 1992 general election the government promised to launch a new initiative for London-wide business promotion: in fact, it established two bodies – London First and London Forum – then merged them in 1993 under the chairmanship of a hotel entrepreneur, Lord Shepherd. His London First recruited a membership of quangos, trusts, training and enterprise councils, private groupings such as the Confederation of British Industry and the chambers of commerce, and some individual businesses such as British Airways, property companies, and Shepherd's own Grand Metropolitan hotel chain – companies with a tangible stake in the economic performance of London. It joined forces with the Corporation of London, the City of Westminster and the London Docklands Development Corporation to establish an inward investment bureau. As part of its commercially oriented notion of 'voice' it jointly commissioned – at a rumoured cost of £1 million (eight people working for nine months) – a brand marque for the capital city, aptly described by the journalist Michael Bywater as 'three ghosts rising like pestilence above the word LONDON which itself appears to be floating in a little splodge of pus'.

Logos, glossy brochures, and canapé launches galore could not dispel the basic problem of legitimacy which surrounded London's patronage elites. Unlike the growth coalitions of Manchester or Glasgow they had no nexus to the local political class but were implanted by government. Whitehall did not intend them to function as lobby organisations; it gave a cold shoulder when London First attempted to press for a cross-London main-line rail link instead of the government's preferred extension of the Jubilee Line to Docklands. There could be no appeal to popular opinion because the names and faces of the quango elites were unknown to the public at large. Profiled in the listings magazine *Time Out* (28 April 1993), they were overwhelmingly male, white and middle-aged. The Training & Enterprise Councils, lead players in the economic partnerships, were among the most secretive and least accountable of all London's 272 quangos (Skelcher and Stewart 1993).

Ministers did have their political mandate. The alternative strategy to the issue of London's 'voice' was to provide it themselves, as the Scottish Secretary did for Scotland. From 1992 the government invested an increasing amount of ministerial time and attention in London. The Secretary of State for the Environment, John Gummer, issued an invitation on glossy paper to Londoners to join him in drafting what he called a new prospectus: 'London needs a coherent and widely shared vision of what can be done and what can be achieved. I want civic and business leaders in London to come together to set an agenda for change, building on the strengths of our great capital city' (DoE 1993). In his four years at the Department of the Environment he valiantly pursued themes of environmental quality, urban design, and the use of the Thames. But there were limits to how far any minister could be involved in the affairs of the single city without prejudicing his or her responsibilities for the country as a whole. And with London so comprehensively alienated from the government of the day, the basic issue of legitimacy remained.

Opinion polls since 1986 had consistently shown that a majority of Londoners desired an elected government of their own. This sentiment gathered in strength: a

Table 5.3 *The Democratic Deficit*

Public opinion in 1994 on the need for an assembly –
London compared with other parts of the UK

	% support	% oppose
Scotland	72	22
Wales	58	37
England	51	44
London	63	28
North West	61	36
Yorks & Humberside	53	43
North East	53	41
Midlands	50	45
South West	49	47
East Anglia	46	49
South East	42	54
Britain	54	41

Source: ESRC Local Governance Programme, Public Opinion & Local
Citizenship Survey, University of Strathclyde and University of Glasgow.

nation-wide poll of attitudes towards regionalism and devolution in 1994 put
Londoners ahead of the Welsh and every other English region and second only to
the Scots in their desire for an elected voice (Table 5.3). In the run-up to the 1997
general election, the Labour Party reaffirmed its commitment to re-establish a city-
wide elected government. The title of its paper – *A Voice for London* – reflected an
emphasis on structures of representation and accountability, rather than administrative overhaul (Labour Party 1996). The emphasis was all the stronger after
Labour's election victory, when Tony Blair as prime minister boldly endorsed a
proposal to introduce a directly elected executive mayor for London alongside the
new assembly, a fundamental innovation for British local government (PP 1997).

One aspect of the Green Paper was less innovative (Figure 5.3). 'We have made
it clear that we do not propose to abolish the City Corporation. In recent years the
City Corporation has sought to play a much more positive role in order to promote
inward investment and fund schemes and studies for the benefit of London as a
whole. The Corporation has assured the Government that it will continue to
develop this work and has accepted that it must respond to the need to improve its
electoral arrangements' (PP 1997: 2). This was very different from Labour's 1992
manifesto commitment to abolish and dismember the City.

When Tony Blair made his historic contribution to the *London in the 21st
Century* debates, outlining Labour's 1997 commitment to give London a directly
elected mayor, he had beside him on the platform at Central Hall Westminster the
world's most famous mayor, Pasqual Maragall of Barcelona. On the drape in front of
him (because it had co-sponsored the debate) was the crest of the City of London,
with its tradition of mayoral government stretching continuously back to 1191, the

Figure 5.3 Corporation of London. *A gryphon defends the ancient boundary of the City of London on the site of Temple Bar*

world's oldest. It would have been neat to make the connection. Labour might have seized its historic opportunity to give the ancient office real civic meaning, as Herbert Morrison (1935: 160) once dreamed. Leaving aside the subtle cumulative effect of banquets observed by William Robson (see page 101 above), why did it not do so? The explanation lies partly in the account given here of the Corporation's civic leadership over the decade of balkanisation. But in part it reflects a dawning recognition of the economic importance of the Square Mile for London and the country as a whole. That is the topic for our next chapter.

PAVED WITH GOLD

PAVED WITH GOLD

Two enduring characteristics observed by economic historians are the strength of the London economy and its diversity. Three centuries ago the economy of early modern London was already the motor for economic growth in the rest of Britain – particularly through its demand for coal (Wrigley 1967). Its internal diversity was tangible in the separate worlds of City merchants and lawyers, sailors and artisans in the eastern hamlets, the landowners, rentiers, politicians, functionaries and retailers of Westminster, the warehousemen, musicians and courtesans of the south bank.

The economy of modern London – at £75 billion, comparable in size to the GDP of Russia or Saudi Arabia – accounts for 20% of UK GDP and exerts an influence on national economic performance unlike no other region, for better (Michie 1997) or worse (Hutton 1995). It has shown an ability to innovate and create new markets over the very long run. This dynamism owes something to the favoured position of the capital within a unitary state constitution (Robson 1986; Garside and Hebbert 1989), but something also to local circumstance – the early modern footprint of the City, Westminster, Southwark and their diverse suburbs, still visible in the maps of economic districts prepared by wartime planners (Forshaw and Abercrombie 1943) or in 1996 by Peter Hall and fellow-consultants (Llewellyn-Davies 1996). London's strongly differentiated spaces have provided a hospitable environment for competition and innovation.

> Although Clerkenwell and Smithfield today do not make clocks and instruments or slaughter animals, their old workshops and storerooms have been converted to accommodate design studios and software consultants, who form an interdependent, competitive environment which the residents of the eighteenth and nineteenth centuries would have understood. Flexible specialisation, communities of skill, and the speedy circulation of information remain important features of the metropolitan economy (Daunton 1996: 7).

Breaking the economy into broad headings of activity, we can distinguish six sectors with their corresponding geographies. London is, first, a capital city. The monarchy, the legislature, the executive are clustered in an arc round St James's Park in the City of Westminster: the palaces of the royal family on the Mall, the core of the state bureaucracy along Whitehall, the Houses of Parliament beside Edward the Confessor's Abbey, and major departments of state along the Embankment and down Victoria Street. Political parties, interest groups, lobbyists and consultants pack into the streets beyond Parliament Square, while most embassies are disposed in a broad band of converted terraced houses from Kensington

Gardens up to Regent's Park. Public administration in itself is significantly less important for London than for many other capitals, accounting for little more than a twentieth of GDP, a declining proportion. As a seat of international governance London ranks behind Washington, Brussels, Tokyo, Paris, and Bonn/Berlin, with only 30 international agencies and 400 intergovernmental and non-governmental organisations. The UK civil service has been relocating staff out of the capital for more than three decades: 55 000 posts were moved in 1962–79 as part of a planned locational strategy for regional development (Marshall, Alderman and Thwaites 1991) and a further 11 500 in 1979–89 as a by-product of budgetary decentralisation. From over 500 000 jobs in the 1950s, central government and other capital city institutions (notably justice and international diplomacy) today employ approximately 350 000 people. But as in private sector corporations, back-office functions have dispersed while higher (and better-paid) decision makers remain in town, and their penumbra of lobbyists and media communicators continues to grow. Capital city status accounts also for central London's concentration of research institutions, higher education, teaching hospitals, and the ancient complex of legal universities, the Inns of Court, which extend along the western boundary of the City from the Temple to Clerkenwell.

Second, London is a resort, one of the world's great centres of consumption, luxury, leisure, art, museums, sport and vice (Figures 6.1 and 6.2). Its thousand years at the centre of power have left deep sediments of antiquities and national monuments, and historical memories at every turn. All roads lead to London. Formerly the landed classes flocked here each year to spend 'the season' in the proximity of the court. That pattern of residential rotation survives among the global super-rich who keep houses in Belgravia or Kensington and patronise the long-established gunmakers, art dealers, tailors and vintners of the West End. For the ordinary tourist, London used to be a stuffy place, preoccupied with its own business and snobberies (James 1883; Olsen 1986). The modern city has put chairs on its pavements and learned to please. In 1995 it attracted 21 million visitors and they contributed £7 billion to the metropolitan economy: the sector accounts for a direct employment total of 220 000, rising to more than 500 000 if account is taken of indirect jobs and of employment in the shops of the central area (LTC 1996). It underpins London's extraordinary variety and richness of cultural life. Overseas tourists go equal thirds with home visitors and resident Londoners to fill theatre seats. They contribute a tenth of total of retail expenditure in the capital – Oxford Street shops are their top destination, followed by Knightsbridge, Regent Street and Covent Garden. Visitor traffic is highly localised with a polygon defined by the top ten attractions, each drawing between one and seven million visitors in the course of the year: the British Museum, the National Gallery, Westminster Abbey, Madame Tussaud's waxwork collection, the Tower of London, the three great South Kensington museums (Natural History, Science and Victoria & Albert), and the Tate Gallery. In scale, visitors' London resembles the preindustrial metropolis, a city of perhaps 10 square miles centred on Trafalgar Square.

Figure 6.1 Heritage. *Japanese tourists pose beside the Roman brickwork of London Wall on Tower Hill. Like many of London's major tourist destinations, the setting is tatty, inconvenient, overcrowded, and tainted with the odour of McDonald's*

Figure 6.2 Pseudo-heritage. *But in a city as diverse (and safe) as London the enterprising tourist can always find her own photo-opportunities and 'knowledge'*

More localised still, because of the boundedness of the Square Mile, is the third and most powerful component of the London economy, financial and business services. It employs 600 000 people directly and draws business command and control functions which are estimated to employ a further 200 000. London has the headquarters of 220 of the UK's top 500 companies, 118 of the European top 500, and 64 of *Fortune* magazine's ranking of the world's 500. The importance of business and financial services for the metropolitan economy explains the curious outcomes at the end of the previous chapter. The Corporation of London has become a special district for its stewardship.

In its last testament, the Greater London Council gave a very different perspective, placing manufacturing at the heart of the economy, and 'reclaiming production' as the core of its strategy for enterprise and growth (GLC 1985b). The manufacturing and goods-handling sectors have suffered a long decline. In 1951 more than one and a half million people worked in London's factories. Today manufacturing employs about 300 000 and contributes a sixth of the capital's output. Deindustrialisation has left its mark on working-class London, leaving intractable problems of unemployment and dereliction.

A capital city, a pleasure resort, a financial centre, and a manufacturing region: the list is incomplete without a fifth element which has always been an ubiquitous part of the London life and labour, but the most elusive. The black economy of London is the great unknown. It includes tax evasion, off-the-book sales, intercompany barter, moonlighting, welfare benefit fraud, cash-in-hand work and trading, the vice and drugs industries, dealing in stolen and smuggled goods, gangsterism. What does it all add up to? Definition and estimation are notoriously difficult: macroeconomists (measuring the mismatch between cash in circulation and declared earnings) have offered figures of up to 22% of UK GDP whereas the findings of micro-sociological research, based on actual patterns of family expenditure, tend to be in the 2–3% range (Pahl 1990; Smith 1986). The profile and scale of irregular activity in the New York and Parisian economies has been well researched: London's remains very obscure. Sassen and Gordon believe it to be far less significant than in New York, estimating (from comparison of the population and employment censuses) that it occupies only 2% of the workforce (Fainstein et al. 1992: 126). One would expect a higher figure, given the capital's concentration of features associated with informalisation (Barthelemy 1990; Williams and Windebank 1994; Thomas and Thomas 1994); its construction, tourism, personal and business services, and rag trade; its well above-average proportion of self-employed workers – the main source of undeclared business turnover – and distinctively dense immigrant concentrations, giving potential for clandestine labour markets; the uniquely high proportion of street trading in its retailing sector; its status as an international crossroads. London's fame as 'the world's coolest city' acknowledges a vibrant club scene but also, tacitly, a compliant drug economy. The black economy may be statistically elusive but Londoners can glimpse it any day in the billwads of street traders. And in death, the passing of minor crooks can stop the traffic with a cortege on the scale of a state funeral: marching band, horse-drawn bier with black plumes, top-hatted funeral director, hearses full of floral tributes, and a procession of limousines full of mourners in sunglasses.

In a long perspective, the underworld of the East End, the upperworld of the royal palaces, the institutions of state, and the diversions of the rich have been constants within the London economy, whereas its financial and manufacturing roles have been more variable and fickle, reflecting shifts of markets and technology, and the cyclical effect of long waves of development. For the remainder of this chapter we will take a broad historical perspective on those dynamic aspects of the London economy, the trading, mercantile, banking and industrial sectors, following the interplay of fortune and design in their evolution. At the end of the chapter we will return to the most difficult question of the parts and the whole, the interconnectedness of the metropolitan economy.

World's Market (1)

The economic geography of London begins with the river and the sea. Modern visitors are surprised at the space and emptiness of the Thames. What amazed the novelist Henry James when he took a riverboat trip down to Greenwich in 1883 was 'the duskiness, the blackness, the crowdedness, the intensely commercial character of London' (James 1883: 219). The masts and funnels of shipping, trade advertisements, crowded narrow streets, trucks and barrows gave the City a nautical vitality. Aylmer Vallance's book *The Centre of the World* (1935) drew the contrast with other European capitals:

> Paris, Berlin, Rome – these cities, with their banks and Bourses, are the focal points of a markedly national life. London is a port; the river that brings cargoes of wool and rubber, hides and wheat and timber, 'peacocks and ivory', and all the silks and spices of the Orient to its docks, brings also North Sea fish to within a stone's throw of the Bank of England, and carries to its financiers, its stockbrokers and its merchants an ever-present sense that their lives are touched daily with the ebb and flow of sea-borne commerce (1935: 12).

The sea-port was a pervasive influence despite the difficulty – to which we return in Chapter 8 below – of getting a sight of it behind the high walls of the docks, or the warehouses shoulder to shoulder along the tidal Thames. James Bird (1957) noticed how office workers from the insurance companies and banks of the Square Mile used to line up along the western parapet of London Bridge in the lunch hour to watch the loading and unloading of international cargoes in the Pool of London.

Forty years later the Thames has been opened up for view and a promenade with pubs, cafés and cultural attractions runs all the way along the south bank from the Tower to Westminster (Figure 6.3), but the only cargo visible on the river is the capital's rubbish going down for landfill on the estuary. The economy of the Square Mile has dematerialised. The departure of Hudson's Bay fur pelts from Upper Thames Street, fish slime from the cobbles of Lower Thames Street, the aroma of pepper, cloves and cinnamon from the brickwork of Wapping and Bermondsey leaves a smart, post-modern environment for 'dealing in deals' (Budd and Whimster 1992).

Historically, the financial markets of the modern City originated in sea trade, just as the commodities and futures markets were a by-product of warehousing. The modern insurance market stays close to the coffee house in Tower Street which Edward Lloyd made in 1688 a centre for merchants and ship-owners to exchange information and spread their risks. The Stock Exchange began as a coffee-house gathering of ship-owners, merchants and financial backers. The history of the modern financial City begins in the commercial boom of the eighteenth-century port of London, whose trade doubled in 1700–70 and again in the 25 years to 1795, largely by shipment of West Indian sugar, rum, dyewoods, and spices to satisfy the consumer demand of Britain's prosperous middle classes. Two thirds of national imports and exports came via the hypercongested shipping moorings of the Pool of London. The scale of commercial turnover within the Square Mile, together with its enclave status, assisted the development of a financial superstructure. Where West End banks dealt with landowning clients and lent

Figure 6.3 The Pool of London. *Crammed with shipping until the 1960s, the Pool now has only the cruiser* Belfast *in permanent mooring as a tourist attraction. Beyond rise the towers of the financial district*

on mortgage, City banks originated in the world of trade and the merchant's bills of exchange. Many were founded by overseas mercantile families such as the French Huguenot Cazenoves, the Dutch De Zoetes, the Barings and Schroders from Lutheran North Germany, and the Rothschilds, Jewish and from Frankfurt. The City's growing importance as a financial centre was linked to the decline of eighteenth-century Amsterdam, from which – as the French invaded the Netherlands in 1795 – London received a flight of capital just as Amsterdam had in its time from Venice (Marx 1930: 838). By the outbreak of the Napoleonic Wars London was the pre-eminent centre in Europe where finance was practised as an activity in its own right, independent of trade (Kynaston 1994).

The Industrial Revolution and the policy of free trade after the Reform Act of 1832 consolidated both the financial and the mercantile facets of the London economy. While the industrial north expanded its own port capacity at Liverpool, Manchester, Hull and Newcastle, London remained the gateway for a third of Britain's total exports and imports, particularly the colonial trade with India, Australia and New Zealand (the first Colonial Wool Sale took place in 1821, and the first refrigerated consignments of Australian and New Zealand meat and butter arrived in 1880–2). Through their command of colonial resources London's wharfiers and traders developed the Thames into a global commodity entrepôt: the world's wool, tea, hides, copper, coffee, cocoa, spices, and rubber were shipped and warehoused along its banks, traded on the City commodity exchanges, then reshipped for export.

Later, Victorian Britain saw its youthful manufacturing dominance eroded first by the competition of Germany and America, then by a growing line of newly industrialising nations within Europe and beyond. The same period established the Square Mile as the economic hub of what could now, for the first time, be described as a single 'world economy', unified by steam-power, telecommunications, and capital flows. Manufacturing eclipse and financial zenith were not unrelated. City banks and finance houses provided capital for the development of manufacturing in the new industrial powers, and credit to finance the imports of primary products from the underdeveloped world, much of it under British colonial control. For the Square Mile, these were – as Kynaston (1995) calls them – the golden years. At the turn of the twentieth century more than half the world's trade was financed in sterling: more than half the stocks quoted on the Stock Exchange were overseas securities, and approaching half the world's shipping tonnage was British. The country's declining earnings from manufacturing exports were more than offset by the growth in invisible earnings from shipping, insurance and brokerage, as well as the revenue accruing to the world's greatest creditor nation. Wherever trade was conducted, the 'bill on London' would serve for payment. The threads of the entire world's web of trading and financial settlements ran through London (Hobsbawm 1968: ch. 3).

After 1900 the US dollar began to erode sterling's status as the reserve currency in international trade. The number of foreign banks within the Square Mile fell sharply after 1910 and remained low for the next half-century. The New York money market was already on its way to replacing London's when the First World War plunged Britain from creditor to debtor status. From then, its share of invisible earnings followed the downward slope of manufacturing. The geographical centre of finance and banking had shifted across the Atlantic to make New York, and not Aylmer Vallance's London, the true 'Centre of the World'. For the next half-century of industrial and imperial decline, the City of London would play a diminished role on behalf of the shrinking bloc of countries who traded in sterling (MacRea and Cairncross 1991; Rose 1994). On the rebound, merchant banks diverted more attention to modernising British industry, pulling it southwards in the process. The London clearing banks also consolidated their grip; this period marked the demise of regional financial systems within the UK.

Though eclipsed as a world financial centre, the City remained important in commerce. Telecommunications allowed London traders to rely less upon the physical traffic through the port than on logistics and control at a distance, shipping, storing and selling consignments in the light of the best commercial intelligence about markets world-wide. Vallance was close to the mark in his romantic emphasis on the ebb and flow of seaborne commerce in the Square Mile. Ship and aeroplane charter, insurance, brokerage, entrepôt warehousing and eso-teric commodity specialisms were facets of an international trading community which remained its global role after the First World War, despite the rupture of the important Anglo-German connection and the protectionism of the 1930s. But London commercial houses were severely affected by the Second World War and the period of state control which followed it (Michie 1992: ch. 2).

In 1950, the intrepid traveller Freya Stark (cited in Russell 1994: 14) was to describe a walk along the pavements of the City of London as 'one of the most romantic things in the world; the austere and unpretentious doors – the River Plate Company, or Burmah Oil, or affairs in Argentina or Ecuador or Hudson's Bay – they jostle each other and lead away to strange places, and create a feeling of being all over the world at once among the messenger boys and the top hats . . . in Moorgate'. In fact the Moorgate of 1950 – bomb damage apart – was severely depleted, with its intelligence networks broken, and the world trade in many markets transferred to state-appointed boards, or about to be internalised within multinational corporations. The commercial city never fully recovered from this setback. But its legacy of expertise and internationalism remained, and would play a crucial role in the recovery of the London economy in the 1980s.

MADE IN LONDON

A hundred years ago another intrepid traveller, the humourist R. Andom (a pseudonym for A.W. Barrett) announced a voyage of exploration into untoured territory within a 6-mile radius of Charing Cross. *Industrial Explorings* (1896) was a travelogue of Piano-Land (Brindmead's factory in Kentish Town), Rope-Land (J.T. Davis, Rope-Maker of Coborn Road, Bow) Tram-Land (North Metropolitan Tramways factory, off Leytonstone Road), Candle-Land (Price's Patent Candle Co. works in Battersea), Gas-Land (West Ham Gas Works, Stratford), Paper-Land (McMurray Paper Mills, Wandsworth), Soap-Land (Edward Cook & Co., Leamouth), Mineral-Water-Land (Idris & Co, Pratt Street, Camden Town), Match-Land (Palmer & Son, Old Ford Road, Bow), Rubber-Land (Abbot Anderson & Abbott, Limehouse), Wire-Land (Bullivants, Millwall), and Sweet-Land (Clarke Nickoll & Coombs, Hackney Wick).

Though several of the companies were major exporters – Price, Idris and Bullivants manufactured for world markets – R. Andom had to do his exploring in back streets and side turnings. Industry did not dominate the townscape of the capital as it did cities of the Midlands and the North. The importance of manu-facturing in London was largely unregarded by visitors and researchers. Peter Hall's seminal study, *Industries of London since 1861* (1962) directly challenged readers' preconceptions with data from the 1861, 1921 and 1951 Census of Production:

> At all three dates the capital was clearly the most important single seat of manu-
> facturing industry in the country, accounting for between one in six and one in seven
> of all manufacturing workers in 1861, over one in six in 1921, and over one in five in

1951. Manufacturing occupied nearly one in three workers in London in 1861, over one in three in 1951. These are important and striking facts. They flatly deny the traditional assumption about London, implicitly underlying many of the references to it in economic geographies or economic histories, that it came into existence as a major manufacturing centre after the turn of this century, perhaps even after 1918 (Hall 1962: 23; see Schwarz 1992).

Despite its collective weight the London industrial economy was untypical in most respects. It had a bipolar structure, with a small number of large firms (brewing, printing, newspapers, metal foundries) and a large number of small ones (Green 1996). Agglomeration favoured small businesses and independent artisans and tradesmen. Enterprise thrived on proximity: proximity to the City for credit, the port for materials, the manufacturing districts for inputs and the metropolis for markets. The basic lines of the industrial geography had already been laid down in the eighteenth century, with river-based industries taking and transforming materials to the south and east of the City, and the varieties of specialised craft production – engraving, jewellery, watchmaking – to the north and west. During the Industrial Revolution a succession of basic industries collapsed or relocated under pressure of competition from the emerging factory systems of the Midlands and north of England: Wandsworth lost its clothing industry, Lea Valley copper and brass production went to Birmingham, china works and potteries departed to Staffordshire, cutlery was overtaken by Sheffield and shoe-production by the East Midlands. But their place was taken by industries answering metropolitan demand: engineering trades to serve the mechanical requirements of the commercial heart of empire – its demand for ropes, trams, rubber, cables, gas; luxury trades to cater for the growth of consumerism at all levels, with pianos and soda-water for the gentry and candles, soap, sweets for the masses.

District specialisms created diverse labour markets, with a broad gradient of skill from east to west. Having escaped the full impact of the factory system, the London labour market had a unique diversity of skill and artisanship, evident in the astounding range of specialities listed in the trades columns of the annual *Post Office Directories* for the London postal area: at its peak in the early years of the twentieth century it had over 2600 pages of business entries densely printed at 250 entries to the page, from absorbent cotton wool manufacturers to zincographic printers. 'Without the traditional self-consciousness of the North's specialized industrial towns,' wrote the geographer O.H.K. Spate (1938: 432) 'every industry was represented within her borders; and in many she was great'. In retrospect we can see some characteristic strengths and weaknesses in the turn-of-the-century economy. With its encyclopedic diversity, it was a better milieu for invention than for standardisation and mass production.

A minor invention which might be taken as a parable for London manufacturing was the musical instrument patented by Charles Wheatstone in 1844 as the 'concertina', an ingeniously compact hand organ, with button-operated reeds set into hexagonal bellows-plates. Its popularity grew steadily as an inexpensive substitute for the parlour piano (though Wheatstone aimed higher, seeing it as a substitute for the violin) and by the turn of the century London had ten manufacturers producing the instruments. But true to the spirit of competitive enterprise, almost every maker introduced his own improvements to the arrangement of buttons and reeds. Apparently identical hexagonal squeezeboxes were unplayable to someone who had bought a rival system, a 'Jeffries duet', say, instead of a 'Wheatstone English', 'McCann Duet' or 'Davies Anglo'. The idiosyncratic failure of London's concertina manufacturers to standardise their product consigned it the margins of musical history, while the German Hohner company (founded in 1857) mass-produced accordions and mouth-organs for the world.

Peter Hall and Paschall Preston (1988) trace the same pattern in the key group of late nineteenth-century innovations which laid the technical basis for the modern era: alternating current, the electrical light, internal combustion. Many of the original inventions had been made in the capital, in fact the patents underpinning the technologies of the telegraph, electrical measurement, dynamo, cryptography and electronic timekeeping belonged to the very same Sir Charles Wheatstone, combining his family musical instrument business with a distinguished academic and research career at King's College. The glass light bulb with incandescent filament was an invention of Sir Joseph Wilson Swan of University College. But at the development stage of each of these facets of electrical technology, the initiative passed to Germany and the United States, to firms large enough to develop, manufacture and market on a mass scale. Westinghouse and General Electric were products of American commercial capitalism, Siemens and AEG were the result of the Prussian government's strategy of amalgamating 39 pioneer companies into two corporate giants. Britain had no industrial strategy and City of London banks were notably reluctant to finance the fledgling electrical industry (Kynaston 1994: 408). So, the electric traction which revolutionised London's transport was developed by US firms, who financed and built the Underground. The first London company to organise a factory on the 'American shop' system was the German electrical giant Siemens. The glass light bulb company launched by Sir Joseph Wilson Swan, with its headquarters on Cheapside and factory at Ponders End, was merged with and absorbed by the Edison empire, and Britain remained a net importer of bulbs right up to the First World War. New York and Berlin surged ahead with electrification while London struggled with a confusion of utilities which included, in 1900, '65 different undertakings, 49 distinct supply systems, 32 different voltage levels for transmission and 24 for distribution, and 70 different systems for charging and pricing' (Hall and Preston 1988: 145). An industrial structure dominated – relative to the USA and Germany – by small-scale, competitive, specialist family enterprises, was ill-equipped to develop new technologies, and slow to adopt them (Hobsbawn 1968).

At the outbreak of the Second World War London presented a very different picture, with a complete coverage of electrical supply linked to the national grid, and a perimeter infrastructure of motor highways designed for road haulage. Most

Figure 6.4 Ford Motors, Dagenham. *London's largest manufacturing plant in acres and employees, Dagenham was designed as a remarkably self-sufficient production complex, with body and assembly plants supported by blast furnaces, coke ovens, power plant, foundry, forge, and engine works. Photograph by kind permission of the Ford Motor Company Ltd*

homes were electrified and there were already around a quarter of a million private motor cars on the roads. The most significant change was in the scale and visibility of manufacturing industry. No longer tucked away in obscure back streets where only comic journalists would venture, the white, floodlit facades of the new industry dominated every approach to the capital, as we saw in Chapter 3 above. This interwar industrial architecture was monumental, at least on the front elevation. The style was trans-Atlantic and so was much of the ownership. What London had lost in the shift of invisible earnings from the City to New York it regained by the arrival of US brand names such as Firestone, Gillette, Heinz, Hoover, Kodak, Johnson & Johnson, NCR and Quaker Oats (Hamilton 1991). Largest of the newcomers was the Ford Motor Company, relocated from Trafford Park, Manchester, in 1931 by Henry Ford's son Edsell (Figure 6.4). The company brought south 2000 workers, whom the London County Council eventually accepted as tenants to fill some of unlet stock on its vast Becontree estate (Home 1997; see page 56 above).

The attractions of a London location for international business had already been apparent from before the turn of the century: inward investment met up with and reinforced the outward push of London companies from sites in the congested centre (Hall 1962). Ebenezer Howard, recognising these factors in the 1890s, had been confident he could attract industrialists to new urban centres on greenfield sites in the Home Counties, providing an economic base for his Garden City experiment at Letchworth in 1904. But the First World War gave a powerful boost to decentralisation within the region. Factories producing armaments and war equipment clustered particularly in Middlesex to the north-west, in what was until then the only undeveloped sector within the 5–7 mile radius of Charing Cross (a by-product of transport geography, because the Euston and Paddington lines offered the fewest suburban stopping services). After the Armistice these fully serviced sites, transformed into 'trading estates', provided the starting point for a huge industrial sector stretching westwards on either side of the Bath Road from Acton towards Slough. A second sector of expansion was northwards up the Lea Valley, where the Enfield Small Arms Factory had expanded during the First World War, developing new industrial sites and creating a large, predominantly female workforce to be re-employed by newly arriving firms after 1918. As we saw in Chapter 3, the potential of these areas was enhanced in the 1920s when, to relieve postwar unemployment, dual-carriageway arterial roads were built to reduce the congestion along the most heavily trafficked trunk routes out of London, and a start was made on an orbital road system, the North Circular Road, which ran conveniently by two of the largest new former munition factory estates, at Wembley and Park Royal. Suburban factories soon colonised the frontages of the new roads, most spectacularly along Great Western Avenue and the Great West Road, but also (for example) along the Lea Valley axis of the Great Cambridge Road, southwards by Croydon along the Purley Way, and to the east along the Southern Arterial Road. The social impact of these suburban transformations is vividly conveyed by Porter (1994) and Weightman and Humphries (1984).

The composition of the outer London factory belt was analysed in detail by Smith (1933) and Hall (1962). About half the companies settling in the new industrial areas were transfers from inner London. West End and East End seeded different compositions of radial industry, reflecting the preponderance of bespoke trades and craft skills, on one side, and mass production and cheap labour, on the other. As industries moved outwards, expanding in scale from workshop to freestanding factory, their geographical structure retained some imprint of the initial divisions of labour within the preindustrial nucleus of City, Westminster and surrounding parishes. The electrical and automotive industries developed towards the west, taking with them aircraft production, London's fastest-growing industry in the 1920s. The precision engineering industries, originating in the scientific instrument makers of inner north London, had the additional westward pull of the military training and testing grounds in Surrey and Berkshire. Conversely, the City fringe and river-frontage industries of clothing, furniture and chemicals developed out to the east sectors (Green 1991; Martin 1966).

Overlying this evolutionary effect was the revolutionary impact of Americanisation. The old imperial capital had become, in Weightman and Humphries' (1984: 46) words, the happy victim of a new form of economic colonisation. One in two

Figure 6.5 Guinness Brewery. *The Park Royal brewery, complete with railway sidings, playing fields, workers' club and model housing. The immense brick flanks, vertical ribbing and high frieze show the hand of Sir Giles Gilbert Scott, architect of Liverpool's Anglican cathedral and Battersea Power Station*

jobs created by inward investment in interwar Britain was with an American company in the London region, but their impact extended far beyond direct job creation. They accelerated the geographical shift to the suburbs, teaching conservative British businessmen new ways to read the map. The Reading-based property company who bought the derelict armaments factory at Park Royal after the First World War had intended to use it for scrap metal sorting, the land being polluted and the location semi-rural. It was Heinz, the American food giant, which recognised the potential of an industrial site located beside the Grand Union Canal, the main railway lines to the West Country and the Midlands, the Underground, and the main road to the West End. Heinz's arrival in 1925 laid the basis for a hygienic food processing and distribution complex which soon included the Guinness brewery (Figure 6.5), United Biscuits, and packaging manufacturers; by 1939 Park Royal was the largest industrial estate in the south of England, employing 70 000 people.

Americans also pioneered the shift from workshop, skilled and predominately male production to the large-scale shopfloor with a female-operated production line; they spread the gospel of scientific management and the use of press, cinema and billboard advertising to stimulate consumer demand. Henry Ford participated directly in London's Fordist revolution by bringing an exhibit of a car-assembly line

146

to the Wembley British Empire Exhibition in 1925, shortly before the decision to transfer production from Manchester. London met all the locational requirements for assembly-line industry, with plentiful flat, drained land to east and west, little tradition of labour militancy, rich component-supply networks, and maximum accessibility to showrooms and final markets. In the 1930s these lessons were being applied by British big business in a short decade of growth under a national policy regime of cheap money, protectionism (the tariff wall known as 'Imperial Prefer-ence') and electrification (thanks to the establishment of a government monopoly on wholesale power through a Central Electricity Board, linking local supply systems into a National Grid). An impressive symbol of the shift to large-scale production in London was Battersea Power Station, designed in 1932 by Sir Giles Gilbert Scott, architect of Guinness's Park Royal Brewery and Liverpool Cathedral: a monolithic monument to the new era of giant industry on the banks of the Thames.

Meanwhile in the nooks and crannies of inner London, the older traditions of small-scale manufacturing and craft production developed new patterns of linkage with big firms. John Martin's (1966) meticulous industrial geography of London depicted the huge manufacturing tract at a continuous density of over 300 operatives per square kilometre extending from the West End to the edges of nineteenth-century London, with tentacles extending further along the river valleys, and indents of exclusively residential areas on the heights of Dulwich, Highgate, and Putney:

> The greatest unity is probably in the industrial landscape. There are no industrial estates. Right through the tract, in Camden Town and Hackney, in Vauxhall, Camberwell and Deptford, industry is largely in adapted premises. These are of astonishing, indeed bewildering, variety, ranging from converted houses, shops and warehouses to mews premises, former cinemas and ballrooms, church halls and chapels and even former horse-tram depots. Working conditions are typically cramped and single-storey factories are the exception' (Martin 1966: 82).

A vigorous subcontracting economy linked the new world of the whitewashed factories on the radial roads to the ramshackle, competitive, low-rent world of the veneerers, polishers, model makers, electroplaters, tool makers, jig makers, paint sprayers, who carried on in direct line of descent the London tradition of craft workshops (Hall 1962).

In his pioneering study of the industrialisation of the Lea Valley, Smith (1933) argued stoutly that there was no conflict between London's electrically powered factories, producing proprietary articles for domestic consumers, and the export staple industries of the Midlands and North. This argument became harder to sustain as protectionism hit the areas worst affected by unemployment while boosting the already prosperous south. Import tariffs encouraged the growth of London companies catering for mass consumerism, on top of a final surge of inward investment from US companies ducking under the tariff wall. The growth was self-reinforcing, for every factory stimulated labour demand, which triggered migration, reinforcing the housing boom, which in turn renewed demand for London's fastest-growing industrial outputs, building materials, furniture, furnishings, consumer durables and convenience foods. However, London's dynamism in the 1930s gave no stimulus to regions bearing the brunt of the depression. The Royal Commission on the Distribution of the Industrial Population confirmed the effect on the geography of British manufacturing. In the six years between 1932 and 1937 Greater London had captured no less than 83% of factory-building in the country as a whole. Data on openings and closures of factories employing 25 or more people in 1932–6 revealed that in the country as a whole there had been 2688 births and 2207 deaths, a net increase of 481, of which London had 479, the rest of Great Britain . . . two!

The Commission's report, published in 1941, recommended drastic measures to halt London's growth. Here were the origins of the green belt which has kept postwar London within strict bounds, and of the planned satellite towns which drew off many of its growth industries and young skilled workforce. Other legacies of Barlow were a system of grants and incentives to attract firms into peripheral regions of high unemployment, and administrative controls to discourage factory building in south-east England. These strong measures took effect in a postwar world with a very different dynamic of industrial location to that which had created the interwar suburban factory boom. Congestion of the continuously built-up metropolis – the problem which most exercised Barlow – was curing itself by the spontaneous shift of industrialists towards larger, lower-density plants in out-of-town locations. As everywhere, firms have been drawn by access to the national highway network and by the flexibility and efficiency of low-density units on greenfield sites. Industrial sites within the built-up area were to become more attractive for storage and handling of goods, and for retailing. In London these generic trends were reinforced by regional policies diverting investment from south-east England to the north, and by the clearances and controls of the land-use planning system, which by misfortune swept away the 'non-conforming' incubator premises of small-scale manufacturing just when its machinery was getting quieter, cleaner, and more neighbourly (Vigor 1975). The cumulative impact on the London economy – well analysed in local detail by Buck, Gordon, Young and others (1986) – can be summed up in a single word: deindustrialisation.

At first all seemed well. In the 1950s, one London worker in three was employed in a factory. Despite the controls against expansion of existing premises and strong incentives to relocate elsewhere, new firms always seemed to spring up to take the place of the old – the problem which exercised policy makers was the apparent irrepressibility of London manufacturing (Hall 1962, 1963). The interwar industries of outer London were still in an expansion phase that masked the decline of the older craft manufacturing in the inner parts. As late as 1961, half of the jobs in the London suburbs were in manufacturing, on top of which the central area was experiencing a steep increase in public and private office employment, unforeseen by Barlow and Abercrombie (Goddard 1975). The surge of white-collar employment

Figure 6.6 Park Royal. *Derelict light industrial units await the regenerative effects of Assisted Area designation and Objective 2 status under the European Regional Development Fund*

was driven by management changes and mergers in the domestic economy which mirrored the Fordist transformation of blue-collar factory work in the interwar years. The trend to concentration within British industry reinforced demand for corporate headquarters in the capital. In the words of an influential pamphlet of 1962, *The Paper Metropolis*: 'With London the dominant centre of almost every aspect of national life, what city, asks the board of directors, could possibly confer greater prestige – if the question is ever asked' (TCPA 1962: 17).

The curve of employment, though, was levelling and would soon begin a remorseless downward slope. A London location had suited big business in the 1930s, but three decades later, the pack was on the move to places with lower costs, higher capital subsidies, or both. Roy Porter (1994: 347) gives the litany of closures and redundancies affecting all the largest factories in outer London; Belling (Enfield), GEC (Willesden), Thorn–EMI (Hayes) British Aerospace (Hayes), British Leyland (formerly AEC – Park Royal), Lucas (Acton), Hawker-Siddely (Kingston). London was 'at the eye of the storm' (GLC 1985b: 3) in the national crises of deindustrialisation and urban unemployment, suffering, in round terms, a haemorrhage of half a million factory jobs in 1965–75, the same in 1975–85, and a further quarter of a million in 1985–95 (Figure 6.6) (see Hall 1989: ch. 3).

When the Greater London Council was established in 1965 its aims had been to keep the lid on industrial and office floorspace while encouraging the outmigration of families and firms through assisted colonisation schemes. But these postwar planning axioms were in full collapse even as the Greater London Development Plan went through the process of public enquiry in the early 1970s. The 1966 and 1971 Censuses had shown up some ominously American correlations of selective outmigration, immigrant concentration, rising unemployment and welfare need. First the Greater London Council, then the London Boroughs, then central government switched to a new policy agenda based upon the retention of population, regeneration of the employment base, and reclamation of land left derelict by industrial closures (Buck, Gordon and Young 1986).

Unemployment and dereliction were so directly linked to industrial closure that it was natural for London's rising generation of New Left activists to seek a remedy through intervention in the board room. The movement known as 'local Socialism' encouraged experimental approaches to economic policy, forging direct links between local government and the workplace. For London, this thinking climaxed under the radical Labour administration of the GLC in 1980–6 (Pratt 1994). The council's 600-page *London Industrial Strategy* set out a neo-Marxist strategy for 'reclaiming production' through local state intervention in industry, based on local government's powers of procurement, its ownership and regulation of land, its pension investments, its (limited) capacity for discretionary expenditure, and its political ability to mobilise worker and community participation (GLC 1985b).

The GLC was abolished before it could put this plan into effect, but the wider forces of change – anatomised in Sassen's (1991) comparative study of London, New York and Tokyo – made it as improbable that London would recover as a factory location as that cargo ships would return to the Pool of London. The trends were universal and irresistible. Looking over the long run, the golden age of 1930–60 would come to seem anomalous: 'A few years when technology made factories and London look as if they were natural bedfellows rather than nodding acquaintances' (Elliot 1986: 91). Though the anti-industrial bias of the policy system had been fully reversed, and London offered sites and subsidies to compete with any other region in Britain, demand remained elusive: in the Docklands, non-operational docks expensively filled in by the GLC for factory sites attracted negligible commercial interest despite world-wide promotion (Ledgerwood 1987; Hebbert 1992b). London was no longer matching itself against the other UK regions, but against low-cost production sites in the southern hemisphere. The emergence of business corporations with a global span, and the acceleration of ether-based transactions and information flows, were setting a radically new context for urban regeneration, even in a city so accustomed to see itself as the nerve centre of the world economy. The keyword was *globalisation*: 'not internationalisation, whose building blocks are firmly national, but globalisation, a universe with its own rules, which has genuinely burst out of national boundaries' (Hutton in Budd and Whimster 1992). The challenge for London at the end of the twentieth century was not to recover its old employment base, but to carve out a fresh role in the universe. And more by fortune than design, it succeeded.

WORLD'S MARKET (2)

London stands today in a unique position in the world economy. It has the world's busiest international airport and is the world's most popular tourist destination. It competes with Paris as Europe's largest city and with New York as the world's largest centre of entertainment and culture. It is ranked as the most popular global business location, and in a capitalist world its capital markets are paramount (CoL 1995; Llewellyn-Davies 1996). London has not had such a taste of pre-eminence since 1900 and the experience is unfamiliar. Forebodings of irreversible economic decline remain a very recent memory (Hoggart and Green 1991: 220–32).

The recovery had a long gestation. In 1958 the City was the first European financial centre to relax exchange controls, a process completed in 1979. That encouraged a revival of international activity within the Square Mile, beginning with an upturn in the number of overseas banks (Coakley 1992). Recovery continued in the 1960s through the development of the 'eurobond', an informal market in fixed-interest securities which grew up outside the restrictive and regulated environment of the Stock Exchange. It attracted financial institutions from all around the world, particularly from oil-rich OPEC countries debarred from US markets after 1973. Federal restrictions on foreigners lending and borrowing in the USA also stimulated London's 'eurodollar' market. Originally a form of interbank dollar lending within the cluster of City-based European banks, this was developed by merchant bankers into a major source of international medium-term credit. The success of eurobond and eurodollar markets greatly revived the external standing of the City. Even before British entry into the European Common Market in 1976 London had positioned itself as Europe's primary gateway to international financial markets. Its overseas earnings were to increase tenfold in 1976–86. As the process of globalisation began to bite, and multinational companies broke loose from domestic capital markets, issuing equities directly to the international investor, London was the optimal trading environment: large by European standards, but less dominated by domestic factors than the even larger markets of New York and Tokyo (Michie 1992: 140–2).

A further lesson of eurodollar and eurobond success was that they both circumvented the traditional restrictive practices of the Stock Exchange and the clearing banks. They showed that London was still large and loose enough to allow innovations that might not have occurred in more tightly supervised financial centres (fringe bank failures in the 1970s were the other side of this coin). The scale of eurodollar and eurobond activity destabilised traditional City institutions and set in train a demand for further deregulation. From 1979, under Mrs Thatcher's premiership, the case for liberalisation of the City received support from Westminster. So the scene was set for the epochal event of October 1986, London's 'Big Bang'.

Globalisation has made every financial centre's rules and practices out of date, forcing change sooner or (as in Tokyo) later. What was distinctive about the Big

Bang was that the trading system changed at a stroke, as the name implies, and it occurred earlier than in other European centres, giving London the advantage of timing. The reform, which was actually precipitated by a legal challenge rather than government action, lifted restrictions on entry to the stock market and replaced face-to-face dealing on the floor of the Exchange with an electronic share-price display system, allowing screen-based trading.

Big Bang's impact was fundamental. Long-established stockbroking partnerships merged and were swallowed into broad-based investment banks, many of them entering the UK securities market from overseas. The eurobond market returned to the fold of the Stock Exchange. Foreign equities activities doubled in 1986–91 and again in 1991–3. The somewhat closed, clubby world of the City was invigorated by new arrivals from Wall Street and Tokyo, with their information systems designers and office architects close behind them. Through the crash of October 1987 and the recession of the early 1990s London continued to develop and consolidate its position against intense competition from other European centres, as the dominant market in the hours between the close of trading in Tokyo and the opening of New York.

London has over 600 000 jobs in banking and financial services; boosterists tell us it is 'the largest such concentration in the world' and 'larger than the total population of Frankfurt' (CoL 1995). The gross figure groups two essentially different types of activity with distinct locational tendencies: the provision of retail services to the holders of bank accounts, mortgages, pensions, consumer credit and insurance policies, and provision of wholesale services to other financial business or corporate investors. Because of its concentration of headquarters, London had a more than proportional share in the 1980s expansion of the domestic financial sector, but this workforce began to decline after 1990 through office mechanisation and the relocation of clerical and data-processing activities to lower-cost locations. Wholesale finance, on the other hand, has continued to gravitate to the centre. Dealers move towards the widest and deepest market. The global reach of information technology has reinforced the pulling power of the few centres where turnover is deep enough to be measured in thousands of millions and wide enough to span the entire range of financial products and services. Three centres of global finance dominate their respective time zones. But powerful domestic economies shape the regulatory environment of the Tokyo and New York markets. The City of London is the paramount wholesale market; in this sense it has recovered in the 1990s the position it held in the 1890s as 'the only true world centre' (CoL 1995: xviii).

The gravitational pull of London's wholesale financial markets is evident in the tally of foreign commercial banks published annually in *The Banker* since 1966. In three decades the total of banks with a full London office has grown from 88 to 428 (*Banker* 1996) Tokyo has less than a quarter of that total, New York less than two-thirds (Llewellyn-Davies 1996). At the head of the list are the nine foreign banks listed in Table 6.1 which employ more than 1000 City staff. Note that Deutsches Bank, Dresdner Bank, Swiss Bank Corporation, Credit Suisse and the Union Bank of

Table 6.1 *Foreign Banks in the City*
(Banks with over 1000 Staff in 1996)

Citibank	4000
J.P. Morgan	2400
SBC Warburg	2700
Union Bank of Switzerland	2500
Goldman Sachs	1700
Deutsche Morgan Grenfell	1500
Bank-America Corporation	1250
Banque Paribas	1200
ING Barings	1200

Source: The Banker, November 1996.

Switzerland have centralised their wholesale activity in London rather than Frankfurt or Zurich. The majority of overseas banks maintain only a small office, but their presence in London is dictated by the same need to perform core investment and banking functions in the markets with greatest liquidity.

The global standing of the City rests partly on its conventional strengths in international bank lending, underwriting, bond trading, foreign exchange trading and investment management, partly on a continual invention of new financial products. Some of the innovations – swaps, cross-exchange equity trading, currency options – are abstruse. In 1995 the collapse of Barings, the City's staunchest family business, bankers to the Queen, showed the extent of ignorance within the senior financial community about markets on which a single trader could lose $1.4 billion (Fay 1996). The main sectors of activity are presented to the lay reader, in ascending degree of detail, by Clarke (1991), MacRae and Cairncross (1991) and Michie (1992).

The London foreign exchange market is the largest in the world, with a daily turnover estimated to account for 30% of global exchange transactions, equal to those of New York, Tokyo and Paris combined. It has no central meeting place but is scattered through some sixty dealing rooms in the Square Mile and Canary Wharf. A derivative market in short-term currency options and futures accounts for most (80%) of the trading on LIFFE, the London International Financial Futures Exchange. Located above Cannon Street station until it can move into its new premises beside the Bishopsgate Institute (Figure 1.5), LIFFE offers banks and finance houses a means to manage their risks and hedge against potential exchange rate fluctuations. In 1996 it had an average *daily* turnover of £160 billion. Chicago's derivatives market is even bigger but deals in dollars, where LIFFE is global, offering derivatives in seven currencies: sterling, US dollars, yen, Deutsche-marks, Italian lire, Swiss francs and ECUs.

The London Stock Exchange is smaller than Tokyo and New York but more international. There, foreign equities account for only about a tenth of turnover; in London their total value surpasses the domestic share market. Once again, it is a wholesale market dominated by institutional business, and the average transaction in international equities is five or six times larger than in the domestic market (LSE 1996). When New York City launched municipal bonds for the foreign institutional investor (the first US city to do so) the target group was German banks but the flotation was made in London. Many transactions involve a buyer and seller from the same overseas country – a trading system designed for the wholesale transactions of corporate customers allows, say, an Italian bank to buy shares in an Italian company faster and at lower cost in London than in Milan.

The London insurance market has always dealt in extraterritorial hazards, symbolised by the ship's bell, rescued from a wreck, which stands beneath the soaring atrium of the Lloyd's building and rings for a loss (Figure 6.7). Lloyd's, specialising in the reinsurance of large-scale and unusual risks, is a successful survivor of the City's commercial era, performing a significant wholesale role which parallels those of the London securities and foreign exchange markets. More than half its turnover is from overseas. In particular, London still retains just under a quarter of the world market for marine insurance and well over a third of the market in aviation risks. Other commercially originated sectors which survived the lean years and have expanded on the back of globalisation are ship and aircraft broking, the commodities markets (notably the London Metal Exchange) and the trade in commodity futures (now part of LIFFE).

The web of international wholesale markets is supported by business services which reflect the same process of specialisation: in law, accountancy, and surveying a 'City' office is synonymous with an international corporate clientele. It is no coincidence that the Square Mile physically abuts the legal quarter of the High Courts (on the Strand), the Inns of Court (where lawyers train and have their chambers) and the Central Criminal Court at the Old Bailey. City law firms have a long involvement in the markets and have been active in their modernisation, for example in the creation in 1994 of the City Disputes Panel to arbitrate in the area of wholesale finance. Law is itself big business in the City. The legal profession is stratified, with mainstream corporate deals (in excess of, say, £100 million) handled by the big five firms of Slaughter & May, Linklaters & Paines, Allen & Overy, Freshfields, and Clifford Chance. A further 15 medium-sized firms tend to deal in specialised, niche work. Between them the top 20 firms have 8700 fee earners in the City. Their earnings are not published, but the magazine *Legal Business* attributed to the largest, Clifford Chance, a fee income of £200 million in 1996. City law firms have recently developed global networks of offices to extend their reach to clients, and deploy in foreign markets the unique concentration of expertise in financial instruments acquired in London since 1980. One of London's most marketable exports is its expertise in privatisation of public utilities and assets. City merchant banks and lawyers now sell to the world the skills developed under Thatcherism (Hoare 1997). Similar patterns of professional service development are evident among the chartered surveyors (acting as both estate agents, and investment managers) and the accountants. The six largest accountancy firms – Coopers & Lybrand, KPMG, Ernst & Young, Arthur Andersen, Price

Figure 6.7 Lloyd's Building. *Architect Richard Rogers purportedly hung lifts and technical services on the outside of the insurance market's tower to facilitate repair and replacement. Be that as it may, the visual impact of his silver ducts and pipes is exhilarating, especially under violet anti-pigeon floodlights. The spectacle has helped to draw increasing numbers of tourists into the closed business world of the City*

Waterhouse and Touche Ross – are estimated to have 29 000 City professionals between them (CoL 1995: 6).

THE CITY IN THE CITY

'Concentration', wrote Anthony Sampson in the *Anatomy of Britain* (1965: 393),

> is the most important characteristic of the City: within the Square Mile, although only 5,000 live there by night, 400,000 work by day. Apart from the newspaper industry on the western edge, none of them makes anything except money. The propinquity of the financial offices, their steady rubbing, shaping and polishing, has provided the 'sensitive mechanism' (to use a favourite City phrase) on which their reputation rests . . . The inner square has an intense atmosphere which no visitor can fail to notice. Nearly everyone wears a dark suit and carries an umbrella, and discount brokers or gilt-edged stockbrokers still wear top hats. The city is a village is a favourite saying: the streets and bars are full of people meeting, recognising, discussing each other. They are pressed closely together by their work, and isolated from the rest of London or the country.

The accuracy of Sampson's portrait of the City was confirmed statistically in a study commissioned by the Corporation of London in the mid-1960s, involving detailed logs of face-to-face, mail and telephone contacts. The consultants' most striking finding was the frequency of face-to-face meetings and the fact that people almost always went to them on foot. Contiguity and accessibility were paramount (Dunning and Morgan 1971).

Thirty years on, computers have transformed City offices and dealing floors, the 'shiny Victorian drinking saloons down small alleyways' described by Anthony Sampson compete with sushi bars and brasseries, and more of the money makers in dark suits are cosmopolitan or female. But the essentials of Sampson's portrait of City life are instantly recognisable. Commuting by car is almost unknown. City workers walk the dense streets from station to office, and they use the street to get to appointments during the working day, typically walking to meetings in indoor clothes (no coat) with papers tucked under the arm (no briefcase). Ten years of electronic trading revolution have not in any way reduced the need for face-to-face meeting: the more global the market, the greater the need for word-of-mouth information, personal contact and the proverbial handshake. Nowhere else in Britain retains such an intensely urban character and such a strong habit of pedestrianism. The police cordon established after IRA bombs in 1992 and 1993 has enhanced the sense of the Square Mile as an enclosed, walkable precinct, albeit at a cost of worsened traffic congestion outside the boundaries.

The compactness of a 2000-year-old urban core is fortuitously well suited to the operation of a globalised financial service centre. Two thousand years of history, on the other hand, do imply severe restraints on the availability of land for office development. Site ownership is fragmented, building heights are controlled (to protect views of St Paul's), and the City contains 550 protected historic buildings and 23 street environments with statutory protection as Conservation Areas. Sharon Zukin reminds us that London is not the only world city to find difficulty accommodating the bulky, disruptive architecture of modern financial service buildings (in Budd and Whimster 1992: ch. 8), but the issue was especially acute in the Square Mile, at once a working business district and an historic urban core, ringed by the West End and by residential communities (pages 88–9 above). In the early 1980s neither planners nor developers appreciated the scale of the transformation that was about to occur (Duffy and Henney 1989). The Corporation of London actually tightened its heritage controls in the lead-up to the Big Bang. The effect was to displace office development to the City fringe, over the tracks and platforms of railway stations (Liverpool Street, Cannon Street, Fenchurch Street), onto warehouse sites across London Bridge, former newspaper buildings along Fleet Street, and – as we shall see in Chapter 8 – to the derelict quays of Canary Wharf, a mile and a half to the east in the Docklands. But even while these schemes were under construction, the Corporation recognised their threat and relaxed planning controls within the core, authorising the construction of floorspace which more than matched the total available in Canary Wharf.

The immediate result was oversupply and a spectacular property crash. The medium-term consequence was a marked improvement in occupation costs relative to other business centres and a jump in users' expectations of the quality of office accommodation available in London. The most important long-term outcome of Big Bang property turbulence was undoubtedly Canary Wharf's emergence as a secondary office district, acting in relation to the City as Battery Park does to midtown Manhattan (Gordon 1996). The moment of proof was the inability of the City – despite the best efforts of its lawyers and lobbyists – to prevent the departure of its largest overseas bank to a prestigious quayside office tower designed by Sir Norman Foster at Canary Wharf. Others will follow.

The City's reaction to Canary Wharf echoed episodes of fractious opposition to economic growth outside its walls in earlier centuries (pages 28–9 above). In a sense, more was at stake from the overspill of financial services than ever before. Insofar as banks on the Isle of Dogs undermined the only surviving monopoly of the Square Mile, they removed the City's sole line of defence against a government committed to abolition of its Corporation. The victory of Labour under Tony Blair in May 1997 brought commitments to radical constitutional change, including devolution of the unitary state, and reform of the House of Lords. But as we saw in the previous chapter, the City of London was spared. It will survive – with a reformed system of business voting – as an independent jurisdiction, providing a high quality of local public services for the core financial services district, rather in the manner of an American Business Improvement District (BID). Canary Wharf and other fringe areas will play a supplementary role which is more complementary than competitive, allowing London to perform its global role to the full without destroying the scale and fabric of its historic core.

Connections

This happy ending, if that is what it is, corresponds with a growing recognition of the motor function of the financial and business services sector within the London economy. The best estimate for the various forms of international wholesale activity in the Square Mile in 1995 is a total employment of 150 000 and an annual output of £10–15 billions, with sustained growth on all fronts. By definition, the sector is not a heavy consumer of raw materials; the intermediate inputs which it consumes are business services, involving multiple flexible linkages into the host economy (CoL 1995: 2–7). Similarly, the corporate headquarters attracted by the markets are good customers to have. The logic of globalisation obliges firms to shed non-core functions and buy them in *ad hoc*. 'Outsourcing' and 'delayering' imply demand for independent suppliers. London has provided a fertile seedbed for business services. The ready availability of skills combines with the convenience for multinational clients of a legal framework which allows short and flexible contracts, permitting highly skilled teams to be be recruited and dissolved, and an English-speaking city with frequent air connections to every other centre.

Just up the road from the Bishopsgate Institute is the district of Shoreditch. Ten years ago it was a quiet area of shabby workshops linked to the declining furniture trade, with a high level of vacancy and dereliction, matched by unemployment on the neighbouring housing estates. Today, the Victorian workshops are brilliant with halogen lamps, their hoists and pulleys have new paint, and chic bars and cafés have appeared on every corner. Like other industrial districts of the inner ring it has reverted to its nineteenth-century role of direct economic linkage to the Square Mile, and is being colonised by firms meeting the core economy's demand for public relations, marketing, design, equipment rental, headhunting, software consultancy, photography, displays, promotions, catering, flowers, artworks, events. There seems to be a sympathy between risk-taking in the markets and the daring of artistic creativity. The growth of world business sharply boosted London's arts, culture and entertainment sector, already well rooted in capital city and leisure economies described at the start of this chapter. The cultural industry was estimated to have a turnover of £7.5 billion and overseas earnings of £3.9 billion (PP 1997) and to employ as many as 250 000 people in 15 000 enterprises (LTEC 1996; see Table 6.2). The motor lay in the linkage of media and design sectors with the financial service core, whether as corporate inputs, or to meet the demand – implicit in the word 'yuppy' – of its young workforce for an urban life-style based on conspicuous, lavish and fashionable spending (Thrift and Williams 1987). A new wave of designer restaurants, bars, boutiques and clubs entered the cabbies' Knowledge: 'hip' and 'cool' were back after a 30-year absence.

Meanwhile, what of manufacturing? In 1980 factory workers had outnumbered employees in banking, finance, insurance and business services by 100 000. Ten years later they were already outnumbered by 400 000. All other world cities display the same steep inversion, definitively analysed in Saskia Sassen's (1991) monumental comparative study of London, Tokyo and New York. Various factors

Table 6.2 *Creative Industries in the London Economy*

	Turnover (£m)	Employment (000s)
Performing arts	423	11.2
Radio & television	1839	34.6
Film	360	11.8
Publishing	2720	88.9
Music	395	29.2
Visual arts	530	9.1
Crafts	48	3.5
Design	800	15.0
Advertising	325	10.4
Arts funding bodies	26	0.8
Total	7466	214.5

Source: LPAC (1991) *London World City: The Position of Culture,* Appendix 1 p. 36. Statistics compiled from various sources around 1990.

were at work in the intersection of global market growth and local manufacturing collapse: the physical competition of offices and factories for space, inflation of operating costs, or a less tangible process of 'devalorisation' of factory work within a high-profit, office-oriented system (Sassen 1994). The complexity of these relations is shown in recent work by Dan Graham on London's manufacturing sector. The haemorrhage of employment was relentless and extreme, for the capital lost 240 000 jobs in 1985–95 while the UK as a whole had a net gain of 484 000. However, when output is measured instead of jobs it appears that London was close to the UK average, and over the same period the productivity of (almost) all its manufacturing sectors increased at one and a half times the rate of the rest of the country. London's manufacturing sector has not so much declined, as refocused and specialised, upgrading its equipment and skill base (Graham and Spence 1995, 1997).

At the end of the twentieth century London had a tenth of its workforce in manufacturing, and with 330 000 workers was still the largest industrial concentration in Britain. The sector accounts for about 17% of the output of the capital. What remains after three decades of decline is a hard core of productive industry with a geographical motive for being in London: the most important sector is paper, printing and publishing, accounting for over a third of the manufacturing output and a quarter of employment. Others are electrical engineering and electronics; food drink and tobacco; mechanical engineering; and the clothing industry (LTC 1996). Except in the inner districts around the central area, manufacturing's overall geography has changed very little, preserving its corridor distribution east along the River Thames, north up the River Lea and the valleys of lesser tributaries, and all around London on the arterial roads of the 1920s. In keeping with Sassen's (1991) theory of the economy of global cities, a low-wage, labour-intensive clothing industry survives right on the doorstep of the financial district (Figure 6.8).

Figure 6.8 Middlesex Street, E1. *Just beyond the medieval boundary of the Houndsditch, the financial services district abuts the East End rag trade quarter. By day, Petticoat Lane market mediates the two worlds, selling cheap fashion to City clerical and secretarial staffs*

The deregulation of land-use controls in the 1980s did allow some displacement of bluecollar by whitecollar work, weakening the ability of local authorities to protect their factories and workshops. But competing for space with a high-value office sector gave some London industrialists a productivity advantage by allowing them to release investment capital through relocation – the most spectacular example being the 1980s dispersal of newspaper industry from its historic location along Fleet Street. 'Elbowing-out' or 'crowding-out' may be spurious metaphors in a metropolis of London's size and complexity. There are, for example, 6500 rentable workspaces under railway arches, and demand is buoyant: for every arch beside a main line terminus being converted into a brokers' winebar or gym, you may find another down the line being cleared of scrap, plumbed, wired and fitted out as a workshop. What matters is the regulatory context. Current policy – central and local – re-establishes an explicit commitment to London manufacturing, identifying particularly the potential of industries which incorporate high-quality services and design, and capitalise on the city's role as a centre of culture, medicine and education (GoL 1996; LTC 1996). The image, again, is one of structural complementarity. The London economy in the late twentieth century is doing what it has always done best, exploiting the diversity of its parts.

It would be misleading to end with an image of equilibrium. The strong performance of the London economy is marred by a labour market which excludes 300 000 unemployed residents from the city's prosperity. The social and ethnic composition of London are as diverse as its economy and are changing as fundamentally. So far we have considered London as a place and a centre of activities. It is time to consider Londoners themselves.

CHAPTER 7

LONDONERS

LONDONERS

A curious by-product of the institutional confusions in 1986–97 was a sudden glut of data when the Government Office for London and the London Research Centre produced separate but overlapping statistical yearbooks (GoL 1995; LRC 1995). The image presented in these publications was disconcerting. London appeared as the wealthiest region in Britain and one of the wealthiest four in Europe, but also as a sink of poverty and unemployment, with the four most deprived local authority areas in England, and 750 000 households living below the poverty line of £125 per week: a city in whose inner districts almost half of children live in a household with no earner. An empirical profile drawn up for the benefit of potential inward investors could convincingly place it in the first rank of productivity and livability; a profile aimed at welfare funding agencies would show a city in the bottom rank for poverty and social exclusion. The Association of London Authorities illustrated this ambivalence by issuing a two-colour booklet with rose-tinted glasses to read it by. When you took the glasses off, you saw a very different London. That was at the start of a successful campaign to win recognition of the capital as 'the largest concentration of unemployment in the EEC'.

The ambivalence reflects the degree of social inequality within London. Since the incorporation of the suburbs 30 years ago the capital's social structure (like its politics) has resembled the country at large except in having a disproportionate share of the richest and poorest groups. Several factors in the past two decades have combined to widen the gap between those extremes (Hamnett 1994, 1996). A polarised social structure has acted like a lens, magnifying the regressive effect of tax and benefit trends that were redistributing income on the national scale. The specific process of deindustrialisation described in the previous chapter caused joblessness and created the conditions for casualisation and downward pressure on pay for menial work. The reward systems of the booming international financial sector, based on percentages of immense volumes of monetary transactions, brought astronomical increases in the pay and bonuses of certain categories of workers after Big Bang (for them, the streets of the City *were* paved with gold). The rise of a post-feminist generation of professional and managerial women doubled the earning power of middle-class households with two or three incomes, of whom there are many in the capital. London's persistently above-average house-price inflation squeezed the household budget of renters while rewarding owner-occupiers with untaxed capital gains. For all these reasons the gap between rich and poor widened faster in London than the rest of Britain (Green 1994; Edwards and Flatley 1996); faster than in New York (Fainstein, Gordon and Harloe 1992: ch. 5).

Londoners traditionally looked to the educational system to mitigate the social effect of poverty. In the modern city it seems rather to have aggravated it. In the 1990s the government began to publish comparative tables of the examination performance of schools and education authorities in England and Wales. London authorities polarised: in the 1993 national exam league table, three were among the top ten, six were in the bottom eight. The dichotomy shows up in the capital's labour force. One in five of the workforce has a degree (the national figure is one in eight), but London falls progressively behind the rest of the country in terms of workers with non-degree qualifications, trade apprenticeships, GCSEs, and other training: over half of young Londoners have no qualification at all. So, employers cannot recruit the staff they need, and residents cannot find the work they want – that is, if they do want it, for there was disturbing evidence that one in three working-age men in inner London had withdrawn from the workforce. In the booming high-skill economy of 1995, over 25% of young London males had been unemployed for more than two years (LTC 1996).

The mismatch between supply and demand in the London labour market was linked to a strong increase in commuting from the Home Counties into the city. In 1981 520 000 people crossed the green belt to work in London, in 1991 the daily flow had increased to 670 000. The proportion of jobs taken by in-commuters, approximately one in five, continued to rise in the 1990s. Within the Square Mile it was one in three. The phrase 'social exclusion' – coined in France to describe the diminished citizenship of blacks in outer suburbs – applied vividly to the economic inactivity of largely black districts traversed twice daily by the stream of mainly white participants in the metropolitan economy.

A million Londoners on welfare. The figures of poverty and social exclusion throw a shadow across the page. It is not easy to reconcile them with the community-centred picture given in Chapter 4. The scale of inequality, and the rate at which it has increased, and the degree of correspondence with ethnic divisions, all appear portentous. They imply a city of dystopia where inequality, crime, violence, fear, and social control are locked in a vicious circle, with the urban riot and 'white flight' as its climax. Peter Hall's great historical panorama of urban thought, *Cities of Tomorrow* (1988, uncorrected in the updated edition of 1996), ends with a deeply pessimistic postscript on black riots in Brixton (1981) and the Broadwater Farm Estate, Tottenham (1985), portents of an urban 'underclass' as alienated as its American counterpart, if not more so.

Comparative work on social and racial polarisation in London and New York does not support such pessimism (Fainstein, Gordon and Haloe 1992). All things considered, the apocalyptic streak is remarkably absent from Londoners' attitudes as glimpsed in opinion surveys, or by their revealed preferences in choice of living, shopping, schooling and mode of transport, or through the tone of coverage of London stories in the media. Conviviality, civility and the urban public realm may have deteriorated (Young 1995) but they have not by any means disintegrated, even in Hackney where a third of the population receives supplementary welfare benefit:

least of all in Hackney (Butler 1996). The theme of social breakdown, a subtext throughout the debate over GLC abolition (see page 117 above), had gone missing when an elected metropolitan government was re-established 15 years later. Rightly or wrongly, Londoners do not perceive themselves as sitting on an urban tinderbox.

At the core of social polarisation is a conundrum: if things are so bad, why aren't they much worse? As this book goes to press the government-funded Economic and Social Research Council is launching a major research project by Peter Hall, Ian Gordon and others which may begin to shed more light on the dynamics of metropolitan society. For the moment we shall approach it elliptically, with a descriptive account of Londoners themselves, beginning with their racial and cultural diversity. Almost half the entire ethnic minority population of Britain lives in London. We shall take a guided tour of the peoples of the capital and their distribution within its space, before returning to the conundrum of inequality and conviviality at the end of the chapter.

THE WORLD IN A CITY

'I do not at all like that city' wrote the cleric Richard of Devizes in 1185. 'All sorts of men crowd there from every country under the heavens. Each brings its own vices and its own customs to the city' (in Bailey 1995). The novelist Ford Madox Ford loved London for that reason. It was a permanent world fair, 'a great slip-shod, easy-going, good-humoured magnet' (*The Soul of London*, 1905). This cosmopolitanism is another historical constant. Like other capital cities its magnetism has a double reach, drawing multitudes of young, ambitious Dick Whittingtons from the provinces and the Celtic nations, alongside a much smaller but more distinct settlement of foreigners from overseas (for example, despite the perception of the Victorian city as a melting-pot, the census recorded only 60 000 foreign-born residents in an 1881 population of 3.8 million). With prosperity, the domestic migrant may move up, out and away. Modern London consistently draws young people from all parts of the UK and loses them after the age of 45 (with their young offspring) to other regions, particularly the growth areas south of the Avon–Wash line (LRC 1995: 48). Wrigley (1967) noted a similar escalator effect in the seventeenth century, when one English person in six was found to have spent at least part of his or her life there. But having put down roots in the city and built their community infrastructure and places of worship, London's non-indigenous populations have always been less likely to disperse beyond its limits: that effect may have been accentuated in modern times by the bounding constraint of the green belt. Instead, established communities develop longitudinal patterns of return migration and replenishment with a home country or, as it may be, with a diaspora.

So the evolution of multicultural London has been additive, building like a coral reef on communities with a strong degree of historical continuity and resilience. But perhaps a coral reef is the wrong metaphor for a demography as magnetic and dynamic as London's. The 1991 Census found that 22% of the population had migrated from overseas: three births in every nine were to a mother born outside the United Kingdom. The capital has immigrant communities over 10 000 strong from 37 different countries (Coleman and Salt 1996; LRC 1995). 'World city' it certainly is.

A leading authority in immigration in London is the father of social geography, Emrys Jones (Hoggart and Green 1991: ch. 10). Welsh speaking, he forms a link with the oldest minority in the capital. During the week the Welsh community is dispersed and invisible, but at the weekend it gathers in the 11 Welsh places of worship, or at the London Welsh Club on Gray's Inn Road, or on the touchline of the London Welsh Rugby Club at Richmond. Drapery and milk supply were two particularly Welsh niches in the London economy. The drapery connection survives only in the name of the West End department stores of John Lewis, Peter Jones and D.H. Evans. The nineteenth-century link between Cardiganshire farm families and milk rounds continued until the emergence of the large milk distribution companies in mid-century. In inner London, many Welsh-owned diaries stayed on as general grocery stores. The slow penetration of supermarkets (page 90 above) allowed these small family groceries to survive longer in London than other British cities – long enough for the grocer Reeses and Joneses to sell a going concern to the Patels and Singhs in the 1970s or 1980s.

The Jewish presence in London is almost as ancient as the Welsh, but has a stronger functional continuity and geographical presence. Jews were prominent in the trading economy of early medieval London until expelled by Edward I in 1290. Oliver Cromwell reopened London to Jewish settlers, who joined with Protestant Huguenots expelled from France, and Dutch entrepreneurs to lay the basis of the bourgeios capitalist economy in the City of London. The Huguenot and Walloon communities provided seven of the 24 founder directors and the first governor of the Bank of England; Jewish dealers founded the embryonic Stock Exchange in Jonathan's Coffee House in Change Alley. The Bevis Marks synagogue on the eastern edge of the Square Mile was founded in 1656 and the present building – handsomely panelled, with great brass chandeliers – has been in continuous use since 1701. Descendants of the original Sephardic congregation are still active in both the synagogue and the financial markets of the City.

While Sephardic (Mediterranean) Jewry links to the world of finance, the Ashkenahzi (North European) diaspora connects to trades in precious metals, stones, and jewellery which are quartered in Hatton Garden just beyond the western edge of the Square Mile. Yiddish is spoken on the morning flights between London City Airport and Antwerp: these orthodox merchants in gabardine are following an ancient trade route. For most of the nineteenth century the European Jewish presence in London was a seamless part of the city's strong functional linkage to the Hanseatic and Baltic trades and the economy of Germany. Until 1880, Germans were the largest immigrant group in London, with a community more than 20 000 strong, accounting for over a third of all foreign-born residents.

From 1881 to 1905 the pogroms in Russia and Poland brought a sharp rise in the Jewish population, and a new type of immigrant: rural, impoverished, rich in culture but not in formal education. Like the earlier influx of Irish peasants after the Potato Famine of the 1840s, it was an exodus driven by the instinct for survival. The Irish had clustered around the docks, the railway stations, and the rookeries of St Giles between the City and Westminster. Their manual labour built and maintained the physical infrastructure of Victorian London. Yiddish-speaking Jews settled on the eastern edge of the City at Whitechapel, already established as a textile quarter by seventeenth-century Huguenot refugees. The subsequent trajectories of Irish and Jewish settlement in London differed greatly.

The Jewish influx was large, involving hundreds of thousands. Some proceeded on to New York, others remained to work their way up and out of the East End, primarily through the garment industry (the 'rag trade'). The streets of the inner East End are still Britain's most important textile trade quarter, and have a residual elderly Jewish population, but the initial intense residential concentration has dispersed to the London suburbs. Ultraorthodox Hasidim are concentrated in a small area of Stamford Hill on the northern boundary of the borough of Hackney. Eastward migration from Whitechapel led to the interwar suburbia of Ilford, in the borough of Redbridge, while a larger and more prosperous suburban community settled in the 1920s in Edgware and to the north of Hampstead Heath in the modern boroughs of Finchley and Barnet. Their established presence made north London the main destination area for the smaller but important influxes of European refugees from Nazism before 1939 and Communism after 1945.

In 1994 a 6-square-mile *eruv* (a ritual enclosure for the purposes of orthodox Sabbath observance) gave physical definition to this area: demarcated for some of its length by seven metre poles linked with wire, the *eruv* covers Golders Green, Hendon, the south part of Finchley, and Hampstead Garden Suburb, and contains eight synagogues. Invisible for the most part, it is only of interest to a minority of perhaps 10 000 orthodox residents in a population of 140 000 which may be a third to a half Jewish and is largely liberal or non-observant. The planning application for the *eruv* – rejected by the local authority, permitted by the Secretary of State – was as controversial as it was unusual. Many residents disliked the connotation of a North American style ethnic enclave: more characteristic of London is a pattern of clustering within a mixed and varied suburban setting – what Stanley Waterman (1989: 3) calls 'concentration without segration'. The ecology of settlement reflects the extent to which British-born Jews have made the city their own. Four generations on, the Ashkenazi families who arrived in destitution in the 1890s are prominent in many spheres of London life: finance, law, property, politics, the arts, learning, medicine – and taxicabs.

London's Irish resembled the Jews in their high level of religious observance and collective identity, but not in their drive for economic advancement. As in North American cities, Irish solidarity developed through the channels of local politics. They improved their living standards through trades union and municipal action.

Irish working men were prominent among the 'old Labour' elites which controlled political life in inner London until displaced by 'new left' bed-sitter radicals in the 1970s and 1980s. Though thousands of individual Irish did advance in their professions and move to the suburbs, the centre of gravity of the Irish population is still a broad band of working-class districts in the inner to middle ring of London. There are significant concentrations all around south and east London, but the density thickens to the north and west: between 6% and 9% of the resident populations of the boroughs of Islington, Camden, Hammersmith & Fulham, Ealing and Brent was born in Ireland (north and south). Kilburn is the heart of the Irish community. With its overt Republican support in the pubs and its heroically high attendance of teenagers and young adults at Sunday morning mass it seems more Irish than Dublin. The cultural communities of parish church and pub have been continually replenished by a two-way migration flow which has run strongly and uninterruptedly through the creation of the Irish Republic in 1922, two world wars, and twenty years of the troubles in Northern Ireland. The placards of civil engineering contractors still carry Irish names: FitzPatrick, Joyce, O'Leary, McBride, McGhee, McGrath, Murphy, Noonan, Riney, Ryan. A hundred years ago gangs of Catholic Irishmen dug the holes in London's roads for tramlines and hydraulic mains; today they are doing the same for fibre-optic cabling.

Along the Edgware Road Irish Kilburn and Jewish Hendon represent very different patterns of settlement. The Oxford geographer Ceri Peach (1996) uses them as archetypes. The 'Irish' model is blue collar, manual labour dominated, council house tenured, inner city; the 'Jewish' model, white collar, self-employed, owner occupied and suburban.

Somewhere between the two are the Italians. They started arriving in London a little earlier than the Yiddish-speaking north European Jews, and had built up to a population of 10 000 by 1900, most strongly concentrated in an Italian quarter between Farringdon Road and Leather Lane, just beyond the north-west boundary of the City of London. The London Italians tended to be self-employed: organ-grinding on the streets, lens-grinding in the optical instrument and watchmaking quarter of Clerkenwell. Ice-cream making and vending were, of course, Italian specialities, and so was market gardening, which developed in the 1920s into a major industry in the valley of the River Lea to the north-east of London, the largest concentration of glasshouses in Britain. In the mid-1950s a second surge of immigration linked to the spread of Italian restaurants and cafés took the population up to its present estimated level of 75 000, of whom 30 000 were born in Italy. Modern Italian settlement is dispersed widely around London, but keeps a series of long-established focal points around the centre of London: the provisions merchants of Soho, Farringdon and Finsbury; St Peter's Church, Clerkenwell Road (built 1863 – the first overseas Italian church in the world); and the Italian Hospital in Holborn.

The phasing of Polish settlement in London broadly matched the Italian, with a low-level presence in the nineteenth century and a small north London community in the 1930s, and large-scale settlement after the Second World War. Unlike the Italians, they were political emigrés, and many were professionals. In the 1940s 150 000 Poles came through Britain, lodging mainly in Hammersmith, Earl's Court and South Kensington. By the early 1950s a maturing community of about 33 000 was distributed through the inner ring of suburbs. Brockley was the site of the first Polish parish, founded in 1951; the large-roomed late Victorian villas of that part of London were typical of the areas settled by Poles: Brixton, Balham, Clapham and (to the north of the river, the largest concentration) Ealing. The community sought to maintain its identity through language classes, dancing lessons and the network of ten parishes around London. As settlement shifted further outward, to Finchley and Willesden in the north and Croydon in the south, it strengthened the cluster of bookshops and cultural resources in the original destination areas of inner west London: the Polish Social and Cultural Centre (founded 1974), the Polish Airmen's Club, the Polish Institute, the Sikorski Museum (Merriman 1994: 157–60).

Another dispersed population with nucleated services is the Chinese community. The original, legendary 'China Town' (so named by George Sims in 1902) sat between Limehouse and Poplar by the Pennyfields entrance to the West India Docks. East India Company crews first settled there in the 1780s, forming the basis of a nineteenth-century Chinese quarter which developed – as in San Francisco – restaurants, a laundry industry and a notorious undergrowth of opium dens. The community declined rapidly after the Second World War. Seamens' Union rules penalised recruitment and settlement of Chinese sailors. The physical fabric of Pennyfields was bombed by the Luftwaffe, bulldozed by London County Council slum clearance, and finally swept away in the 1980s in the grandiose road schemes of the London Docklands Development Corporation. Meanwhile, the seed of modern Chinatown had been planted in a few Cantonese restaurants opened in Soho for GI trade during the Second World War. As postwar migration from Canton and Hong Kong developed in the 1960s, Chinese shopkeepers, clubs, agents and stallholders progressively colonised the attractive district of dense eighteenth-century streets between Shaftsbury Avenue and Leicester Square. In the 1980s the quarter was given a facelift, a ceremonial arch and decorative lighting to mark its standing as the largest Chinatown in Europe (McAuley 1993: 5–22).

Cypriot immigration to London began in 1925 when the island of Cyprus became a British colony. The men were recruited as waiters by French Soho restaurateurs, the women worked in the garment industry, and the families made their homes in multioccupied housing in Camden Town. McAuley puts the size of the community in 1941 at 10 000 (1993: 169). From the end of the war through the late 1960s immigration continued steadily at around 4000 a year. There were sharp upward fluctuations after Cypriot independence in 1960–1 and the Turkish invasion and partition in 1974–5. The dual-ethnic structure of the island was reproduced in the diaspora, with Muslim Turks alongside Greek Orthodox, each with their systems of cafés based on villages of origin. Cumulatively, Cypriot London developed into a substantial community with its own garment industry, shops, and business services. The settlement model was 'Jewish' in its high level of self-employment and upward and outward mobility, but instead of the leapfrog progress of the Jews from inner city to outer suburb, the Cypriots crept incrementally out along the radial roads of north London, the Turks towards Islington, Hackney, Stoke Newington, and northward into Enfield, the Greeks along Turnpike Lane towards Wood Green and Palmers Green. The growing prosperity of the main community on the old drovers' road of Green Lanes shifted its centre of gravity by 5 miles northward to Harringay, leaving a trail of fixed social capital – churches, factories, clubs – stretching all the way back to Camden. A second, smaller Greek Cypriot colony established in cheap rented accommodation in Fulham in the late 1940s followed a westward vector towards Richmond, and is mirrored on the southeast of London by a secondary Turkish Cypriot axis extending from Lewisham and Catford towards Bromley.

The star-shaped migration pattern of the Cypriot communities has generously distributed the benefits of their presence in London, for each radius is marked by wonderful shops, open early and late, with fresh greengrocery piled in boxes to the front, and vats of olives, sacks of nuts, and trays of baclava within. The Cypriots make active use of their radial corridors:

> There is a regular traffic along the 29 bus route: Camdenites going to Haringey for the specialist shops, people from Wood Green going to the long established travel agents in Camden, and everybody going to Fonthill Road on a Saturday morning for the cut price fashions produced by the many Greek–Cypriot dress manufacturers there (Merriman 1994: 102).

The presence of Irish, Cypriot and Chinese minorities in London evokes chapters in the history of British imperialism. Economically, the Empire's primary foundation was the West India trade – based on the triangular traffic of goods from England, slaves from Africa and sugar and cotton from the Americas. In the late eighteenth century, when this trade was at its most prosperous, it brought to London a significant Afro-Caribbean presence, 'upwards of 20 000 Negroes' according to a witness in a court case in 1768, in fact probably closer to 15 000 (Gerzina 1995: 5). There was the nucleus of a settled and prosperous community of free blacks, but most were dispersed as personal servants, military bandsmen, sailors, or beggars and street poor. London's black population declined after the Napoleonic Wars and the ending of the triangular trade and for the next century and a half had just a fragmentary presence. The black GIs who arrived with the American army in the 1940s caused as much of a stir in London as in rural East Anglia.

THE EMPIRE IMPLODES

In one of her short stories the author Doris Lessing looks at the passengers around her on the modern Underground, delighting in 'its variety, its populations from everywhere in the world, its transitoriness', and remembers how different it was when she first came to London in the 1950s:

> In that other London there were no foreigners, only English, pinko-grey as Shaw said, always *chez nous*, for the Empire had not imploded, the world had not invaded, and while every family had at least one relative abroad administering colonies or dominions, or being soldiers, that was abroad, it was there, not here, the colonies had not come home to roost (1992: 84)

Fifty years later, the population of London is – in round terms, allowing for substantial undercounting (see Coleman and Salt 1996) – a quarter black or Asian. The implosion of Empire occurred in a series of clearly defined waves. The Caribbean wave began in the late 1940s and peaked in the early 1960s. The Indian wave peaked after 1970. The most recent major influx, from Bangladesh, began in the early 1980s and peaked before 1990. Settlement from the New Commonweath – so called to distinguish it from the old ex-colonial dominions of Canada, Australia and New Zealand – has transformed the overall population of London, and specific districts all the more: in Northcote Ward, Ealing, only one person in ten is white (Peach 1996: 14). Though there were strong migrations from New Commonwealth countries to the industrial towns of the West Midlands and the North, nowhere else has London's degree of ethnic mix and variety. Overall, the capital has 45% of the entire non-white population of Britain, and a growing proportion of these are born and bred indigenous Londoners. As the geographer John Western (1992: 237) found in a fine account of the Barbadian community, 'Londoners' is how they see themselves.

The Caribbean migration to London was a direct response to labour market shortages of the early 1950s. As the long postwar boom began, employers found themselves squeezed by the continuing demands of military service, on the one hand, and by the planners' policies of decentralisation to new towns, on the other. In 1956 London Transport sent its first recruiting team to Barbados. The catchment was extended to Trinidad and Jamaica in 1966. The National Health Service recruited directly from the West Indies, as did the British Hotels and Restaurants Association (Glass 1960; Merriman 1994: 8). The flow began at around 1000 year, rising to 20 000 in 1956 and 45 000 in 1960 until it was curtailed by the Commonwealth Immigrants Act of 1962. Thirty years later there is a sizeable return migration to the West Indies, as the early generation of migrants comes into retirement pensions or realises the capital value of London home ownership.

The initial geography of settlement reflected Caribbeans' restricted access to the housing market. They were excluded from public rental housing by a points system based on length of residence, and in the days before the Race Relations Act 1965 a *Whites Only* sign was a common sight in the windows of boarding houses and bed and breakfast establishments. So West Indians followed contact chains to the bedsit zones of grand Victorian houses subdivided by private landlords: Dominicans to Paddington, Montserratians to Finsbury Park, Jamaicans to Brixton, and Barbadians and Trinidadians to West Kensington. They colonised these rooming-house districts in a climate of racial tension which climaxed in the Notting Hill riots of 1958, white riots against black settlers, ending in a conclusive Caribbeanisation of the district (Glass 1960). The geographical patterns laid down in these early years have proved remarkably stable. Brixton remains the epicentre of the black music industry (and the drug trade) and the Notting Hill Carnival through the streets of West Kensington in the last weekend of August is the greatest annual celebration of black identity in Europe.

West Indian settlement overlaps with a Black African community less than half in number, miscellaneously drawn from all of Anglophone Africa, particularly Somalia and Nigeria. The African migration began later than the Caribbean and was based more on individual fortune-seeking than corporate labour recruitment. The main influx coincided with the opening up of council housing to immigrants and a surplus of difficult-to-let property on the run-down council estates of inner London. Black Africans found their niche in the eastern inner ring of boroughs: Hackney, Lambeth and Southwark. In Liddle Ward in Southwark they account for more than a quarter of the population. Harlesden, Kensal Rise, Stockwell, Lewisham, Walthamstow, Finsbury Park, and Mare Street, Hackney, are centres which sustain black market stalls, hairdressers, restaurants and travel agents. But they are localised concentrations within a pattern of wide and increasing dispersal, particularly of West Indians; even at their highest concentration, in Roundwood Ward, Willesden NW10, Black Caribbeans account for less than a third of the local population. Trevor Lee's study *Race and Residence* (1977) showed that black segregation was already declining in the 1960s. That process continued strongly over the next two decades, and with it have come substantial advances into owner-occupation and salaried employment, particularly for women. Males have been less successful in the labour market, though their level of participation is still better than the new Asian minorities from Bangladesh. Peach has followed their progress from the 'Irish' future which seemed likely in the 1960s to a position in the 1991 census which 'does not differ dramatically in terms of housing tenure, jobs or residential segregation from the white population. It has an exceptionally high proportion of black and white households and in this way appears as one of the most integrated groups' (Peach 1996: 23).

A handful of Asians settled in London through the medium of the East India Company in the eighteenth century and the British Raj in the nineteenth. Large-scale Asian migration to London began a decade after the Caribbean influx. First came Punjabis and Gujuratis; then a migration of professional and commercial Asians leaving the newly independent African states by choice or (from Uganda) by force; lastly, an intense flux of Bangladeshis, mostly from the rural region of Sylhet. With the exception of the Pakistanis, whose main destination region was the north of England, London attracted more than its proportional share of every sort of Asian, encapsulating within its own population the immense linguistic and religious diversity of the subcontinent: Bengali, Gujurati, Hindi, Punjabi and Urdu. Twenty years on from the peak year of immigration, the new generation of London-born

Indians is already prominent in universities and in share of professional and skilled technical recruitment. National data (Church and Summerfield 1996) show the Indians to have the highest savings rate, the highest proportion of income from salaries of self-employment, the lowest dependency on welfare benefits, and the highest rate of owner-occupation: in a word, they are most 'Jewish' of the New Commonwealth migrants.

Because of its professional and entrepreneurial element, Asian immigration broke the conventional pattern of racial exclusion in London's ring of interwar suburbs. In Southall in west London, where three quarters of the housing is owner-occupied, whites became the ethnic minority (25%) within the largest Asian quarter in Europe. The basis was laid by Punjabi Sikhs but the community is diverse, with Hindu, Muslim and Sikh faiths alongside Christian. The mile of independent ethnic retailing in Southall Broadway and High Street is the most striking example of Asian settlement putting new life into a stagnant suburban centre: other instances around London are the parades of sari, sweet and jewellery shops in Tooting High Street (Wandsworth), and Barking Road (Newham). Asian shopkeeping extends to tens of thousands of small tobacconists, newsagents, chemists and corner shops, sustaining the pattern of independent retailing which we saw in Chapter 4 to be such a marked feature of London districts. Retail statistics (page 93 above) cannot convey the contribution to the quality of life in London made by its courteous and cheerful Gujurati shopkeepers, despite the long working hours and low return of local shopkeeping.

London's least entrepreneurial and most concentrated Asian population is from Bangladesh. A small pocket of Sylhetis was established in Tower Hamlets during the nineteenth century as 'lascars', labouring seamen. After the Second World War some remained to work in the Jewish-owned rag trades of Whitechapel. Expansion from a nucleus of predominately male immigrants began as wives joined them during the 1970s. The 1981 census recorded 9808 Bangladeshi-born immigrants in the borough: the total size of the community was variously estimated at 14 000, 18 000 or 24 000 (Eade 1989: 27). It expanded rapidly throughout the 1980s and 1990s by immigration (largely female) and a high rate of organic increase that reflected the attitudes of a Muslim traditionalist community towards child bearing and contraception (Church and Summerfield 1996: 60). In the 1980s, while every other London borough lost population, half by more than 5%, Tower Hamlets grew by 7.5%. With neighbouring Newham to the east, it has the highest fertility rate in Britain, enough to more than compensate for extremely low reproduction levels in the bed-sitter zones of Westminster, Kensington, Hammersmith and Fulham to the west. Overall, London's population in the mid-1990s is enjoying a natural increase (births minus deaths) of 40 000 a year (LRC 1995: 45), reversing eight decades of continuous demographic decline. The epicentre of this recovery is in Tower Hamlets.

The only comparable mushrooming of an ethnic minority was the the settlement and growth of the Jewish population a hundred years previously. There were close parallels in the geographical location of the Jewish and Bangladeshi settlements in Whitechapel and Spitalfields, in the economic basis provided by sweatshops of the rag trade, and in the political response of right-wing agitators, exploiting the defensive fears of white East Enders. In Whitechapel, the huge East London Mosque – built with a £1 million grant from the Saudi Arabian government – stands back to back with the Fieldgate Street Synagogue (Figure 7.1). An even more famous symbol of ethnic succession and displacement is the Neuve Eglise ('new church') on the junction of Fournier Street and Brick Lane, one of eleven built in Spitalfields by Huguenot Protestants in the late seventeenth century when *they* were the fast-growing population on the eastern fringe of the City. That original congregation declined as the French-speaking minority intermarried and became absorbed, until in 1809 the church was taken over by the London Society for Promoting Christianity among the Jews. In Victorian times it served as a Methodist chapel until the influx of north European Jews to Spitalfields at the turn of the century. In 1898 it was converted into the Great Synagogue. From the 1960s the Jewish congregation dwindled, and the building closed again. It was reopened in 1976 as the London Jamme Masjid, one of the largest mosques in the capital, with capacity for 4000 worshippers in its prayer hall.

Each evening on the busy roads to the east of the City, clothes dealers dodge traffic wardens as they load up the fashion products of East End sweatshops for distribution around the country or across the Channel. Despite the commercial bustle along its main road frontages, the Bangladeshi quarter is not, or not yet, locked into a 'Jewish' model of settlement. Comparative statistics on ethnic minorities (which now exist in plenty, thanks to the introduction of an ethnic question into the decennial census and other government surveys) place the community at the opposite extreme to Indians on every measure. With the Pakistanis, Bangladeshis come lowest in terms of level of qualifications, male activity rate, and hourly pay rate; they come highest in terms of their concentration in council housing, and their dependence on child benefit, income support, council tax benefit and other welfare transfers (Church and Summerfield 1996). The combination of direct migration from rural Asian poverty, large families, and small council flats gives the community – and the borough in which they have settled – a living density that is unique in any British city, and contributes significantly to the poverty profile of the capital as a whole. The pressures are intense, but remembering the succession of arrivals and absorptions described in the last few pages they are surely also temporary and transitional. The settlement is recent, the population is young, its GCSE and A-level grades are low but rising steeply: their predecessors in the Whitechapel ghetto of the 1890s have shown the way.

COSMOPOLIS

In his account of the settlement and achievements of the Huguenot refugees, published in 1867, Samuel Smiles praised London as 'the world's asylum, the refuge of the persecuted of all lands' (in Merriman 1994). London's role as a refuge has

Figure 7.1 Synagogue and Mosque. *Fieldgate Street, E1. A hundred yards to the left, the Whitechapel Bell Foundry has been casting bells for Christian worship since 1570 (some say 1420)*

been as important for immigration as its Empire or its port. The Reading Room of the British Museum offered a safe haven for Mazzini, Marx, Garibaldi. Sun Yat-sen fled here after his unsuccessful rebellion against the Manchu dynasty in 1895, and the Metropolitan Police secured his release from the Chinese Embassy in Portland Place when he was kidnapped there on the personal orders of the Emperor. The Inns of Courts gave Nehru and Gandhi their training in the rule of law. The greater a community's degree of international dispersal, the greater the importance of a world city as a focal place for political activity, often reproducing in microcosm the ideological divisions of the home country: the divisions may be all the deeper for the stateless diasporas – Armenians, Assyrians, Kurds – who have no home country.

There has recently been a very sharp increase in the number of refugees seeking asylum in the United Kingdom. Their origins match the ethnic trouble spots of late twentieth-century history – Nigerians, Afghans, Bosnians, Kurds, Somalis, Tamils. Refugees in flight are likely to fly to the world's largest international airport. Numbers rose from around 4000 a year in 1985–8 to 44 000 in 1991 and have since fluctuated in the 15 000–40 000 range. Each year a few thousand are granted permanent asylum or 'exceptional leave to remain' and a larger number melts into the pool. Official Home Office estimates are that 145 000 illegal immigrants entered and remained in England and Wales in 1981–91: statisticians allocate that figure to local authorities on a pro rata basis, giving London a formal total of 24 000. 'Anecdote' says the London Research Centre (1995: 49) 'would indicate that this may be considered a severe under-representation'. In fact, the capital absorbs at least 90% of refugees to Britain. Most arrive at Heathrow and head for London: in very exceptional circumstances – for example, Vietnamese boat-people and Bosnian victims of Serbian genocide – the Home Office will take in hand the reception and settlement of a large and politically sensitive refugee influx, distributing it around the country; but an informed estimate is that for 1000 Bosnians assisted to settle in the provinces under the Special Refugee Action scheme, 13 000 came spontaneously to London. Many Vietnamese dispersed under the earlier scheme eventually made their own way back to the capital.

Where people end up in London depends partly on housing vacancies, partly on established patterns of chain migration – new arrivals following pioneers, and community facilities following in turn. Some communities gravitate to the privately rented accommodation sector, others to the difficult-to-let stock of council flats. Diverse areas attract diverse populations; Southall, where 60 languages are spoken in the primary schools, has 5000 of the 8000 refugees in the borough of Ealing. Administrative action tries to spread the load: the Refugee Arrivals Project at Heathrow and Gatwick Airports, a voluntary body which meets in-comers and secures them temporary accommodation, distributes them through the London boroughs on a rota basis; some inner London boroughs house homeless in bed and breakfast accommodation in the suburbs; once established in a council tenancy there are mechanisms for transfer from borough to borough.

Employment is a further factor in the geographical distribution of minorities. With or without a work permit, new arrivals will follow their contact chain into a niche of the labour market. The employment of Spanish and Portuguese as hospital porters has a clear origin in National Health Service recruitment. Latin Americans have a large part in the office-cleaning sector while Ghanaians sit in the huts as car-park attendants, Nigerians stack the shelves of 711 stores, Tamils do the same for the *Europa* chain, Eritreans chop meat in the Indian meat markets of Balham, Ethiopians drive minicabs. London's small Maltese community have always been part of the criminal economy, for reasons explained by Geoff Dench (1975).

Concentrated upon London, the immigrants are widely dispersed within it. A recent refugee group such as the Somalis are distributed in every borough in London, keeping a concentration of support facilities in their original point of contact around the dockside in Tower Hamlets. The Armenian Centre at Ealing provides a strong core of support for a longstanding diaspora community which is both dispersed and internally divided (Talai 1989). A centre at Hammersmith performs a similar role for the Kurds, one of the more fractious diaspora communities in London, whose spread in north-east and south-east London echoes that of the Turkish Cypriots. The axis of settlement for London's 17 500 Latin Americans lies more to the south and west, with clusters of services in Kensington and Chelsea and further west in Kilburn, where Latin America House is an important meeting point and source of help for newcomers. On Sunday afternoons the strands come together on Clapham Common for the *Liga Latino Americana de Futbol*. One of the most dispersed and elusive communities are the Filipino servant class who work, sometimes in conditions of virtual slavery, for the wealthy international households of the West End and outer suburbia.

Overlapping with the previous groups is the huge population of students and visitors in London – particularly young adults from New Zealand, Australia and Canadians – working for a few months to enjoy the city and accumulate enough ready cash to tour Europe. Pubs, restaurants and insurance companies are major sources of employment, and so is the National Health Service. This short-stay population accounts for the majority of the 53 300 from the three countries in the 1991 Census. Earl's Court with its large-roomed red-brick mansions, ideal for shared living, is the long-established contact centre for Australians in London. Rising rentals have forced this engaging and gregarious group of short-term migrants into a wide band of bed-sitting-room country in subdivided houses in the inner ring of west and south London.

Further out, and further up the economic spectrum, is the expanding population of international business workers. The scale of global corporate activity, and the popularity of a London posting create sufficient demand for extensive support services for the constantly changing population of executives and their families. The Japanese Embassy estimates that for every 13 of the 25 000 nationals in and around London, one is a permanent resident. Facilities for the international professional class tend to be located either in the diplomatic quarter beyond the

West End or in a western arc of comfortable and quiet residential suburbs extending clockwise from Wimbledon to Barnet: N3, N12, NW11, NW4, SW19. Each morning, nine minibuses tour the west of London, collecting children for the Japanese High School (Hoshuko) in Creffield Road, Acton W3. The largest Japanese concentration lies within the *eruv* of Golders Green and Hampstead.

Globalisation has also brought a growing population of the international super-rich who come to London to spend money made elsewhere, notably Latin America, the Gulf and the former Soviet Union. Quarters around Hyde Park – Mayfair, Belgravia, Knightsbridge, Kensington and Bayswater – are no longer part of the regular continuum of property available to Londoners in regular employment. Shopping streets that lead north from Hyde Park, such as Queensway and the southern end of Edgware Road, are almost entirely Arabised. Since 1995 the downstairs tables at Whiteley's casino have been taken over by Russians, displacing the Arabs upstairs.

Some of the national groups can draw upon services established decades – even centuries – ago for merchants and seamen compatriots who came to do business in London. The Germans and the Dutch have long-established churches in or near the Square Mile. The Norwegians and Swedes, now distributed mainly in the western suburbs, drive east on high days and holidays to their old churches at the dockyard gates in Rotherhithe. International migration has brought a revival of numbers for the congregations of the cluster of Orthodox churches near the embassies in the inner western belt: the Greek cathedral of St Sophia in Bayswater, W2, the Bulgarian Orthodox in Ladbroke Grove, W11 and Serbian Orthodox in Lancaster Road, W11, Copts, Arabic Orthodox and Russian Orthodox in Kensington. New Armenian refugees join the congregation in the church of St Sarkis built by Calouste Gulbenkian in a quiet square off Kensington High Street in 1920. The main denominational effect of recent immigrant and refugee influxes has been the rapid growth of Islam in London. By 1995 there were more than 50 mosques, eighteen of them with a capacity of more than 500, and a further eight with a capacity of more than 1500 (Figure 7.2).

SOFT CITY

In a speech to the Brent Conservative Association in 1973, the right-wing politician Enoch Powell MP predicted that in 20 or 30 years the population of inner London would be 'at the absolute theoretical minimum one third to one half coloured, but on all rational grounds of expectation preponderantly and in some cases exclusively coloured' (cited in Lee 1977: 2). Powell was correct about the theoretical minimum but the expectation that it was 'rationally' bound to trigger white flight and ghettoisation was off the mark. Quite the opposite has happened in London. Instead of ghettoising, the immigrants have diffused towards the suburbs. Instead of fleeing the polyglot city, the white British have been attracted back into it. That preference

178

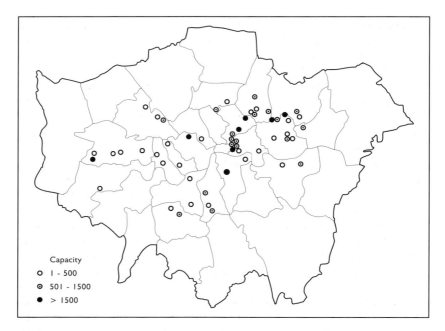

Capacity

○   1 - 500

◉   501 - 1500

●   > 1500

Figure 7.2 The Mosques of London. *Immigration and natural increase have favoured Islam in the late twentieth century just as they did Roman Catholicism in the mid nineteenth. Like the photographs of Docklands in the next chapter, this map is sure to be outdated by new development. Original compilation, from Alawiye and Alawiye (1995)*

has been greatest for the professional and salaried classes with purchasing power. In the early days the sociologist Ruth Glass (1964) and the novelist Monica Dickens (in *The Heart of London* 1961) both noticed the uneasy sympathy, within the ecology of large, decayed houses of areas like Notting Hill, of the white bohemians, beatniks and young professionals, and the new poor of black Caribbeans, both groups standing apart from the indigenous Cockney community. The aftermath of the Notting Hill riots opened up West Kensington to the blacks and also to the bohemians. As the immigrant wave spread over London, so did the resettlement of the terraces and villas of eighteenth- and nineteenth-century London by British non-tabloid readers.

Jonathan Raban's book *Soft City* (1974) presents a predatory picture of these middle-class pioneers, romanticising their neighbours as they drive them out of house and home. Gentrification may have this ruthless edge in the terraced streets of Chelsea, Fulham and Wandsworth, where one in four work in the banking and financial sector (Jones 1993), but Battersea, Hammersmith, Finsbury Park, Bow or Lewisham present a much more typical picture, with a mix of housing types and tenures that allows each district to echo the overall ethnic and social variety of the city. The word 'gentrification' – with its implication of a consolidated stake as a freehold owner-occupier – hardly conveys the variety of renting, subletting, sharing, squatting, cooperating and other strategies pursued by young professionals for their foothold on the London scene. Cosmopolitanism is half the attraction of the city, and the key to much of its creative energy (Hannerz 1993; Butler 1996). A clearly defined belt of suburban homogeneity stretches around the southern and eastern edges of the city through the boroughs of Barking, Havering, Bexley, Bromley, Croydon, Sutton, Richmond and Kingston, where over nine out of ten residents (eight in Croydon) are white. But elsewhere, ethnic mixing is the norm. Ethnic matching follows. High proportions of British-born Black and Asian Londoners have white partners: maybe as high as one in two Caribbean men, one in three Caribbean women, and one in five male Indians or African Asians (Berrington 1996; Berthoud and Beishon 1997).

The heterogeneity of London's social geography leads us back to the questions posed earlier in this chapter. Statistics depict the borough of Newham as 'the poorest urban area in Northern Europe' (LTC 1996). But any visitor from, say, Liverpool or Glasgow who sees the thronged pavements of East Ham High Street, the vitality of local shops (and lack of empty premises or gap sites) all through the borough, and the continual self-improvement of thousands of terrace houses (Figure 2.9), must feel that the statistics are missing something. Perhaps it is the unenumerated economy of transactions within ethnic communities. Perhaps it is an informal sector too pervasive, dense and complex for the taxman and the welfare agencies to police. London has real poverty and need, but it does not have the waxen-faced, down-at-heel misery of the older industrial cities, with their desolated housing estates where churches, pubs and shops are vandalised and boarded up and the tissue of social life seems utterly eroded.

The proof lies in Londoners themselves. Despite high unemployment, and though they live at the highest densities in any British city, and have twice the national rate of overcrowding, they are the healthiest and sturdiest urban population in Britain. London districts have consistently and significantly lower levels of mortality from all major causes of death except breast cancer. The standardised mortality ratio has been falling since 1980 and is (remarkably for a dense metropolis) well below the national average. Studies of morbidity from the Health and Life Style Survey find that Londoners on the whole experience less illness and better health, mental and physical, than the rest of urban Britain (Benzeval, Judge and Solomon 1992). London's suicide rate, once significantly higher than the rest of the country, has fallen steadily at a time when the national rate is rising (Congden 1996). Though health levels vary between richer and poorer parts, the complete picture indicates that the worst poverty in Northern Europe is not to be found in this dense, polyglot city.

Londoners' private lives are full of anxieties about neighbours, the sound of their music, the smell of their cooking, the behaviour of their teenagers. Little of this can be reflected in the public discussion of ethnicity, a subject hedged around by

180

Figure 7.3 The Global Corner Shop. *Rastafarian shopper; Middle Eastern shopkeeper; fresh produce from the world over, freighted into Heathrow; late opening; Cockney banter; globalisation has reinforced London's village quality*

taboos, particularly within the Labour Party. At times – waiting for a late bus, for example – the multiculturalist optimism of the left seems disingenuous. Yet London does wonderfully demonstrate the meaning of conviviality (Figure 7.3). A contributor to the Museum of London's 1995 exhibition *The Peopling of London* summed it up in terms of her local high street, Blackstock Road, Finsbury Park, on the N4-N5 border:

> Here in a hundred yard stretch can be seen an Irish pub, Indian newsagents, food shop and restaurant, a Greek–Cypriot delicatessen, a halal butcher, a variety of West Indian businesses, a West African restaurant with a taxi-service above, a Chinese take-away, a Lebanese flower shop, a Jewish-run ironmongers, an Italian restaurant and a Spanish-run off-licence. It is this rich mix of cultures rubbing alongside one another that characterizes contemporary London and adds so much to its vitality (Merriman 1994: 13).

CHAPTER 8

A NEW GEOGRAPHY

CHAPTER 8
A NEW GEOGRAPHY

The previous few chapters have described radical experiments in London's system
of government; a metropolitan economy fundamentally reoriented to the global
service sector; a population stabilised in number but transformed in kind; and the
melding of all these ingredients in the confines of a city of fixed physical limits.
The result – only gradually becoming apparent at the century's close – is a profound change in the geographical structure of London. The change centres on the
Thames and the redeveloped port. The story of Docklands brings together all the
strands of the previous three chapters with a large pinch of accidental circumstance: if anything in London's history was more by fortune than design, this
eastern renaissance was it.

THE WORKING RIVER

The Thames dictated the old geography of London. Not concentric in structure, it
was a classic example of a sectoral city of the kind analysed by Homer Hoyt, with
its port and industry along the banks of the river to the east, the royal court and
well-to-do London to the west, and an alternating pattern of high- and low-status
districts dictated by the physical relief of hills and rivers to north and south. The
downstream Thames was grimy, utilitarian, commercial and – residentially –
repellent to all except those who could live nowhere else. The upstream Thames
was arcadian, fashionable, a place of pleasure and conspicuous consumption, and a
residential magnet: at Chelsea, Chiswick, Richmond and Twickenham, the river
was a scene to be admired (Willmott and Young 1973). All of London's geography
pivoted on the contrast between the two worlds, captured almost photographically
by James Bird in his study of the Port of London (1957: 92):

> A great human geographical contrast may be observed beneath the northern
> approach to Tower Bridge. Westwards is the promenade in front of the Tower of
> London. Here thousands of tourists bent on visiting the Tower take their ease
> between views of the Tower battlements and the Traitors' Gate on the one hand, and
> the river and Tower Bridge on the other. A Beefeater's information kiosk against the
> bridge is their eastern limit; for as the tourist thinks to move under the bridge he
> glimpses the canyon-like, lorry-ridden thoroughfare of St Katharine's Way. On the
> south-east corner below Tower Bridge is a coffee-stall where dock workers may take a
> snack. The tourist blinks at the blackness of St Katharine's Way; the docker stares
> back stolidly. The tourist goes back to the Tower, and one more visitor to London
> turns his back on its port.

One of the great themes of seventeenth-century town planning was the idea of reorienting cities so that visitors, instead of turning their backs on the port, could promenade on open quaysides lined with public buildings. In Paris, Bordeaux and fortified naval bases such as Rochefort and Brest, Louis XIV created a civic image of sea power that was to influence the layout of port cities the world over: Amsterdam, Copenhagen, St Petersburg and Havana in Cuba all show it (Konvitz 1978). Every plan for London after the Fire incorporated open quaysides (Figure 2.5), and the King's first proclamation of 29 September 1666 laid down the principle of a fair new river frontage (Knowles and Pitt 1972: 29). But as we saw in Chapter 2, these designs were never implemented. The Thames remained secreted behind buildings all along its banks and over London Bridge: in 1765 a French visitor surmised that the failure to open up the river might be due to fears about the English tendency to suicide (Morton 1951: 171).

At the end of the eighteenth century the building of enclosed docks might have provided the opportunity – as in Continental cities – to appropriate the waterfront for public use. But instead it had exactly the opposite effect, thanks – not for the first time in this book – to the tenacity of City vested interests. The Master Lightermen, incorporated by Act of Parliament in 1556, opposed the docks because they would reduce the carriage of goods on the river. They secured a clause in the 1799 parliamentary bill for the West India Docks (where Canary Wharf now stands) allowing lighters to enter and discharge or receive goods without paying any toll. This 'free water' privilege enabled the owners of riverfront wharves to get access to maritime cargoes without incurring the cost of dock warehousing or dock quay dues. So instead of releasing the river frontage, the growth of the enclosed dock system – 700 acres of impounded water and 31 miles of quays by the end of the nineteenth century – stimulated a secondary growth of wharves and warehouses all along the Thames.

It took cholera and the crisis of London's sewage system to partially realise Charles II's vision of a promenade in the form of Sir Henry Bazalgette's Embankments (built 1868–74) combining parts of the Circle Line with a promenade, avenue, and receptor sewer all the way from Chelsea to Westminster. But Bazalgette stopped short of the City boundary, and the plane trees, lampposts and cast iron benches of the Victoria, Albert and Chelsea Embankments were a unique 3½-mile interlude in 70 miles of waterfront dominated by the dirty, utilitarian, workaday business of goods-handling and manufacturing. Two-thirds of the ships arriving in the Port of London found their berth in the river and not in the enclosed docks. And more than half of the cargo from ships that did moor inside the docks was loaded onto lighters and taken out onto the Thames again to be landed on a riverfront wharf in the black, crowded, intensely commercial environment that so amazed Henry James when he saw it from a Greenwich riverboat: 'Few European cities have a finer river than the Thames, but none certainly has expended more ingenuity in producing an ugly river front . . . A damp-looking dirty blackness is the universal tone' (James 1883: 219). Joseph Conrad described it all the memorably

> ### Joseph Conrad on 'the waterside of watersides'
>
> It is to other watersides of river ports what a virgin forest would be to a garden. It is a thing grown up not made. It recalls a jungle by the confused, varied and impenetrable aspect of the buildings that line the shore, not according to a planned purpose but as if sprung up by accident from scattered seeds. Like the matted growth of bushes and creepers veiling the silent depths of an unexplored wilderness, they hide the depths of London's infinitely varied, vigorous seething life. In other river ports it is not so. They lie open to their stream, with quays like broad clearings, with streets like avenues cut through thick timber for the convenience of trade. I am thinking now of river ports I have seen – of Antwerp for instance; of Nantes or Bordeaux, or even old Rouen, where the night watchmen of ships, elbows on rail, gaze at shop-windows and brilliant cafés, and see the audience go in and come out of the opera-house. But London, the oldest and greatest of river ports, does not possess as much as a hundred yards of open quays along its river front. Dark and impenetrable at night, like the face of a forest, is the London waterside.
>
> *The Mirror of the Sea* (1906: 107)

with the eye of a sea-captain: it was the only great port where you risked sticking your topgallant yardarm through a warehouse windowpane (Conrad 1906: 108).

During the nineteenth and early twentieth centuries, wharfage spread westwards along the Thames, pushing back that upstream world of lawns and leisure: not until Putney on the south side and Brentford on the north did 'willow tree succeed the hard-working crane' (Herbert 1947: 48). The Thames was the longest and largest of London's mixed-use corridors, a watery street served by a huge fleet of around 400 tugs and 7000 barges, most of them dumb (motorless) lighters, flat-bottomed to sit on the mud, and swim-ended to ride the ebb and flow of the tide.

James Bird (1957) analysed the different types of wharfage activity along the banks. Around Wandsworth, the shorelines were dominated by wharves for public utilities (gas and electricity generation) and widely spaced yards for bulk cargoes, shipped from barges: asphalt, coal, cattle feed, chemicals, cement, oil, paint materials, marble. Buildings were single-storey sheds. The multistorey warehouses lining the waterfront of the Square Mile, and a mile or so downstream, took in high-value goods linked to the commodity trades of the City: teas, furs, bristles, mica, shellac, drugs, essential oils, lychees, lotus nuts and other exotic imports. There were also several specialised wharves for newsprint and paper, supplying the presses of Fleet Street newspapers, and on the south bank of the Pool of London, above Tower Bridge, a series of huge refrigerated warehouses for imported provisions: wine, meat, eggs, butter, canned foods, fruit juices. Downstream from Shadwell and Rotherhithe bulk handling dominated again – softwood, granite, sand, coal – along with ancillary industries to the port: marine engineers, ship repairs, barge makers, rope and cable makers. Downstream of the Lea mouth, the Essex shore was dominated by industrial bulk wharves linked to Thameside factories: sugar, paint, soap, chemicals, flour, cable, oilseed.

The free water clause had a double effect. As well as spreading commercial activity along the waterfront, it weakened the profit base of the docks. Until 1830 they had a monopoly on all vessels entering London with tobacco, rice, wine and brandy, but thereafter they were exposed to the full effect of competition. By 1898 the dock companies were getting dues on less than 20% of the goods discharged in their waters. All the rest went over the side into lighters for transfer to river wharves or for direct delivery to consignees. The leakage was a fine stimulus to commerce but fatal to companies already exhausted by the suicidal rivalry for traffic between the systems of the London and St Katharine Docks (which owned and expanded the Royal Docks), the Surrey Commercial Docks, and the East and West India Dock Company (plunged into receivership two years after the opening of its Tilbury Docks in 1886). In 1908–9 Winston Churchill intervened as president of the Board of Trade, supervising a merger of the dock companies into the Port of London Authority (PLA), with responsibility for the enclosed docks and the management of the entire port system from Teddington to the estuary, and deep dredging for the sea approaches. The PLA inherited an unwieldy and unremunerative dock system based upon casual labour – the daily call at the dock gate continued well into the 1960s – along with a bitter industrial relations tradition, and an arcane, esoteric set of specialised trades and restrictive practices developed in self-protection from the worst effects of casualisation (Pudney 1975). It also inherited the free water clause and a competitive relationship with the 300 riverside wharves. However, its estate included Tilbury Dock (1886) on the Essex marshes, an unconstrained site opposite Gravesend, at the limit of sea pilotage. Tilbury held clear attractions for the port authority. Twenty-six miles downstream of London, it was less vulnerable to the leakage effect of the free water clause. Unconstrained by built-up areas and labour traditions, it would eventually become the focus for the twentieth-century modernisation of the port, with profound consequences for London (Bird 1957; Brown 1978).

Tilbury was vast and empty at the turn of the century. Joseph Conrad (1906: 116) predicted that its moment would come. Originally built as a railway dock, with just a cinder track for provision waggons, it had room to adapt to the twentieth-century growth of road haulage. In 1929 the dock entrance was widened and the berths deepened so that its could take the largest ocean-going ships. A large riverside passenger terminal was opened in 1930. Almost undamaged during the war (perhaps because intended by the Germans as the beachhead for invasion) Tilbury took the lead in the postwar adoption of new labour-saving technologies. Roll-on–roll-off (ro–ro) facilities introduced by the army for wartime landing craft became the basis for regular service for freight road connection to Europe in the 1950s. The dock was one of the first to embrace palletisation and containerisation in the 1960s. Container technology brought radical efficiency gains, emptying and loading ships in a fraction of the time and labour required for conventional cargos, and handling ten times the tonnage per berth. Above all, containerised traffic went over the PLA quays and not over the side into lighters (Pudney 1975).

Tilbury was not a competitive outport as Bremerhaven was to Bremen, or Cuxhaven to Hamburg. As part of the PLA system, it cross-subsidised the older docks and allowed the entire system to remain fully operational throughout the first half of the twentieth century. In fact 1964 was the all-time peak for cargo in the Port of London, with a traffic of 61.3 million tons, and 500 ships a week on the river. The same year saw the first postwar modernisation (as opposed to repair of war damage) of the docks on the Isle of Dogs with the installation of new sheds and cranes for the Scandinavian trade in the West India and Millwall Docks, followed by a stylish new terminal for the Fred Olsen line. But within two decades the upstream port – London Docks, Surrey, West and East Indias, Millwall, and the 3-mile-long Royal Docks – was all of it dead, along with the entire complex of lighterage and wharfering which it sustained.

Seven container berths were built at Tilbury Docks in 1968–9. They had the capacity to handle seven eighths of the whole non-bulk traffic of the Port of London. However, containerisation was as much the occasion of dock closure as the cause. The upstream docks could have been selectively modernised and non-container traffic retained, as in the river port of Antwerp, which captured a good share of London's former trade. Two factors encouraged the PLA to move out of town: labour and property. Though daily hiring at the dock gate had ended in 1966, decasualisation had not put labour relations on a modern footing. The unions refused to come to terms with the basic container philosophy of door-to-door delivery without 'stuffing' and 'stripping' by dockers, and 24-hour working was resisted until 1971. Besides, decasualisation had imposed direct costs on the port. The PLA had become 'employer of last resort' for registered dock workers. Until its abolition in 1989 a Dock Labour Scheme ensured employment and sick pay whether or not there was work to do. In the late 1970s the Authority was paying more than 1000 dockers to go home without work each day, and because of the high average age of the workforce (49 in 1980) it incurred over £1 million annually in sick costs.

Then there was the notion of potential value in ownership of a huge wedge of real estate so close to the heart of London. In 1969–70 the Port of London ran at a loss of just under £2 million. The national dock strike which closed British ports for three weeks in July 1970 coincided with the publication of ambitious plans for a marina, residential village and prestige hotel (London's third largest) on land in St Katharine's Dock, just where James Bird's tourist had peered into the black canyon of St Katharine's Way. The PLA had disposed of the site at a low industrial valuation to the Greater London Council. As the authority woke up to the asset potential of its estate, a series of further sales – including its monumental headquarters building on Tower Hill (Figure 8.1) – helped the Port of London to financial recovery while Liverpool headed for collapse. The authority's strategy was to dispose of its loss-making upper docks so as to finance expansion either at Tilbury or on the silts

Figure 8.1 Port of London Authority Building. *'Pomp and Circumstance' in Portland Stone. Tower Hill tourists are surprised to be told that this exuberant Edwardian monument, designed in 1912 by Sir Edwin Cooper for the newly established Authority, is nowadays just another private office block*

of the estuary, where there were ambitious plans ('Operation Trumpet') for a modern port to rival Rotterdam. Hesitantly, with several reprieves, it proceeded to pull out of London. The East India Dock was closed in 1967, the London and St Katharine's in 1968, the Surrey Docks by stages in 1968–70, and the long, slow rundown of the West India and Millwall Docks began in 1970. The Royal Docks continued in operation during the 1970s but with heavy losses (£25 000 per day in 1978) until their traffic was transferred to Tilbury in 1981.

Thirty years ago the Port of London handled 65 million tonnes of cargo out of a national total of 319 million. Despite the closure of the upstream docks it still keeps its place at the top of the league table of British ports for tonnage of goods, handling (in the mid-1990s) around 50 million tonnes of cargo a year, about a tenth of the national total. The stripped-down port of Tilbury, plus a few remaining river wharves, is complemented by the rapid growth of ports around the mouth of the Thames – the Medway, Dover, Ramsgate and Felixstowe Docks – which hardly existed in 1965 but now between them handle 30 million tonnes a year. Meanwhile, Britain's leading port by value of goods has grown up on the further side of London. Besides being, by a large margin, the world's busiest international passenger airport, Heathrow carries a steadily increasing share of air cargo; no longer used exclusively for consignments that are urgent, valuable and unbulky, it has replaced the Port of London for much machinery, most of the fruit and many of the vegetables sold at London's wholesale markets. In 1995 it shipped a million tonnes of cargo with a value of £38 billion (supplemented by a further 300 000 tonnes through London's other airports at Gatwick, Stansted and Luton). The economic complex of lightermen, shippers, wharfingers, hauliers, dealers and brokers along the banks of the Thames has metamorphosed into the offices and depots of logistics companies on the western side of Heathrow Airport, juggling and balancing the streams of global freight so deliveries come and go just when they are needed, without the warehousing that had dominated the old waterfront.

FROM DOCKS TO DOCKLANDS

The closure of the upstream docks and ancillary wharves released an immense windfall of building land stretching across five boroughs into the commercial heart of London. The opportunity was initially too large to grasp. The property industry was sceptical about market prospects east of Tower Bridge, an area of nationalised public utilities and municipalised housing estates, which was off the edge of the main *Geographia* map of central London, and did not form part of the cabbies' Knowledge (in fact they were reluctant to accept fares there). The instinctive conservativism of property developers was reinforced by that of London's planners. The *Greater London Development Plan* issued in 1969 and approved in 1976 assumed that the enclosed docks would remain operational, with the possible exception of the Surrey Docks. For redevelopment of bankside industry and warehousing the plan looked for provision of housing with 'appropriate civic, cultural and educational uses'. It had no concept of 'Docklands'. The Greater London Council had complex arrangements for planning the Thames waterfront, involving three joint committees, one for strategy, the second for advice and the third for projects, but they covered the whole length of the river without distinction between east and western sectors. The future of the docks and wharves was hardly mentioned in all the intense controversy surrounding the London plan (page 76 above).

However, as dock and industrial closures took effect, the area attracted more than its share of plans, designs and proposals (Ledgerwood 1987). After great controversy a plan was agreed by a Docklands Joint Committee representing the Greater London Council and the boroughs. Its approach was strictly utilitarian. It assumed that all non-operational docks would be filled in – a process already begun in the Surrey and London Docks – to provide land for council housing and industrial estates, low-density, low-income land uses. No attempt was made to exploit the potential of the waterfront as a new urban frontier, as Antwerp, Tokyo and Vancouver were doing (Konvitz 1978: 186). There was an unspoken political assumption that nothing should disturb the historic pattern of municipal landlordism in the East End, though the planners' own studies had shown it to be a key factor behind the outmigration of firms and families. The boroughs quashed an attempt by Horace Cutler, the Conservative leader of the Greater London Council from 1977, to inject a visionary note with a bid to hold the 1988 Olympic Games in the Royal Docks. The bias of private developers and industrialists against sites east of Tower Bridge remained intact. It was poignant, but entirely typical, that the professional team working to promote Docklands on behalf of the joint committee was based right outside the area in Blackfriars Road. While they toured Europe and America distributing promotional leaflets about 'the biggest industrial development in the world' with the familiar motif of a helicopter's eye view of the Isle of Dogs, decline and dereliction tightened their grip (Hebbert 1992b). At the turn of the decade, Simon Jenkins (1981) painted a bleak picture of these 'disused wastes . . . under siege from planners for ten years. Their population has already been decimated by economic collapse and the young are escaping by every route they can find. A journey through their city takes us past a series of dejected walls, warehouses and vandalised housing estates. In between are raw patches where the city's skin has been ripped away, first by bombs and then by senseless demolition' (Figure 8.2). The Docklands did not make a good advertisement for town planning.

THE JEWEL IN THE CROWN

As in so many other aspects of this story, the 1979 election of Mrs Thatcher was a turning point. The Conservatives seized upon an idea of using the Isle of Dogs as a

Figure 8.2 Nelson Dry Dock Rotherhithe, mid-1980s. *Even without floating detritus, grey weather and a low camera angle the task of regeneration was formidable: but so were the opportunities (cf. the opening page of this chapter). Reproduced by kind permission of the LDDC*

test case for an 'enterprise zone', based loosely on a proposal by Peter Hall for a deliberate experiment in deregulation or 'non-plan' (Hall 1982). They combined it with a Labour Party proposal to apply *ad hoc* appointed bodies – development corporations, modelled on those which had built the postwar new towns – to the task of urban regeneration. In December 1979 provisions for Urban Development Corporations and Enterprise Zones were squeezed into the parliamentary time-table, and the next year, after some delays over legal challenges, the London Docklands Development Corporation (LDDC) began work (Brownill 1990). Unlike its predecessor the Docklands Joint Committee, it made its base in Millwall Dock at the heart of the Isle of Dogs, in the Fred Olsen shipping terminal – a fine early building by Norman Foster. Fundamental changes of policy were signalled. The infilling of docks, already well advanced in the Surrey and London Docks, was to stop. The LDDC discovered that keeping the wet docks would be cheaper than filling them with household waste and rubble, and it recognised for the first time the magnificent landscape potential of these huge expanses of water. Substantial investments were made to upgrade the physical environment of Docklands. They took down corrugated iron and chain-link fencing, removed the fences and walls that screened the docks from view, planted trees and shrubs inside the development area and on approach roads, opened up public access along the river front and along dock quaysides, and laid out new ornamental canals within the infilled Surrey and London Docks.

Despite their closeness to central London the docks had always been a closed world – concealed, esoteric, covert, almost enigmatic are the words used by their portraitist John Pudney (1975: 6). The LDDC struggled to dispel this sense of remoteness from the rest of London. It could improve local access – laying a cheerful red-brick road through the middle of the Isle of Dogs, for example – but the major transport connections lay outside its boundary, and had become entangled in political disputes between the GLC and central government. The GLC was committed to a full-scale extension of the Jubilee Line into Docklands, the government believed that conventional buses would serve the purpose. But by good fortune, key individuals within LDDC, London Transport, and the GLC were willing to work through the political impasse and promote an intermediate, light-rail option. The political leadership was cajoled into allowing officers from the three organisations – and the Departments of Transport, Environment and Industry – to form an *ad hoc* group to analyse the public transport choices for Docklands. They found that a light-rail scheme, though more costly, would have a powerful impact on land values and employment potential of sites along the route. The Canary Wharf site might provide 1600 jobs if it was on a bus route, but 6000 with a rail link to Bank and Stratford (ten years later that figure was about right). Most importantly, they recognised the potential that a high-technology, driverless rail link could make to Docklands' image as a place of the future. On the eve of the 1982 Conservative Party conference the Chancellor of the Exchequer was persuaded to commit £77 million to the project. It was soon the key feature in publicity for the Isle of Dogs Enterprise Zone, 'a lively modern business zone . . . [with] new vistas, tree planting, water activities, landscaped open space, red brick roads and a new high technology rail link forging the future across the docks'.

The emphasis on liveliness and modernity reflected the continuing difficulty of stimulating investors' interest in the areas east of the Tower. The Docklands – sometimes described as the jewel in Mrs Thatcher's crown – was a genuine experiment in market freedom. Previous plans for the area had (altogether unsuccessfully) attempted to set targets and specify land uses. The new regime saw its task differently. It laid down the infrastructure and prepared sites for disposal – with significant tax concessions inside the Enterprise Zone boundary – but there were few preconceptions as to what should occur. The hands-off approach produced a curiously piecemeal environment. Unlike the best contemporary waterfront projects such as Barcelona or Boston (which looked back to the celebrated reclamation of Chicago's waterfront in 1904–8), the Docklands had no overall philosophy for the massing and scale of buildings, or for the layout of public spaces (Gordon 1996). Examples of young, exhilarating architecture were mixed in with the mediocre and the crass (Williams 1990). Two admired schemes were on adjacent quays in West India Dock. Heron Quays was a development of offices and workspaces designed by Nicholas Lacey in a racy yacht-club style, with single-pitch roofs, colourful red and purple cladding, and lightweight structures cantilevered over the water's edge. Advertised at its opening in 1985 as 'the business heart of the Enterprise Zone', its architecture captured 'the ethos of the Enterprise Zone – masts and spars, steel and glass, sometimes glitzy, sometimes brash, often evocative . . . exciting and challenging'. Just to the north on the parallel quay of Canary Wharf, the post-modernist Terry Farrell had made a lively conversion of a banana warehouse into a film studio for Limehouse Productions. However, these were the high points of Enterprise Zone design.

Academic studies of the first decade of Docklands bitterly criticised its aesthetic incoherence (Punter in Thornley 1992; Edwards 1992) and the market-driven disregard of social policy (Brownill 1990; Ambrose 1994). In retrospect, a more telling criticism might be that the government-appointed development corporation had not fundamentally shifted the ingrained geographical preconceptions about the potential of the former dock area. With strong encouragement from the Secretary of State Michael Heseltine, leading national housebuilders had been prevailed on to bring their standard suburban product into the Beckton marshes, north of the Royal Docks. But two thirds of the private investment was by overseas companies – Dutch, Swedish, Danish, Japanese, Kuwaiti – and several of the British schemes were by developers from the provinces, or young new companies such as Kentish Homes, who built London's first private-sector high-rise flats on the western side of the Isle of Dogs, to an outrageously eclectic design by the architects CZWG. The mainstream of the property sector continued to see the Docklands as a low-density business area similar in style to the emerging industrial landscapes of the urban fringe: trees, water, ample car-parking, crinkly tin sheds, offices and workshops for the business service and media sectors, some warehousing, and the occasional larger plant such as the relocated printing presses of the Fleet Street newspaper industry. In a word, as a convenient backyard to the real London west of the Tower.

Fortune, and not design, produced a very different outcome.

CANARY WHARF

At this point in the narrative we need to backtrack to that moment in Chapter 6 when globalisation began to take effect in the financial markets of the City. As office demand picked up in the early 1980s, the Corporation of London had reinforced its policies for conservation within the Square Mile, while the GLC reinforced its policies for community areas all around it. The Big Bang was approaching. International bankers knew that it would stimulate automation and information-based dealing, which in turn required large, modern office units, flexible in plan, with deep floor-plates to accommodate state-of-the-art technology in suspended ceilings and underfloor cabling. Such space was hard to find in the Square Mile. Nomura, the Japanese finance house, got it by taking the the General Post Office Headquarters at 1 St Martin-le-Grand (Sir Henry Tanner, 1895), gutting its Portland stone facade and building what they needed inside. Credit Suisse First Boston scoured the City for two years to find their building. Their chairman, Michael Von Clemm, was Vice-President of the City of London Archeological Trust and President of the US Foundation for Preservation of the Archeological Heritage. He found London's policy of cramming the central business district into the historic core absurd, given the amount of empty space available 10 minutes' drive to the east, in an area where planning permission was apparently guaranteed, along with a 10-year relief from the local property rate and corporation tax. He explored Docklands with his wife, met officers of the LDDC, and urged it to up its sights. He proposed that the bank should lead the way with a £3.8 million conversion of the other banana warehouse on Canary Wharf, next to Limehouse Studios. A mile and a half from the City, the shed had 22 feet depth between its concrete slabs, perfect for dealing floors, and was designed so solidly another two storeys could be added on top.

Though Credit Suisse First Boston was a major player in the Square Mile (first in the eurobond market) it needed to bring other American banks along with it. The top management of Salomon Brothers and Morgan Stanley flew from New York to inspect the Isle of Dogs. An independent Manhattan developer, G. Ware Travelstead, was brought in to devise a scheme. He jacked the scheme up to another scale again, commissioning the architects Skidmore Owings Merrill and I.M. Pei to design a North American style office district crowned by three tall skyscrapers, with over 12 million square feet of commercial floorspace.

The first rumours of the Canary Wharf scheme came in July 1985, dominating the press conference on the LDDC's annual report, which gave no inkling of what was in store. No forethought had been given to the idea of a major office district on the Isle of Dogs; the infrastructure for development on this scale was non-existent. The LDDC could have been blocked it under Enterprise Zone regulations, but instead (somewhat hesitantly) gave approval in the hope that it would provide a physical bridgehead for the larger task of regeneration in the Royal Docks. Central government came down in support of the scheme, partly for fear of losing it to Frankfurt, partly because its sheer scale and *chutzpah* gave such extraordinary vindication of the Enterprise Zone philosophy: its fiscal and financial implications were unprobed. The support of the local council, Tower Hamlets, was bought for cash, a training accord, and the promise of over 80 000 new jobs. Even the City of London offered qualified support, though they also instantly reversed planning policy within the Square Mile, releasing a development surge that would more than match the new centre to the east. However, the uncertainties over infrastructure and investor confidence made it most unlikely that the scheme would go ahead. The initial developers withdrew, and the consent was almost due to expire, when

Figure 8.3 Canary Wharf. *Only North American developers unattuned to the nuances of London geography could have planted 10 million square feet of office accommodation on the Isle of Dogs. The effect of Cesar Pelli's metallic obelisk was magnetic, and much of the empty horizon has been infilled since this 1995 photograph*

the world's largest property company – Olympia and York Developments Ltd – stepped into the breach and signed the master building agreement with the LDDC on 17 July 1987: the Governor of the Bank of England turned the first sod soon after.

Olympia & York, a private company owned by the Canadian brothers Albert, Paul and Ralph Reichman, had built New York's World Financial Center, First Canadian Place in Toronto, and several lesser schemes in North America. Canary Wharf was conceived on a scale unimaginable to any European developer. It made a complete break with everything that had gone before in the Docklands. The £3 billion scheme took shape as a mature urban district, complete with boulevards, squares, fountains and fully grown plane trees: designers of individual buildings were obliged to conform to a building code based on late nineteenth-century concepts of urbanism, with a consistent elevation and cornice line, and shopfronts along the pavement (Davies 1991). The corporate architecture evoked more groans than gasps, but the quality of materials was consistently superb, and the central silver obelisk designed by Cesar Pelli was the only tower in postwar London to win immediate acceptance and affection (SoL 1994; Figure 8.3). The investment in quality was underpinned by tenacious lobbying to shift the mental map of Londoners: by unsuccessful efforts to get the Isle of Dogs (Travelcard Zone

2) into Central London (Travelcard Zone 1), and have its postal code upgraded from E14 to 'D1'; by successful efforts to have it included in the central 0171 telephone area; by curious public relations exercises, such as a commissioned study which demonstrated:

	East London	West London
18-hole golf courses	37	35
1991 school leavers with >5 O-levels	5500	4500

By 1992 the first 5 million square feet of Canary Wharf were complete and ready: the fountains played in Cabot Square, the elegant lawn in the urban park at Westferry Circus awaited sunbathers, a riverbus plied to and fro from Westminster. All that was lacking were tenants. But demand had not recovered after the Stock Market crash of October 1987, and the deregulation of the late 1980s had left London with a glut of office space. Because all the infrastructure was being built (contrary to all the basic rules of planning) during or after the project itself, it paradoxically worsened Canary Wharf's reputation for remoteness. A deep-tunnel extension of the driverless Docklands Light Railway to Bank Station involved four years of computer problems and operational delays. Road access to the Isle of Dogs, never good, deteriorated after the start of work on Canary Wharf in 1988. A new east–west highway had to be smuggled through the planning process under the guise of 14 nominally separate schemes; both the cost (more than £1 billion) and design were controversial, and the immediate effect of construction phase was to aggravate congestion and speed the collapse of the Docklands market (Figure 8.4) (Church 1990).

Olympia & York held out for seven years. At the end of 1993, the eleven banks who had financed Canary Wharf foreclosed and the company went into administration with debts in excess of US$ 20 billion. For Canary Wharf's many critics, its commercial failure condemned it as a white elephant. Others with a longer historical memory were not so sure: the bankrupted Reichman brothers were joining an honourable roll which included the developers of Downing Street (Nicholas Barbon), the Adelphi (the Adam brothers), Kensington Palace Gardens and the Ladbroke Estate (Jenkins 1992).

Their collapse came just as the Docklands Light Railway overcame its teething troubles and the new road access, tunnelled at immense cost under Limehouse Basin, opened for traffic (Figure 8.5). Besides, work was about to begin on the most important infrastructure of all, a £2.7 billion extension of the Jubilee Line connecting Canary Wharf directly to Waterloo, Westminster, and the Stratford terminal of the new high-speed rail link to the Channel Tunnel. The eleven stations on the Jubilee Line were to be architect designed, and none would be more breathtaking than Norman Foster's at Canary Wharf, where 20 escalators would bring passengers from the deep tunnel below the Isle of Dogs into a glass shell that

196

Figure 8.4   Pasteboard Terrace, Junction of East and West India Dock Roads. *Painted hoardings around an empty site on the northern boundary of the Docklands regeneration area neatly summarise the two most serious criticisms levelled at the project: its lamentable quality of urban design (Edwards 1992) and the weak trickle-down or diffusion to adjacent parts of the East End (Ambrose 1994)*

seemed to float in the airy, watery expanse of the West India Dock. Perceptions were shifting. Major companies began to move in alongside the original project backers Credit Suisse First Boston and Morgan Stanley: the *Daily Telegraph*, *Daily Mirror* and *Independent* newspapers, Texaco, Ogilvy & Mather, *Reader's Digest*, BZW, Barclays Bank's investment subsidiary (enticing their reluctant 1950 employees with a £1000 payrise). In 1995 Paul Reichman headed a group of international investors to buy the project back from the banks at a cost of £800 million, and it gathered further momentum. The initial monolithic office complex began to diversify as shops, restaurants and hotels were added. By 1996 the first phase was 80% let, and work was beginning on second-phase projects which would expand the total floorspace to 7 million square feet. Docklands had a major capture when the City's largest foreign bank, having considered sites for a new headquarters in the Square Mile, opted to commission a new tower by Norman Foster to stand alongside his Canary Wharf station. Unsuccessful legal efforts by the Corporation of London to block Citibank's relocation only highlighted the extent to which the Square Mile's historic monopoly of banking and financial services had at last been broken. Enterprise Zone tax reliefs combined with North American enterprise had redrawn the economic geography of London.

Figure 8.5 Royal Docks. *The scale of land still undeveloped in the eastern sector of Docklands can best be appreciated from the flight deck of a plane landing at London City Airport. Reproduced by kind permission of the LDDC*

RISING IN THE EAST

The long-term implications of Canary Wharf are incalculable. First to grasp them, characteristically, was Peter Hall (1991), who had been brought in to Whitehall as policy adviser. He put the transformations of Docklands into historic context. For four centuries the dominant axis of development in London had been westward. This deeply entrenched pattern had been accentuated by deindustrialisation and the shift of the port. The Docklands project – 'simply the greatest piece of urban revitalisation in any city anywhere' – had turned the tide. Postmodernity allowed the Reichman brothers to conjure pure symbolic value with their fountains and granite pavements, breaking the old locational assumptions of the service industry. The eastward shift quite opportunely coincided with the larger trends of European economic integration, which would be oriented to high-speed rail travel and the TGV link through Essex to Stratford and King's Cross. That in turn opened the way to a perception of Docklands as the gateway or beachhead for a far larger regeneration of the corridor of degraded landscapes and depressed industries lying eastwards of London (Figure 8.5). A regional strategy to concentrate growth in this sector could relieve some of the intense development pressure around Heathrow to the west.

Hall's visionary synthesis was developed in further research (Llewellyn-Davies 1993) and crystallised into policy (GoL 1996). By the late 1990s the economic indicators for East London were beginning to show a 'schizophrenic profile' as the old pattern of deprivation began to be overlaid by some of the highest growth rates – across all sectors – in south-east England (Whyatt 1996). In 1997 the incoming Labour government of Tony Blair decided to proceed with a controversial and financially precarious project to celebrate the Millennium by constructing an immense Millennium Dome on the Greenwich peninsula. The scheme had originally been conceived to draw the attention of the world to London's eastern renaissance. But the apparent purposelessness of this immense temporary structure made it a poor symbol. The real message for the year 2000 was that an irrevocable shift had already occurred in London's centre of gravity, dome or no dome.

CHAPTER 9

STILL THE UNIQUE CITY

London: The Unique City is one of the classic portraits of this or any city. It was written by the Danish architect and urbanist Steen Eiler Rasmussen (1898–1990), who began visiting London in the late 1920s and returned for a month each summer to explore and photograph a little more while he pieced together its history in the Reading Room of the British Museum (Figure 9.1).

Rasmussen came with the direct, radical vision of European Modernism. After his first extended stay in London in 1926 he had visited Le Corbusier in his whitewashed studio in a converted monastery at 35 rue de Sèvres in Paris, and gone on to Dessau to see the Bauhaus and meet Walter Gropius's successor Hans Meyer. In cities and buildings Rasmussen always looked for the modernist values of simplicity, directness, fitness for purpose. What was so original about him was that he found these things in the despised, grimy streets of London.

We saw in Chapter 3 the despondent tone of writing and thinking about interwar London. Rasmussen was surprised by this collective inferiority complex: Londoners seemed to be convinced that theirs was not a 'real city' like Paris (1982: 411). However, he did have the good fortune to meet Sir Raymond Unwin, author of *Town Planning in Practice* and architect of Letchworth Garden City and Hampstead Garden Suburb, whose views 'were less banal'. The great town planner took the young Dane for a stride over Hampstead Heath. 'The atmosphere that day was unusually clear. Kites were suspended in lucid skies. We saw the whole of London at our feet and could distinguish Crystal Palace glittering in the sun ten miles away down at Sydenham. What a sight!' As the temperature dropped they returned to Unwin's studio for coffee by the fireside (Rasmussen 1948: 431).

Le Corbusier's vision of a good city was one which allowed apartment-dwellers to look out of their plate-glass windows onto parkland. Rasmussen preferred the London version of the good life: a great metropolis built at low density in single-family homes with a highly articulated public transport network, where you could walk in the park and go home to to your own fireside. He saw how this living pattern was linked to private ownership and management and to the historical dispersal of power within the unwritten British constitution. At a time when most British architects still saw Georgian architecture through Victorian eyes (ugly brick boxes) Rasmussen appreciated its simple, unaffected functionalism. As a town planner, he was one of the first to see London as a planned city, not in the Continental manner of autocratic urban design but through the pervasive regulatory effect of the London Building Acts on building materials, dwelling size,

Figure 9.1 The Unique City. *The standard cast iron telephone boxes of the General Post Office were modelled on the mausoleum of Sir John Soane in Old St Pancras churchyard. Set in a flagged, railed and tree-planted square, they epitomised the combination of individualism and civic order which Rasmussen found so appealing in London. And something of that uniqueness survives still*

road width and estate layout. The narrative of the Great Fire and its aftermath in Chapter 2 above is pure Rasmussen.

The original idea was to convey the lessons of English experience for a Danish readership. *London – Anden Reviderede Udgave* was published in Copenhagen in 1934. But, returning to London as visiting lecturer at the Architectural Association in 1927, where Le Corbusier gripped the young generation of architects (and the more radical their politics the greater its appeal) Rasmussen realised that there was a lesson for British readers as well. His English translation *London: the Unique City* (1937) included a new and direct appeal to beware Continental modernism. He warned that 'the Frenchman, Le Corbusier' – then dallying with Mussolini (Fishman 1977) – belonged to a long tradition of authoritarian monumental design imposed without regard for living conditions of ordinary residents:

> One hardly knows whether to laugh or to cry on seeing a modernistic architecture imported into London, which is far less suitable to the spirit of the age than the Georgian houses of about 1800. There is now a quantity of English books on the latest fashions in foreign architecture, but I have yet to find one English book dealing at length with the standardised type of Georgian town house, the sight of which is one of the most remarkable experiences to the foreigner in London.

After the war Rasmussen resumed his visits to London and closely followed the debate about reconstruction. He welcomed the idea of a green belt and the provision to accommodate the future growth of the capital in new towns – 'the promised land foreshadowed by Sir Raymond Unwin as compact spots of towns against a green rural background' (1948: 425). As mentioned in Chapter 2, the simple policy response to London's immense interwar growth – 'we must stop this' – seemed to him a splendid example of English pragmatism.

He was less sure about the attempts of the reconstruction plans to impose a design on the sprawling fabric of London. He found a strange absence of common-sense in proposals for shops and services. Planners were designating retail precincts without thought to the real patterns of shopping in the high streets and broadways all around London in which, as he observed, peak values were always on main thoroughfares. A related obsession was the concept of segregated neighbourhoods. Rasmussen took wry amusement in the debates over the optimum size of urban neighbourhood, 'the philosophers' stone with which to create a golden *urbanisme* out of leaden towns'. He saw that it was an absurd quest which denied the essential characteristic of metropolitan life, choice of where to work, play, learn and pray, allowing different groups to overlap and interpenetrate. The whole development of London was a continuous object lesson in the experimental, empirical approach to town planning, and the avoidance of pattern-made recipes (1948: 433–5).

London: the Unique City was written as a polemical book to change hearts and minds. The main impact of the first edition was to stimulate the foundation of the Georgian Group and trigger the writing of the first edition of John Summerson's classic text on *Georgian London* in 1945. But Rasmussen was swimming against the current in terms of his larger argument about the modern and functional qualities already to be found in London's urban landscape of homes and neighbourhoods. Opinion was all in favour of the clean sweep, and the replacement of dysfunctional streets with pattern-book neighbourhood units. Distressingly, the black iron railings which he had so much admired in London squares and streets were being ripped out in the name of 'open planning' even where they had survived the cull for armaments foundries (Fox 1995). The Abercrombie plans assumed a clearance of most of the urban fabric portrayed in Rasmussen's poignant photographs of squares and terraces. Equally unfashionable was the nuance in *The Unique City* that London had benefited from fragmentation, checks and balances in its system of governance. The only fear 50 years ago was of a repetition of 1666, when the grand designs of Wren, Evelyn and others for a rational reconstruction had been overridden by the City Corporation's concern for business as usual.

In Chapter 4 we followed the three main strands of the postwar plans for the capital: the redesigning and rebuilding of neighbourhoods as monofunctional residential precincts, the modern road network, and the green belt barring expansion of the built-up area. And more important, we saw how London lived up to its historical reputation of deflecting and absorbing most of the grand design: in the end, only the third objective was fully attained. Rasmussen, who died in 1990, must have been content that Londoners did change their way of thinking and decide to preserve so much of the fabric he liked to explore in the 1920s.

What were the consequences of the collapse of the grand design? Peter Hall has regretted London's inability to modernise the road network as Alker Tripp and Colin Buchanan intended, with fast high-capacity roads defining areas of tranquillity. 'Our failure to handle the problem of the car was the greatest disaster in our postwar planning of London, and it simply reflected the sort of hopeless fudge, up the hill and down again, that has characterised successive policy lurches by governments of different complexions over far too long' (Hall 1994: 6). In the history of London, hopeless fudges have a habit of coming good, and there are several reasons to be grateful for this one.

The arterial network was resisted because of the irretrievable damage it would have done to the web of residential neighbourhoods – village London (Aldous 1980). Its abandonment gave a new lease of life to the 'vast unvisited sequence of intimate single-family cottages with tree-shaded gardens' (Taylor 1973: 10) which Rasmussen explored and photographed in the 1920s. A systematic study of the urban environmental quality of the modern city emphasises just how strong the neighbourhood structure remains to this day, giving legibility, a sense of place and a human scale to the everyday environments of most Londoners (Figure 9.2) (Tibbalds 1993).

London's unmodernised road network has helped maintain a sustainable transport network, and the behavioural habit of using it. In the 1980s – a disastrous decade for urban transport – it was the only metropolitan area with a below-average increase in car-commuting: 5.1% against Manchester's 12.8% (GB 10.6%).

Figure 9.2 Chelsea Houseboats. *A setting for Iris Murdoch in* Under the Net *(1954) and Joyce Cary in* The Horse's Mouth *(1944). The novelistic centre of gravity has shifted detectably downstream in books such as Ian Sinclair's* Downriver *(1992) and Peter Ackroyd's* Dan Leno and the Limehouse Golem *(1994)*

Uniquely, numbers driving to work in the central core *declined* in the 1980s, in both real and proportional terms. Commuting by public transport fell by 2.3% as compared with 6.1% nationally and 8.5% in Manchester, but, uniquely again, London's overall ridership of buses, train and tube increased by 9%, 20% and 43% over the 1981–91 decade. London has the highest proportion of residents (12% in 1991) who walk to work, and one of the highest proportions of people who work at home – rates of 9–10% in Kensington & Chelsea and Camden are matched only in the remoter parts of rural Britain. Inner London boroughs – rich and poor – dominate the ranking of areas with lowest rates of car ownership.

London's high pedestrian densities are channelled into a street net that survives substantially intact from Victorian times. Here and there localised traffic management diverts the flow of vehicles around pedestrian pockets, the largest and boldest being the plastic-ring security precinct inside the Square Mile. But elsewhere, long-distance and local traffic (flowing at more than 2000 vehicles per hour), buses, cyclists and active retail, business and service frontages, including pavement tables and chairs for open-air eating and drinking, still co-exist within the street walls in defiance of all the prohibitions of Abercrombie and Sir Alker Tripp. Cromwell Road, Edgware Road, Whitechapel Road and Walworth Road have the same capacity, congestion and traffic speeds as in the 1930s, but they have survived to an era when, instead of frontage demolition and road widening, the remedy is more likely to be found in traffic restraint, parking or road pricing and reallocation of the carriageway to give priority to public transport, or – as in the recent remodelling of the Strand – to pedestrianism. In the meantime, though traffic jams are unpleasant for pedestrians and vehicle-users alike, better the pollution from idling exhausts than the carcinogenic particulates from urban traffic at speed.

An aspect of London's unmodernised road network which seems to have attracted little notice is the continuing importance of the radial roads as mixed-use corridors. The original intention of the postwar plan for London had been to make deliberate use of the severance effect of modernised landscaped arterial roads to define separation of districts and so – with faulty social logic – community structure. Such a philosophy was applied quite ruthlessly in a city such as Manchester, where municipal planning inverted commercial rationality, uprooting shops and services along the main frontages of the bus routes, and reinstating them in the backlands of council estates. The emptied frontages of the radial roads were first landscaped, then became colonised with billboards, and most recently have been sold off for US-style strip development of warehouse shopping and fast-food outlets.

Parts of the Old Kent Road had this treatment, but most of London's main road frontages avoided wholesale clearance, surviving to provide hundreds of miles of premises which are, by definition, visible for trade and physically accessible, mostly small scale and largely unencumbered by the zoning restraints which applied to 'nonconforming uses' within residential areas. A bus ride in any direction from Trafalgar Square takes you down a radial corridor with certain common characteristics: low vacancy rate of premises, high degree of flexibility and

Figure 9.3 Hammersmith Oarsmen. *Part of the special beauty of the Thames is that it remains tidal for a further eleven miles upstream of Hammersmith Bridge. Recreationists must respect its continual changes of level, tone and mood. May plans to impound the river and cut off the pulse of the sea never succeed!*

functional mixture, frequent occurrence of specialist retail districts (often linked to adjacent workshop industry and import–export warehousing), a predominance of small-scale ownership, and an overwhelming preponderance of ethnic minority entrepreneurship. Rasmussen said the English were not so much a nation of 'shop-keepers' as of 'self-confident tradespeople'. That applies particularly to the new English, or rather British, who colonise the mixed-use corridors which survive and flourish all the way from the City fringes to the edge of the green belt. This permeability is a unique aspect of London's morphology. Commonsense suggests it must have contributed to the patterns of ethnic diffusion described in Chapter 7, but it needs researching.

The most enduring element of the postwar modernisation of London is the green belt. Abercrombie drew the line, it held good, and (in combination with the new towns programme, much admired by Rasmussen) it set the frame for the great postwar decentralisation, planned and unplanned, of jobs and services. Most studies of urban containment have looked at the geographical effects of the green belt in the countryside around London or the wider metropolitan region to which growth has been displaced. As important, but much less well researched, except in terms of price effects, is the contribution which containment has made in refracting growth and development inwards into London. The imposition of the belt clearly helped to reverse the historic trend, deplored by Rasmussen, of middle-class outmigration and social polarisation. London's outstanding quality is its compactness of form and layout. It has a density that allows non-car-drivers to live a full urban life, without – according to surveys – a sense of claustrophobia or overcrowding (Tibbalds 1993: 24). Containment stimulated the recycling of land left derelict by industrial decline and changing freight technology. The eastward shift of the capital's centre of gravity described in the previous chapter would never have begun without the green belt.

What could never have been predicted in the 1930s was the effect of combining a green belt with a powerful, sustained influx of ethnic immigration. The minorities in prewar London were trivial: it was essentially a white Anglo-Saxon city structured by class divisions. London life was riddled with English snobberies about one's relationship to social inferiors, the correct places to live, the right ways to behave. 'If you are forced to live in Bayswater when the other side of the Park is "the Correct Thing" you pine your poor little soul away in envy and talk maliciously of the "Smart Set". One half of London is doing what it oughtn't and the other half is wishing it could do the same' (Allerton 1906). The one blind spot in Stein Eiler Rasmussen's account was that he did not seem to appreciate how much the enchanting English way of life was dictated by snobbery. Postwar ethnic variety has the great merit that new Londoners bring new ways of looking at the map. Not having the blind spots of status preconceptions about postal districts or place names, newcomers are willing to live, work and invest where opportunity arises. The rather stagnant and monolithic social geography of prewar London has given way to a much more interesting and complex ecology. In combination with the green belt, it has spatially dispersed demand within the built-up area, and accelerated the rate of land regeneration and property re-use. Or so it seems from observation: it is another topic deserving research.

We are on firmer ground in considering the institutional effects of containment. Chapter 5 showed how the belt provided a rigid frame for the modernisation of London government. The combination of external containment and internal reorganisation into 33 primary units, with the Corporation of London in their ranks, gave a new and apparently permanent lease of life to Rasmussen's polycentric concept of London government. The London Boroughs have exerted a healthy territorial effect within the metropolis, acting centrifugally as counter-magnets to the powerful international pole of the central area (itself partitioned between five boroughs), but centripetally to protect London's share of population and economic activity against the pull of the outer metropolitan area. GLC abolition reinforced the standing of the primary units, courting risks of parochialism and balkanisation of policy. In practice these risks have been offset, if not eliminated, by the development of new forms of partnership and cooperation. That in turn reflects willingness among local political elites within the green belt to take a London view: the change of perspective is most marked in the City Corporation and in outer London boroughs which 20 years ago resented their annexation into what was then called Greater London. So, urban containment has been good for *The*

Unique City concept of London as a compound entity, an effect which seems unlikely to diminish when London-wide government is returned to local democratic control.

Rasmussen predicted that pattern-made plans would not succeed for London. He was proved right by the failure of two of the three primary aims of postwar planning: comprehensive redevelopment petered out, the primary road network remained unbuilt, but the green belt held firm. This turned out to be the optimal mix. It helped preserve just the qualities which attracted Rasmussen to London in the first place.

The Unique City was not originally written as a tract for Londoners but to express a philosophy about the twentieth-century city. London was the case study for a larger argument about domesticity, public spaces, and the conventional street. For half a century that second strand of argument was completely lost. But in the past two decades designers have begun to rediscover the street, the quarter, the public realm, and the terraced house – key ingredients of Rasmussen's gentle critique of Le Corbusier. Just like the Modern Movement in the first decades of the century, the movement known as the 'New Urbanism' has developed through manifestoes and test-projects (Ellin 1996; Aldous 1992). At the 1996 Congress for the New Urbanism the strands came together in manifesto document – the CNU charter, a declaration of philosophy that aims to set the agenda for the twenty-first century as firmly as the modernist Charter of Athens did for the twentieth. Two years after Stein Eiler Rasmussen's death in 1990, Princeton University Press handsomely republished Raymond Unwin's *Town Planning in Practice* (1909), discovered again as a seminal text. The new urbanists had taken town planning right back to the crossroads where Rasmussen stood in 1926. When the CNU Charter states that 'A primary task of all urban architecture and landscape design is the physical definition of streets and public spaces as places of shared use', it echoes the axiom of German urbanism which Rasmussen learned from A.E. Brinckmann: *Stadte bauen heisst mit dem Hausmaterial Raum gestalten*, or 'Building cities means forming architectural spaces using buildings as material' (Rasmussen 1982: 421). Rasmussen admired London's streets precisely because they combined domestic privacy with a strong, hard-wearing public domain. And they still do. At every scale, from the evenly spaced regional satellites in the green belt, through the internal physical organisation of centres and subcentres, transit systems and green corridors, to the fine grain of neighbourhoods, London presents a pattern-book demonstration – flawed but recognisable – of the principles set out in the Charter of the New Urbanism.

What Rasmussen admired, is still here to be enjoyed. When unaccountable quangos spend millions of pounds inventing and launching a brand marque for London, their market researchers and image consultants come up with the key-words 'heritage, friendliness, diversity, accessibility and creativity'. When writers write about London they return continually to the themes of house in street, small in large, new in old, the world in a village.

Figure 9.4 St Paul's Cathedral. *Sir Christopher Wren's mighty dome no longer dominates the skyline of London as it did within living (postwar) memory, but its aspect close-to is as powerful today as when Samuel Johnson or Charles Dickens trudged up this same pavement of Ludgate Hill*

We began our search for London knowledge at the original central point, Bank junction. We end somewhere 6, 8, 10 miles away, with the words of Duncan Fallowell:

> Other cities are ringed with suburbs of modern residential towers, but London suburbs have mediaeval hearts with Tudor and 17th-century skeletons, 18th-century muscle, 19th-century flesh, 20th-century plastic surgery. It is in the late 19th/early 20th century suburbia – outside the endlessly redeveloped core – that the mysterious labyrinth exists in almost pure form: miles and miles of chimney-potted gables. This is the nearest London gets to purity of form and for the uninitiated it is London at its most terrifying. London doesn't have straight lines. Its space, like that of the universe, is curved. But as with the universe, you can only be inside London. There is no way of standing outside it – because it is not a place but a medium which only ever reveals parts of its parts. Even the ceremonial centre is assembled haphazardly. And here is the magic – this labyrinth is not a prison. It constantly dissolves into fantasy and escape via random paths. All is surprise, fascination and diversion, not too high-octane, rather dreamlike in fact – and everywhere fretted with gardens, trees, more trees: a city half hidden by leaves. *Independent Magazine* (4 October 1996)

FIGURES

TABLES

BIBLIOGRAPHY

Abercrombie, P. (1945) *Greater London Plan 1944*. London: HMSO.

Adcock, A. St J. (ed.) (1935) *Wonderful London*. London: Amalgamated Press Ltd.

ALA (1994) *London's Decade of Decline*. London: Association of London Authorities.

Alawiye, I. and Alawiye, Z. (eds) (1995) *The Muslim Pages*. Middlesex: Greenford Press.

Aldous, T. (1980) *The Book of London's Villages*. London: Secker & Warburg.

Aldous, T. (1992) *Urban Villages*. London: Urban Villages Group.

Allerton, M. (1906) *Towns and Types*. London: W.J.P. Monkton.

Ambrose, P. (1994) *Urban Process and Power*. London: Routledge.

Andom, R. (1896) *Industrial Explorings*. London: James Clarke.

Ashworth, W.A. (1954) *The Genesis of Modern British Town Planning*. London: Routledge & Kegan Paul.

ASI (1989) *Wiser Counsels: the reform of local government*. London: Adam Smith Institute.

Aubin, R.A. (1943) *London in Flames, London in Glory*. New Brunswick: Rutgers University Press.

Bailey, P. (1995) *The Oxford Book of London*. Oxford: Oxford University Press.

Baker, K. (1993) *The Turbulent Years*. London: Faber.

Banker (1996) London calling. *The Banker*, November, 34–57.

Barker, F. and Jackson, P. (1990) *The History of London in Maps*. London: Barrie & Jenkins.

Barlow, I.M. (1991) *Metropolitan Government*. London: Routledge.

Barthelemy, P. (ed.) (1990) *Underground Economy and Irregular Forms of Employment (travail au noir)*. Luxembourg: Office for Official Publications of the European Communities.

de Beer, E.S. (ed.) (1938) *John Evelyn's 'London Revived: Consideration for its Rebuilding in 1666'*. Oxford: Clarendon Press.

Benedetta, M. and Moholy-Nagy, L. (1936) *The Street Markets of London*. London: J. Miles.

Benzeval, M., Judge, K. and Solomon, M. (1992) *The Health Status of Londoners: a comparative perspective*. London: King's Fund Institute.

Beresford, P. (1987) *Good Council Guide: Wandsworth 1978–87* (CPS Policy Study Guide No. 84). London: Centre for Policy Studies.

Berrington, A. (1996) Marriage patterns and inter-ethnic unions. In *Ethnicity in the 1991 Census: Vol. 1 Demographic Characteristics of the Ethnic Minority Populations*. London: HMSO.

Berthoud, R. and Beishon, S. (1997) People, families and households. In Modood, T. *et al.* (eds), *Ethnic Minorities in Britain: Diversity and Disadvantage*. London: Policy Studies Institute.

Besant, W. (1909–12) *Survey of London* (10 volumes). London: A. & C. Black.

Binney, M., Cantell, T. and Darley, G. (1976) Concrete Jerusalem: the failure of the clean sweep. *The SAVE Report*, a special issue of *New Society* 23/30 December 1976.

Bird, J. (1957) *The Geography of the Port of London*. London: Hutchinson University Library.

Bish, R. (1971) *The Public Economy of Metropolitan Areas*. Chicago: Markham Publishing Co.

Bish, R. and Ostrom, V. (1973) *Understanding Urban Government: metropolitan reform reconsidered*. Washington, DC: American Enterprise Institute for Public Policy Research.

Booker, C. and Green, C.L. (1973) *Goodbye London: an illustrated guide to threatened buildings*. London: Fontana.

Booth, C. (1903) *Life & Labour of the People of London*. London: Macmillan.

Boumphrey, G. (1940) *Town & Country Tomorrow*. London: Nelson.

Breheny, M. and Congden, P. (eds) (1989) *Growth and Change in a Core Region*. London: Pion.

Bressey, Sir C. and Lutyens, Sir E. (1938) *Highway Development Survey 1937 (Greater London)*. London: Ministry of Transport, HMSO.

Briggs, A. (1963) *Victorian Cities*. London: Odhams.

Brooke, C.N.L. and Keir, G. (1975) *London 800–1216: the Shaping of a City*. London: Secker & Warburg.

Brown, R.D. (1978) *The Port of London*. Lavenham: Suffolk.

Brownill, S. (1990) *Developing London Docklands*. London: Paul Chapman.

Buchanan, C. (1963) *Traffic in Towns*. London: HMSO.

Buck, N., Gordon, I. and Young, K. (1986) *The London Employment Problem*. Oxford: Clarendon Press.

Budd, L. and Whimster, S. (eds) (1992) *Global Finance and Urban Living: a Study of Metropolitan Change*. London: Routledge.

Burton, J.A. (1974) *The Naturalist in London*. Newton Abbot: David & Charles.

Butler, T. (1996) People like us: the gentrification of Hackney in the 1980s. In Butler, T. and Rustin, M. *Rising in the East: the Regeneration of East London*. London: Lawrence & Wishart.

Carter, E.J. and Goldfinger, E. (1945) *The County of London Plan*. West Drayton: Penguin Books.

CEC (1991) *Green Paper on the Urban Environment*. Brussels: Commission of the European Communities.

Cherry, G. and Penny, L. (1986) *Holford: a Study in Architecture, Planning and Civic Design*. London: Mansell.

Church, A. (1990) Transport and urban regeneration in London Docklands. *Cities* November, 289–304.

Church, J. and Summerfield, C. (eds) (1996) *Social Focus on Ethnic Minorities*. London: HMSO.

Clarke, W. (1991) *How the City of London Works; an Introduction to its Financial Markets*. London: Waterlow.

Clout, H. and Wood, P. (1986) *London, Problems of Change*. London: Longman.

Clunn, H.P. (1932) *The Face of London: the record of a century's changes and development*. London: Simpkin Marshall.

Clunn, H.P. (1970) *The Face of London* (revised edition by Wethersett, E.R.). London: Spring Books.

Coakley, J. (1992) London as an international financial centre. In Budd, L. and Whimster, S. (eds), *Global Finance and Urban Living: a Study of Metropolitan Change*. London: Routledge.

CoL (1944) *Reconstruction in the City of London*. London: B.T. Batsford on behalf of the Corporation of London.

CoL (1951) *The City of London – a record of Destruction and Survival*. London: Corporation of London.

CoL (1959) *Barbican Redevelopment 1959*. Report to the Court of Common Council, London: Chamberlin Powell & Bon, Architects for the Corporation of London.

CoL (1995) *The Competitive Position of London's Financial Services* (London Business School City Research Project: Final Report). London: Corporation of London.

Coleman, A. (1985) *Utopia on Trial: Vision & Reality in Planned Housing*. London: Shipman.

Coleman, D. and Salt, J. (1996) *Ethnicity in the 1991 Census: Volume One – Demographic Characteristics of the Ethnic Minority Populations*. London: HMSO.

Collins, P. (1973) Dickens and London. In Dyos, J. and Wolff, M. (eds) *The Victorian City: Images & Realities Vol. 2*. London: Routledge & Kegan Paul, 537–77.

Congden, P. (1996) The epidemiology of suicide in London. *Journal of the Royal Statistical Society* **159**, 515–33.

Conrad, J. (1906) *The Mirror of the Sea*. London: J.M. Dent.

Coppock, J.T. and Prince, H.C. (1964) *Greater London*. London: Faber & Faber.

Creaton, H. (1994) *Bibliography of Printed Works on London History to 1939*. London: The British Library.

Crowe, A. (1987) *The Parks & Woodlands of London*. London: Quartet.

Cruickshank, D. and Wyld, P. (1975) *London: the Art of Georgian Building*. London: Architectural Press.

Cybriwsky, R. (1991) *Tokyo: the changing profile of an urban giant*. Chichester: John Wiley.

Daniels, P. (1975) *Office Location*. London: Bell.

Daunton, M.J. (1996) Industry in London: revisions and reflections. *London Journal* **21**, 1, 1–8.

Davidson, J. and Wibberley, G. (1977) *Planning & the Rural Environment*. Oxford: Pergamon Press.

Davies, C. (1991) Eastern promise. *Architectural Journal* **194**, 24–5, 58–67.

Davis, J. (1988) *Reforming London: the London Government Problem 1855–1900*. Oxford: Clarendon Press.

Deakin, N. (1983) Who governs London? *London Journal* **9**, 1, 75–7.

Defoe, D. (1974) *A Tour Through the Whole Island of Great Britain (1724–1727)*, Cole, G.D.H. (ed.). London: Dent.

Dench, G. (1975) *Maltese in London*. London: Routledge & Kegan Paul.

Diefendorf, J. (ed.) (1990) *Rebuilding Europe's Bombed Cities*. Basingstoke: Macmillan.

DoE (1989) *Strategic Planning Guidance for London*. London: Department of the Environment.

DoE (1993) *London: Making the Best Better*. London: Department of the Environment.

Dolphin, P., Grant, E. and Lewis, E. (1981) *The London Region: an annotated geographical bibliography*. London: Mansell.

Donoughue, B. and Jones, G.W. (1973) *Herbert Morrison, Portrait of a Politician*. London: Weidenfield & Nicholson.

Duffy, F. and Henney, A. (1989) *The Changing City*. London: Bulstrode Press.

Dunleavy, P. (1981) *The Politics of Mass Housing in Britain 1945–75: a study of corporate power and professional influence in the welfare state*. Oxford: Clarendon Press.

Dunleavy, P., Clegg, T., Crouch, R. and Harding, A. (1985) *The Future of London Government*. London: Greater London Group, London School of Economics.

Dunning, J.H. and Morgan, E.V. (1971) *An Economic Study of the City of London*. London: George Allen & Unwin.

Dyos, H.J. (1961) *Victorian Suburb: a study of the growth of Camberwell*. London: Leicester University Press.

Dyos, H.J. (1968a) The speculative builders and developers of Victorian London. *Victorian Studies* **11**, 641–90.

Dyos, H.J. (ed.) (1968b) *The Study of Urban History*. London: Edward Arnold.

Dyos, H.J. and Reeder, D.A. (1973) Slums and suburbs. In Dyos, H.J. and Wolff, M. (eds), *The Victorian City: Images & Realities Vol. 1*. London: Routledge & Kegan Paul, 359–86.

Eade, J. (1989) *The Politics of Community: the Bangladeshi Community in East London*. Aldershot: Avebury.

Edwards, A.M. (1981) *The Design of Suburbia*. London: Pembridge Press.

Edwards, B. (1992) *London Docklands: Urban Design in an Age of Deregulation*. Oxford: Butterworth Architecture.

Edwards, P. and Flatley, J. (1996) *The Capital Divided: mapping poverty and social exclusion in London*. London: London Research Centre.

Elkin, S. (1974) *Politics and Land Use Planning; the London Experience*. Cambridge: Cambridge University Press.

Ellin, N. (1996) *Postmodern Urbanism*. Oxford: Blackwell.

Elliott, M. (1986) *Heartbeat City*. London: Firethorne Press.

Elson, M. (1986) *Green Belts: conflict mediation in the urban fringe*. London: Heinemann.

Esher, L. (1983) *A Broken Wave: The Rebuilding of Britain 1940–80*. Harmondsworth: Penguin.

Evans, A. and Eversley, D. (eds) (1980) *The Inner City: Employment & Industry*. London: Heinemann.

Fainstein, S., Gordon, I. and Harloe, M. (1992) *Divided Cities: New York and London in the Contemporary World*. Oxford: Oxford University Press.

Fay, S. (1996) *The Collapse of Barings*. London: Richard Cohen.

Fishman, R. (1977) *Urban Utopias in the Twentieth Century: Ebenezer Howard, Frank Lloyd Wright and Le Corbusier*. New York: Basic Books.

Fishman, R. (1987) London: birthplace of suburbia. In *Bourgeois Utopias – the Rise & Fall of Suburbia*. New York: Basic Books.

Fitter, R.S.R. (1945) *London's Natural History*. London: William Collins.

Fletcher, J. (1844) *The Metropolis: its Boundaries, Extent and Divisions for Local Government*. London: The Statistical Society of London.

Flynn, N., Leach, S. and Vielba, C. (1985) *Abolition or Reform? The GLC and the Metropolitan County Councils*. Birmingham: Institute of Local Government Studies.

Foley, D. (1963) *Controlling London's Growth: planning the Great Wen 1940–1960*. Berkeley: University of California Press.

Forman, C. (1989) *Spitalfields: a Battle for Land*. London: Hilary Shipman.

Forrester, A., Lansley, S. and Pauley, R. (1985) *Beyond Our Ken: a guide to the battle for London*. London: Quartet.

Forshaw, J.H. and Abercrombie, P. (1945) *County of London Plan*. London: Macmillan.

Fox, C. (1995) The battle of the railings. *Architectural Association Files* **29**, 50–60.

Fry, M. (1944) *Fine Building*. London: Faber & Faber.

Fulford, M. (1995) Roman London. *The London Journal* **20**, 2, 1–8.

Garland, K. (1994) *Mr Beck's Underground Map*. London: Capital Transport Publishing.

Garside, P. (ed.) (1995) Twenty years of writing on London history 1975–1995. *The London Journal* **20**, 2.

Garside, P. and Hebbert, M. (1989) *British Regionalism 1900–2000*. London: Cassell.

Gerzina, G. (1995) *Black London: Life before Emancipation*. New Brunswick: Rutgers University Press.

Gibbon, Sir G. (1942) *Reconstruction and Town & Country Planning*. London: Architecture and Building News.

GLC (1985a) *Community Areas Policy: a record of achievement*. London: Greater London Council.

GLC (1985b) *The London Industrial Strategy*. London: Greater London Council.

Girouard, M. et al. (1989) *The Saving of Spitalfields*. London: Spitalfields Historic Buildings Trust.

Glass, R. (1960) *Newcomers: the West Indians in London*. London: Centre for Urban Studies and George Allen & Unwin.

Glass, R. (1964) Introduction. In Centre for Urban Studies (ed.), *London: Aspects of Change*. London: MacGibbon and Kee.

Glass, R. (1973) The mood of London. In Donnison, D. and Eversley, D. (eds), *London: Urban Patterns, Problems & Policies*. London: Heinemann, 405–32.

Goddard, J. (1975) *Office Location in Urban and Regional Development*. Oxford: Pergamon.

GoL (1995) *London Facts and Figures*. London: HMSO.

GoL (1996) *Strategic Guidance for London Planning Authorities*. Government Office for London, London: HMSO.

Goldston, R. (1969) *London: the Civic Spirit*. Toronto: Macmillan.

Gomme, G.L. (1898) *London in the Reign of Victoria*. London: Blackie.

Gomme, G.L. (1907) *The Governance of London: Studies on the Place Occupied by London in English Institutions*. London: T. Fisher Unwin.

Goode, D. (1986) *Wild in London*. London: Michael Joseph.

Goode, D. (1990) A green renaissance. In Gordon, D. (ed.), *Green Cities: ecologically sound approaches to urban space*. Montreal: Black Rose Books, 1–10.

Gordon, D. (1996) Planning, design and managing change in urban waterfront redevelopment. *Town Planning Review* **67**, 3, 261–90.

Graham, D. and Spence, N. (1995) Contemporary deindustrialization and tertiarization in the London economy. *Urban Studies* **32**, 6, 885–911.

Graham, D. and Spence, N. (1997) Competition for metropolitan resources: the 'crowding out' of London's manufacturing industry? *Environment & Planning A* **29**, 459–84.

Graves, R. and Hodge, A. (1941) *The Long Weekend*. London: Faber & Faber.

Green, A. (1994) *The Geography of Poverty and Wealth 1981–1991*. York: Joseph Rowntree Foundation.

Green, D.R. (1991) The Metropolitan economy: continuity and change 1800–1939. In Hoggart, K. and Green, D.R. (eds), *London: a New Metropolitan Geography*. London: Edward Arnold.

Green, D.R. (1996) The nineteenth-century metropolitan economy: a revisionist interpretation. *London Journal* **21**, 1, 9–26.

Gutkind, E.A. (1943) *Creative Demobilisation*. London: Routledge & Kegan Paul.

Hall, J. (1976) *London: Metropolis and Region*. Oxford: Oxford University Press.

Hall, P. (1962) *Industries of London since 1861*. London: Hutchinson University Library.

Hall, P. (1963) *London 2000*. London: Faber.

Hall, P. (1964) The development of communications. In Coppock, J. and Prince, H. (eds), *Greater London*. London: Faber & Faber, 52–79.

Hall, P. (1973) England circa 1900. In Darby, H.C. (ed.), *A New Historical Geography of England*. Cambridge: Cambridge University Press.

Hall, P. (1982) Enterprise zones: a justification. *International Journal of Urban & Regional Research* **6**, 3, 416–21.

Hall, P. (1988, 1996) *Cities of Tomorrow*. Oxford: Blackwell.

Hall, P. (1989) *London 2001*. London: Unwin Hyman.

Hall, P. (1991) A new strategy for the South East. *The Planner* 22 March, 6–9.

Hall, P. (1994) *Abercrombie's Plan for London – 50 Years On* (2nd Annual Vision for London Lecture). London: Vision for London.

Hall, P. (1995) Bringing Abercrombie back from the shades. *Town Planning Review* **66**, 3, 227–42.

Hall, P., Gracey, H., Drewett, R. and Thomas, R. (1973) *The Containment of Urban England*. London: Allen & Unwin.

Hall, P. and Preston, P. (1988) *The Carrier Wave: new information technology and the geography of innovation 1846–2003*. London: Unwin Hyman.

Halsey, A.H., Jowell, R. and Taylor, B. (eds) (1995) *The Quality of Life in London*. Aldershot: Dartmouth.

Hamilton, F.E.I. (1991) A new geography of London's manufacturing. In Hoggart, K. and Green, D. (eds), *London: A New Metropolitan Geography*. London: Edward Arnold.

Hamnett, C. and Randolph, B. (1986) Terminal transformation and the flat break-up market in London: the British condo experience. In Smith, N. and Williams, P. (eds), *Gentrification of the City*. London: Allen & Unwin, 121–52.

Hamnett, C. (1990) The spatial and social segregtion of the London owner-occupied housing market: an analysis of the flat conversion sector. In Breheny, M. and Congden, P. (eds), *Growth and Change in a Core Region*. London: Pion, 203–18.

Hamnett, C. (1994) Socio-economic change in London: professionalisation not polarization. *Built Environment* **20**, 3, 192–203.

Hamnett, C. (1996) Social polarization, economic restructuring and welfare state regimes. *Urban Studies* **33**, 8, 1407–30.

Hannerz, U. (1993) The cultural role of world cities. In Cohen, A.P. and Fukui, K. (eds), *Humanising the City? Social Contexts of Urban Life at the Turn of the Millennium*. Edinburgh: Edinburgh University Press.

Hardy, D. and Ward, C. (1984) *Arcadia for All: the legacy of a makeshift landscape*. London: Mansell.

Harrison, M. (1965) *London Growing: the development of a metropolis*. London: Hutchinson.

Hart, D. (1976) *Strategic Planning in London: the rise and fall of the primary road network*. Oxford: Pergamon.

Harvey, J. (1974) *Early Nurserymen*. London: Phillimore.

Hass-Klau, C. (1990) *The Pedestrian and City Traffic*. London: Belhaven.

Hebbert, M. (1991) The borough effect in London's geography. In Hoggart, K. and Green, D.R. (eds), *London: a New Metropolitan Geography*. London: Edward Arnold, 191–206.

Hebbert, M. (1992a) The City of London walkway network. *Journal of the American Institute of Planners* **59**, 4, 433–50.

Hebbert, M. (1992b) One planning disaster after another: London Docklands 1970–85. *London Journal* **17**, 2, 115–34.

Hebbert, M. (1995) Unfinished business: the remaking of London government 1985–2000. *Policy & Politics* **23**, 4, 347–58.

Hebbert, M. and Edge, E. (1994) *Dismantlers: the London Residuary Body*. London: STICERD.

Hebbert, M. and Travers, T. (eds) (1988) *The London Government Handbook*. London: Cassell.

Herbert, J. (1947) *The Port of London*. London: Collins.

Hibbert, C. (1969) *London: the biography of a city*. London: Longman.

Hoare, A. (1997) Privatization comes to town. *Regional Studies* **31**, 3, 253–65.

Hobhouse, H. (1971) *Lost London: a century of demolition and decay*. London: Macmillan.

Hobsbawm, E. (1964) The nineteenth century London labour market. In Westergaard, J. (ed.), *London Aspects of Change*. London: MacGibbon and Kee, 3–28.

Hobsbawm, E. (1968) *Industry & Empire*. London: Weidenfeld & Nicholson.

Hoggart, K. and Green, D. (eds) (1991) *London, A New Metropolitan Geography*. London: Edward Arnold.

Home, R.K. (1997) *A Township Complete in Itself: a planning history of the Becontree Dagenham Estate*. London: Libraries Department, London Borough of Barking & Dagenham.

Howe, G.M. (1972) *Man, Environment and Disease in Britain*. Harmondsworth: Penguin.

Humphries, G. and Taylor, J. (1986) *The Making of Modern London 1945–85*. London: Sidgwick & Jackson.

Humphries, G. and Weightman, G. (1984) *The Making of Modern London 1914–1939*. London: Sidgwick & Jackson.

Hutton, W. (1975) *The State We're In*. London: Jonathan Cape.

Hynes, S. (1976) *The Auden Generation: Literature & Politics in 1930s England*. London: The Bodley Head.

Jackson, A.A. (1974) *Semi-Detached London: Suburban Development, Life & Transport 1900–39*. London: Allen & Unwin.

James, H. (1883) *Portraits of Places*. London: Macmillan.

Jenkins, A. (1986) *Men of Property: Knight Frank & Rutley*. London: Quiller Press.

Jenkins, S. (1975) *Landlords to London: the Story of a Capital and its Growth*. London: Constable.

Jenkins, S. (1981) *The Companion Guide to Outer London*. London: Collins.

Jenkins, S. (1992) Bankrupts who built a city. *The Times* 30 May.

Johnson-Marshall, P. (1966) *Rebuilding Cities*. Edinburgh: Edinburgh University Press.

Jones, C. (1993) *A London Atlas*. London: London Research Centre.

Keene, D. (1995) London in the early Middle Ages. *London Journal* **20**, 2, 9–21.

Kellett, J.R. (1969) *The Impact of Railways on Victorian Cities*. London & Henley: Foulis.

Kennedy, R. (1991) *London: world city moving into the 21st century*. London: HMSO.

King, A. (1970) *Global Cities: post-imperialism and the internationalization of capital*. London: Routledge.

Kirk, J., Ellis, P. and Medland, J. (1972) *Retail Stall Markets in Great Britain*. Ashford: Wye College.

Knowles, C.C. and Pitt, P.H. (1972) *The History of Building Regulation in London 1189–1972*. London: Architectural Press.

Konvitz, J.W. (1978) *Cities and the Sea: Port City Planning in Early Modern Europe*. Baltimore: Johns Hopkins University Press.

Konvitz, J.W. (1984) *The Urban Millenium*. Carbondale: Southern Illinois University Press.

Korn, A. (1953) *History Builds the Town*. London: Lund Humphries.

Kynaston, D. (1994) *The City of London: A World of Its Own 1815–1890*. London: Chatto & Windus.

Kynaston, D. (1995) *The City of London: Golden Years 1890–1914*. London: Chatto & Windus.

Labour Party (1996) *A Voice for London*. London: Labour Party.

Land Use Consultants (1993) *Landscape Change in London's Green Belt and Metropolitan Open Land*. London: London Planning Advisory Committee.

LCC (1951) *Administrative County of London Development Plan: Analysis*. London: London County Council.

LCC (1960) *Administrative County of London Development Plan: First Review Report*. London: London County Council.

Leach, B. (1985) The shires in danger. *Local Government Review* 13 April.

Ledgerwood, G. (1987) *Urban Innovation: the transformation of London's Docklands 1968–1984*. Aldershot: Gower.

Lee, T.R. (1977) *Race and Residence: the concentration and dispersal of immigrants in London*. Oxford: Clarendon Press.

Lees, L. (1973) Metropolitan types – London and Paris compared. In Dyos, H.J. and Woolf, M.J. (eds), *The Victorian City: Images and Realities* Vol. 1. London: Routledge & Kegan Paul, 413–28.

Lessing, D. (1992) *London Observed: Stories and Sketches*. London: HarperCollins.

Levinson, M. (1963) *Taxi!* London: Secker & Warburg.

Llewellyn-Davies (1993) *East Thames Corridor – a Study of Development Capacity and Potential*. London: HMSO.

Llewellyn-Davies, University College London, Comedia (1996) *Four World Cities: a comparative study of London, Paris, New York and Tokyo*. London: Llewellyn-Davies Planning.

Lloyd, D. (ed.) (1979) *SAVE The City: a conservation study of the City of London*. London: SAVE.

LPAC (1994) *Advice on Strategic Planning Guidance for London*. London: London Planning Advisory Committee.

LRC (1995) *London 95*. London: London Research Centre.

LSE (1996) *Fact Book 1996*. London: London Stock Exchange.

LTC (1996) *An Economic Profile of London*. London: London TEC Council.

Lynch, K. (1960) *The Image of the City*. Cambridge, MA: MIT Press.

McAuley, I. (1993) *A Guide to Ethnic London*. London: Immel.

Mack, J. and Humphries, S. (1985) *The Making of Modern London 1939–1945: London at War*. London: Sidgwick & Jackson.

MacRae, D. and Cairncross, F. (1991) *Capital City*. London: Methuen.

McBurney, V. (1995) *Guide to the Libraries of London*. London: The British Library.

McKean, C. (1977) *Fight Blight: a practical guide to the causes of urban dereliction and what people can do about it*. London: Kaye Ward.

Marcan, P. (1993) *The Greater London Local History Directory*. London: Peter Marcan Publications.

Marriott, O. (1967) *The Property Boom*. London: Hamish Hamilton.

Marris, P. (1974) *Loss and Change*. London: Routledge and Kegan Paul.

Marshall, J.N., Alderman, N. and Thwaites, A. (1991) Civil service relocation and the English regions. *Regional Studies* **25**, 6, 499–510.

Marshall, Sir F. (1978) *The Marshall Inquiry on Greater London*. London: Greater London Council.

Martin, J.E. (1966) *Greater London: an Industrial Geography*. London: G. Bell & Sons.

Marx, K. (1930) *Capital* (in two vols, Cole, G.D.H. (ed.)). London: Everyman's Library, J.M. Dent & Sons.

Merriman, N. (ed.) (1994) *The Peopling of London: fifteen thousand years of settlement from overseas*. London: Museum of London.

MHLG (1962) *London Government: Proposals for Reorganisation* (Cmnd 1562). London: HMSO for Ministry of Housing & Local Government.

Michie, R. (1992) *The City of London since 1850: continuity and change*. London: Macmillan.

Michie, R. (1997) London and the process of economic growth since 1750. *London Journal* **22**, 1, 63–90.

Morrison, H. (1935) *How Greater London is Governed*. London: People's Universities Press.

Morton, H.V. (1951) *In Search of London*. London: Methuen.

Moye, A. (1979) *The LCC's Reconstruction of Stepney and Poplar 1945–65* (*Planning Studies No. 5*). London: Polytechnic of Central London School of Environment Planning Unit.

Munton, R. (1983) *London's Green Belt: containment in practice*. London: Routledge.

Nabarro, R. and Richards, D. (1980) *Wasteland*. London: Thames TV.

Nairn, I. (1966) *Nairn's London*. Harmondsworth: Penguin.

Nicholson, G. (1988) Trusting the people. *Architectural Journal* **30**, 35–47.

Nicholson, M. (1987) *The New Environmental Age*. Cambridge: Cambridge University Press.

Nicholson-Lord, D. (1987) *The Greening of Cities*. London: Routledge & Kegan Paul.

Olsen, D. (1982) *Town Planning in London: the Eighteenth and Nineteenth Centuries* (2nd edition). New Haven and London: Yale University Press.

Olsen, D. (1986) *The City as a Work of Art: London, Paris, Vienna*. New Haven and London: Yale University Press.

Pahl, R. (1990) The black economy in the United Kingdom. In Barthelemy, P. (ed.), *Underground Economy and Irregular Forms of Employment (travail au noir)*. Luxembourg: Office for Official Publications of the European Communities.

Parker, C. (1986) *The South London Handbook*. London: The Stockwell Press.

Peach, C. (ed.) (1996) *Ethnicity in the 1991 Census: Volume Two – The Ethnic Minority Populations of Great Britain*. London: HMSO.

Pollins, H. (1964) Transport lines and social divisions. In Westergaard, J. (ed.) *London: Aspects of Change*. London: MacGibbon & Kee, 29–61.

Porter, R. (1994) *London – a Social History*. London: Hamish Hamilton.

Porter, S. (ed.) (1996a) *London and the Civil War*. Basingstoke: Macmillan.

Porter, S. (1996b) *The Great Fire of London*. Stroud: Sutton Publishing.

Powell, C.G. (1980) *An Economic History of the British Building Industry 1815–1979*. London: Architectural Press.

PP (1905) *Report of Royal Commission appointed to Inquire and Report upon the Means of Locomotion and Transport in London*. Vol. I Cd 2597.

PP (1940) *Report of the Royal Commission on the Distribution of the Industrial Population* (chairman Sir Anderson Montague Barlow) Cmd 6153. London: HMSO.

PP (1960) *Report of the Royal Commission on Local Government in Greater London 1957–60* (chairman Sir Edwin Herbert), Cmnd 1164. London: HMSO.

PP (1965) *Committee on Housing in Greater London* (chairman Sir Milner Holland), Cmnd 2605. London: HMSO.

PP (1983) *Streamlining The Cities*, Cmnd 9063. London: HMSO.

PP (1997) *New Leadership for London: The Government's proposals for a Greater London Authority – A Consultation Paper*, Cm 3724. London: The Stationery Office.

Pratt, A. (1994) Industry and employment in London. In Simmie, J. (ed.) *Planning London*. London: Routledge, 19–41.

Pudney, J. (1975) *London's Docks*. London: Thames & Hudson.

Purdom, C.B. (1945) *How Should We Rebuild London?* London: J.M. Dent.

Raban, J. (1974) *Soft City*. London: Hamish Hamilton.

RAPC (1942) *London Replanned: Interim Report of the Royal Academy Planning Committee*. London: Country Life Ltd.

Rasmussen, S.E. (1948) *London: the Unique City* (revised edition with 'Postscripts of 1947 for English readers only' and 'for American readers only'). London: Jonathan Cape.

Rasmussen, S.E. (1982) *London: the Unique City* (revised edition with 'Essay on London new towns modern and ancient: a new and more happy ending, but no end'). Cambridge, MA: MIT Press.

Ratcliffe, P. (1996) *Ethnicity in the 1991 census: Volume Three. Social Geography and Ethnicity in Britain: geographical spread, spatial concentration and internal migration*. London: HMSO.

Reddaway, T.F. (1940) *The Rebuilding of London After the Great Fire*. Royal Fine Arts Commission, London: Jonathan Cape.

Relph, E. (1987) *The Modern Urban Landscape*. Baltimore: The Johns Hopkins University Press.

RFAC (1945) *Observations on the City of London's Report on Post-War Reconstruction*. London: HMSO.

Rhodes, G. (1970) *The Government of London: the Struggle for Reform*. London: Weidenfeld & Nicholson.

Richardson, A.E. (1911) *London Houses from 1660 to 1820*. London: Batsford.

Rivett, G. (1986) *The Development of the London Hospital System 1823–1982*. London: King Edward's Hospital Fund.

Robson, B. (1986) Coming full circle: London versus the rest 1890–1980. In Gordon, G. (ed.) *Regional Cities in the UK 1890–1980*. London: Harper & Row.

Robson, W.A. (1939) *The Government & Misgovernment of London*. London: Allen & Unwin.

Robson, W.A. (1941) *The War & the Planning Outlook*. London: Faber.

Rogers, R. and Fisher, M. (1992) *A New London*. London: Penguin Books.

Rose, H. (1994) *London as an International Financial Centre: a narrative history*. London: Corporation of London.

Rose, M. (1951) *The East End of London*. London: Cresset Press.

Rosenau, H. (1970) *Social Purpose in Architecture: Paris & London Compared 1760–1800*. London: Studio Vista.

Rowat, D. (1980) *International Handbook on Local Government Reorganisation*. London: Aldwych Press.

Royal Fine Art Commission (1945) *Observations on the City of London's Report on Post-War Reconstruction*. London: HMSO.

Rusk, D. (1993) *Cities without Suburbs*. Washington, DC: Woodrow Wilson Center Press.

Russell, J. (1994) *London*. New York: H.N. Abrams.

Saint, A. (ed.) (1989) *Politics and the People of London: the LCC 1889–1965*. London: Hambledon Press.

Saint, A. (1991) Grand designs on London. *Architectural Journal* **194**, 24/25, 46–55.

Saint, A. and Darley, G. (1994) *The Chronicles of London*. London: Weidenfeld & Nicholson.

Sampson, A. (1965) *Anatomy of Britain*. London: Hodder & Stoughton.

Sassen, S. (1991) *The Global City: New York, London, Tokyo*. Princeton, NJ: Princeton University Press.

Sassen, S. (1994) *Cities in a World Economy*. Thousand Oaks: Pine Forge Press.

Savitch, H.V. (1988) *Post-Industrial Cities: politics & planning in New York, Paris & London*. Princeton, NJ: Princeton University Press.

Schofield, J. (1993) *The Building of London from the Conquest to the Great Fire* (revised edition). London: British Museum Press.

Schwarz, L. (1992) *London in the Age of Industrialisation: entrepreneurs, labour force and living conditions*. Cambridge: Cambridge University Press.

Self, P.J. (1982) *Planning the Urban Region: a comparative study of policies and organisations*. London: George Allen & Unwin.

Senior, D. (1966) *The Regional City*. London: Longmans.

Sharp, Dame E. (1969) *The Ministry of Housing and Local Government*. London: George Allen & Unwin.

Sharpe, L.J. (ed.) (1995) *The Government of World Cities: the future of the metro model*. Chichester: John Wiley.

Sheail, J. (1981) *Rural Conservation in Inter-War Britain*. Oxford: Clarendon Press.

Sheppard, F. (1971) *London 1808–1870: the Infernal Wen*. London: Secker & Warburg.

Simmie, J. (ed.) (1994) *Planning London*. London: UCL Press.

Simmons, J. (1973) The power of the railway. In Dyos, H.J. and Wolff, M. (eds), *The Victorian City Vol II*. London: Routledge & Kegan Paul, 277–310.

Simon, Sir E.D., Lady Simon, Robson, W.A. and Jewkes, J. (1937) *Moscow in the Making*. London: Longmans.

Skelcher, C. and Stewart, J. (1993) *The Appointed Government of London*. Birmingham: Institute of Local Government Studies, for Association of London Authorities.

Smallwood, F. (1965) *Greater London, the Politics of Metropolitan Reform*. Indianapolis: Bobbs-Merrill.

Smith, D.H. (1933) *The Industries of Greater London*. London: P.S. King & Sons.

Smith, S. (1986) *Britain's Shadow Economy*. Oxford: Clarendon.

Smyth, H. (1985) *Property Companies and the Construction Industry in Britain*. Cambridge: Cambridge University Press.

SCLSERP (1976) *The Improvement of London's Green Belt*. London: Standing Conference for London and the South East Regional Planning.

SoL (1991) *County Hall (Survey of London Monograph No. 17)*. London: Athlone Press.

SoL (1994) *Docklands in the Making: the Redevelopment of the Isle of Dogs 1981–1995 (Survey of London Parish Volume XLIV)*. London: Athlone Press.

224

Spate, O.H.K. (1938) Geographical aspects of the industrial evolution of London till 1850. *Geographical Journal* **XCII**, 5, 422–32.

Stedman Jones, G. (1971) *Outcast London: a Study in the Relationship Between Classes in Victorian Society*. Oxford: Clarendon Press.

Stowe, J. (1958) *Survey of London* (Everyman Edition, Pearl, V. (ed.)). London: Dent.

Strange, G.R. (1973) The frightened poets. In Dyos, J. and Woolf, M. (eds), *The Victorian City: Images and Realities*, Vol II. London: Routledge & Kegan Paul, 475–94.

Summerson, Sir J. (1963) Urban forms. In Handlin, O. and Burchard, J. (eds), *The Historian and the City*. Cambridge, MA: MIT Press.

Summerson, Sir J. (1966) *Inigo Jones*. Harmondsworth: Penguin.

Summerson, Sir J. (1988) *Georgian London*. London: Barrie & Jenkins.

Swenarton, M. (1981) *Homes Fit for Heroes: the politics and architecture of early state housing in Britain*. London: Heinemann.

Talai, V.A. (1989) *Armenians in London: the management of social boundaries*. Manchester: Manchester University Press.

Taylor, A.J.P. (1965) *English History 1914–1945*. Oxford: Clarendon Press.

Taylor, N. (1973) *The Village in the City*. London: Maurice Temple Smith.

TCPA (1962) *The Paper Metropolis*. London: Town & Country Planning Association.

Tetlow, J. and Goss, A. (1968) *Homes Towns & Traffic*. London: Faber & Faber.

Thomas, D. (1970) *London's Green Belt*. London: Faber & Faber.

Thomas, R. and Thomas, H. (1994) The informal economy and local economic development policy. *Local Government Studies* **20**, 3, 486–501.

Thornhill, J.F.P. (1935) *Greater London: a Social Geography*. London: Christophers.

Thornley, A. (1992) *The Crisis of London*. London: Routledge.

Thorns, D.C. (1972) *Suburbia*. London: MacGibbon & Kee.

Thrift, N. and Williams, P. (eds) (1987) *Class and Space*. London: Macmillan.

Tibbalds (1993) *London's Urban Environmental Quality* (Report to LPAC by Tibbalds Colbourne Karski Williams Monro Partnership). London: London Planning Advisory Committee.

Titmuss, R. (1950) *Problems of Social Policy*. London: HMSO.

Travers, T., Young, G., Hebbert, M. and Burnham, J. (1991) *The Government of London*. York: Joseph Rowntree Foundation.

Trent, C. (1965) *Greater London: its growth and development through two thousand years*. London: Phoenix House.

Trevelyan, Sir G.M. (1959) *A Social History of England*. Harmondsworth: Penguin.

Tripp, Sir A. (1938) *Road Traffic and its Control*. London: Edward Arnold.

Tripp, Sir A. (1942) *Town Planning and Road Traffic*. London: Edward Arnold.

Vallance, A. (1935) *The Centre of the World*. London: Hodder & Stoughton.

Vigor, M. (1975) Industry as a neighbour in urban areas. *Planning Outlook* **17**, 40–52.

VfL (1996) *Revitalising London's Town Centres: a Vision for London Report*. London: Vision for London.

Ward, S. (1994) *Planning and Urban Change*. London: Paul Chapman.

Waterman, S. (1989) *Jews in an Outer London Borough, Barnet* (Research Paper 1). London: Department of Geography, Queen Mary College.

Wates, N. (1976) *The Battle for Tolmers Square*. London: Routledge.

Weightman, G. and Humphries, S. (1984) *The Making of Modern London 1914–1939*. London: Sidgwick & Jackson.

Weinreb, B. and Hibbert, C. (1983) *The London Encyclopedia*. London: Macmillan.

Wells, H.G. (1901) *Anticipations*. London: Chapman & Hall.

Wells, H.G. (1934) *Experiment in Autobiography*. London: Jonathan Cape.

Western, J. (1992) *A Passage to England: Barbadian Londoners speak of home*. Minneapolis: University of Minnesota Press.

Whale, G. (1888) *Greater London and its Government*. London: T. Fisher Unwin.

Wheeler, A. (1979) *The Tidal Thames: the history of a river and its fishes*. London: Routledge & Kegan Paul.

Wheen, F. (1985) *The Battle for London*. London: Pluto Press.

Whitehand, J.W.R. (1990) Makers of the residential landscape: conflict and change in outer London. *Transactions of the Institute of British Geographers* **15**, 1, 87–101.

Whitehand, J.W.R. (1992) *The Making of the Urban Landscape*. Oxford: Blackwell.

Whitehouse, B. (1964) *Partners in Property*. London: Birn, Shaw.

Whyatt, A. (1996) London east: gateway to regeneration. In Butler, T. and Rustin, R. (eds), *Rising in the East: the Regeneration of East London*. London: Lawrence & Wishart, 265–87.

Wilcox, D. and Richards, D. (1977) *London: the Heartless City*. London: Thames Televison.

Williams, C.C. and Windebank, J. (1994) Spatial variations in the informal sector: a review of evidence from the European Union. *Regional Studies* **28**, 8, 819–25.

Williams-Ellis, C. (1928) *England and the Octopus*. London: Geoffrey Bles.

Williams, R. (1973) *The Country & the City*. London: Chatto & Windus.

Williams, S. (1990) *Docklands*. London: Architecture Design and Technology Press.

Willmott, P. and Young, M. (1973) Social class and geography. In Donnison, D. and Eversley, D. (eds), *London: Urban Patterns Problems and Policies*. London: Heinemann, 190–215.

Wilson, A.N. (1993) *The Faber Book of London*. London: Faber.

Winter, J. (1993) *London's Teeming Streets*. London: Routledge.

Wise, M.J. (1956) The role of London in the industrial geography of Great Britain. *Geography* **XLI**, November, 219–32.

Wohl, A. (1977) *The Eternal Slum: Housing and Social Policy in Victorian London*. London: Edward Arnold.

Wrigley, E.A. (1967) A simple model of London's importance in a changing English society & economy 1650–1750. *Past & Present* **37**, 44–70.

Yelling, J.A. (1986) *Slums and Slum Clearance in Victorian London*. London: Allen & Unwin.

Yelling, J.A. (1992) *Slums and Redevelopment: policy and practice in England 1918–1945 with particular reference to London*. London: UCL Press.

Young, K. (1975) *Local Politics and the Rise of the Party: the London Municipal Society and Conservative intervention in local elections 1894–1963*. Leicester: Leicester University Press.

Young, K. (1984) Governing Greater London: the background to GLC abolition and an alternative approach. *The London Journal* **10**, 1, 69–79.

Young, K. (1995) Public space and civility in London. In Halsey, A.H., Jowell, R. and Taylor, B. (eds), *The Quality of Life in London*. Aldershot: Dartmouth, 47–66.

Young, K. and Garside, P. (1982) *Metropolitan London: Political & Urban Change 1837–1981*. London: Edward Arnold.

Young, K. and Kramer, J. (1978) *Strategy and Conflict in Metropolitan Housing: suburbia versus the GLC 1965–75*. London: Methuen.

Zeff, L. (1986) *Jewish London*. London: Piatkus.

Ziegler, P. (1995) *London at War 1939–1945*. London: Sinclair-Stevenson.

INDEX

228

Civil War 21
civil service, *see* central government
Clarke, W 152
Clout, H 86
Coakley, J 150
Cobbett, William 34
Cockfosters 95
Coin Street 90
Colchester 16, 97
Coleman, D 165, 170
Colindale 57
Collins, P 9
commercial development, *see* shops and
  shopping, offices
commons, *see* parks and open spaces
community structure 9, 39, 74, 88–90,
  108–9, 111, 123, 164–80, 203, 205
Congden, P 179
Conrad, Joseph 183–4, 185
conservation of architecture and
  townscape 30, 69, 71, 85, 88, 156,
  203
Conservative Party 50, 93, 101, 107,
  115, 116, 125
Coppock, J T 86
Corporation of London 5, 7, 10, 28, 29,
  38, 47, 50, 57, 65, 70, 101, 102,
  109, 117, 120, 126–8, 135, 183,
  192–3, 203, 207
Corporation of the Suburbs 21, 38
Cornhill 16
Cotton, Jack 85
Coulsdon Commons 57
Council for the Protection of Rural
  England (CPRE) 65, 94
County Hall 62, 63, 75, 80, 81, 101,
  107, 111–17
Covent Garden 29, 32, 83, 84, 85, 118,
  133
Cray, River 95
Creaton, H 9
cricket, *see* sports
crime 136, 163, 176
Crowe, A 44, 57
Croydon 38, 42, 52, 54, 57, 58, 91, 95,
  103, 108, 113, 124–5, 144, 179
Cruikshank, Dan 30
Crystal Palace 9, 200
Cubitt, Thomas 36
Cybriwsky, R 90
Cypriot residents 168–9

Dagenham 58, 110, 143
Daniels, P 113
Darley, G 9
Dartford 94
Davidson, J 95
Davies, C 194
Davis, J 47, 52, 110, 111
Deakin, N 114
De Beauvoir estate 37
Defoe, Daniel 33
deindustrialisation, *see* manufacturing
  industry
demography, *see* population trends
Dench, G 176
deprivation, *see* poverty
Deptford 9, 86, 108, 146
dereliction, *see* vacant and derelict land
Diary of a Nobody 43
Dickens, Charles 9, 46, 209
Dickens, Monica 178
Diefendorf, J 63
Department of the Environment 117,
  121, 122, 124, 126, 191
docks, *see* Port of London
Docklands 14, 113, 114, 117, 121, 149,
  182–198
Dolphin, P 11
Donoughue, B 101
Drury Lane 42, 85
Dublin 167
Duffy, F 156
Dunleavy, P 80
Dunning, J H 155
Dutch residents 138, 177
Dyos, H J 36, 43

Eade, J 172
Ealing 113, 125, 167, 168, 170, 176
Earl's Court 44, 168, 176
East End 30, 34, 40, 63, 77, 80, 81,
  159, 166, 188–9, 194–5, 197–8
East Ham 42, 58, 102, 103, 110
Eaton Square 36
ecology, *see* parks and open spaces
economy 18, 28, 34, 54, 56, 59–60,
  132–60, 184, 188, 192–3, 205–6
  informal economy 135–6, 176, 179
  promotion and inward investment
    125–6, 143, 149, 189
Edge, A 118
Edgware 54, 166, 167